Migranthood

MIGRANTHOOD

Youth in a New Era of Deportation

Lauren Heidbrink

STANFORD UNIVERSITY PRESS
Stanford, California

STANFORD UNIVERSITY PRESS
Stanford, California

Printed in the United States of America on acid-free, archival-quality paper

Library of Congress Cataloging-in-Publication Data available upon request.

Cover design: Black Eye Design | Michel Vrana

Cover photograph: Local family in Chichicastenango, El Quiche, Guatemala. Eddie Gerald | Alamy Stock Photo

Typeset by Kevin Barrett Kane in 10.5/15 Adobe Garamond Pro

for Gabriela, Mateo, and Liliana

CONTENTS

PREFACE

It was unexpected. My father died in a car accident and my mother was left with the four of us to care for alone. We sold the few things that remained in the house—the bed, the dresser, the stove, our *güipiles* [traditional blouses]—so we could pay for the funeral. We still did not have enough, so we mortgaged the house. We buried my father, but not even properly, and we took the rest to pay for my passage. I'm the second daughter; my sister did not want to go, but I did. I wanted to support my family, to help my mother, and to send my little brothers to school . . . I was scared though, worried about getting raped, but I knew I must go. I figured it's better to die trying than to die here not able to contribute. It didn't go as planned. I was caught and returned three times. The debt was heavy; we could not pay it off. The bank took our home and the land underneath it. That was three years ago. Now we live here in my uncle's home. We lost everything—our father, our home, my reputation. My sister says she will try. God willing, she will find better luck.

LETICIA,[1] sixteen years old

The Guatemalan government treats us like we don't belong—even on the lands of our ancestors—and blocks us at every turn. Bad schools, no work, no medical care. They treat us like *indios sucios* [dirty Indians] while they rob gold from under our lands. Believe me, I never wanted to migrate. I'd heard the stories from my cousin—about the dangers of the journey, living in a cramped apartment, working twenty hours a day and never saving—but I had no choice. My mother and sister got sick; the [Marlin] mine contaminated our water and spoiled the crops. They call it *"desarrollo"* [development], but it is not developing our communities; it is devastating them. They are killing us slowly.

JUAN GABRIEL, seventeen years old

I had a nightmare that Manuel was in a warehouse. He was injured; I saw blood. He was calling my name begging me to help him escape. My husband told me it was just me dreaming about the massacre of all of those [Central American] migrants in Mexico. You know, the one in San Fernando that killed so many of us. My husband told me it was just a bad dream, that Manuel would arrive in the United States soon and call us, but I can tell he was worried too. Then I received a call from someone demanding money, [saying] that they would hurt Manuel if we did not send it in two days. We borrowed money from everyone we knew, my brother sent money from California, we sold what we could to send 35,000 quetzales [4,600 USD]. People tell you these things are tricks, that people get some information and take advantage. They say it is probably the cartels or gangs or even the government trying to deceive us. Whoever they are, I know it is real; I feel it in my heart and in my bones. He is a responsible son. He would call if he could. He only wants to care for his newborn. We've searched, now two years, and wait for his call.

ELENA, mother of fifteen-year-old Manuel

LETICIA, JUAN GABRIEL, AND MANUEL are three of a growing number of young people migrating unaccompanied from Central America to the United States. Often dismissed as simple victims of poverty or stigmatized as gang members, these young people are social actors who contribute to the survival of their households through their care, labor, and mobility. Leticia tends to her siblings, works on the family farm, and following her father's untimely death, migrated to ensure her family's survival. In spite of his desire to remain in his hometown of Sipacapa, Juan Gabriel migrated due to the environmental repercussions of a Canadian gold mine that imperiled his mother's and sister's health when it contaminated the soil and local water sources. The U.S. and Guatemalan governments contend that foreign investment—often in the form of extractive industries, free trade zones, and agricultural initiatives—create alternatives to migration through employment opportunities, improved infrastructure, and investment that, in theory, trickles down to communities. For Juan Gabriel, however, the adverse consequences resulting from "development" in tandem with a failing public health system spurred his transnational migration. Manuel, confronted with few economic opportunities and institutionalized racism against Indigenous peoples, migrated to provide for his newborn son, only to be disappeared in Mexico, which, over the last twenty years, has grown increasingly perilous. Amid the proliferation of transnational gangs, corrupt police, and heightened border enforcement through zones of transit, migrating from Central America to the United States has increased in both cost and risk. Now two years since his disappearance, Manuel's whereabouts continue to be a source of anguish to his mother, Elena.

The experiences of young migrants like those of Leticia, Juan Gabriel, and Manuel are regularly overlooked, ignored, or discounted. They are relegated to simplified tropes of children left behind, abandoned, or dependent upon the actions and outcomes of adults. When the media and policymakers acknowledge young people's migratory experiences, their perspectives often are overshadowed by advocates who claim to speak on their behalf. In contrast, *Migranthood* chronicles young people's long-term trajectories of migration and deportation from their own perspectives. Through research with Indigenous children and youth in diverse spaces and geographies—in communities of origin in Guatemala, zones of transit in Mexico, detention centers for unaccompanied minors in the United States, government facilities receiving returned children in Guatemala, and communities of return—young people share how they negotiate everyday violence and discrimination, how they and their families prioritize limited resources and make difficult decisions, and how they develop and sustain relationships over time and space. In other words, their lives are so much more than the migranthood ascribed to them.

Alongside young people's diverse migratory trajectories, *Migranthood* traces how securitized approaches to migration management, often under the guise of "development," is a mode of governance that moves across and beyond geopolitical space. National and regional securitization programs, border externalization policies, and detention and deportation are enlisted to manage desired and undesired migrants, increasingly ensnaring children and youth in this global immigration dragnet. Although cast as objects of policy, not participants, Indigenous youth are not passive recipients of securitization policies, development interventions, or discourses of migranthood. Drawing on the resources of transnational kin, social networks, as well as financial institutions and actors, Indigenous youth enlist a rich social, cultural, and political repertoire of assets and tactics to navigate precarity and marginality in Guatemala. By attending to young people's perspectives, we learn the critical roles they play as contributors to household economies, local social practices, and global processes. In a

new era of mass deportation, the insights and experiences of young people likewise uncover the transnational effects of the securitized responses to migration
management and development on individuals and families and across space,
citizenship status, and generations.

This book is an extension of my ongoing commitment to the Guatemalan
community that began long before I became an anthropologist. In 1999, I traveled to Guatemala for the first time to serve as an election observer. It was the
first free election since the end of Guatemala's thirty-six year armed conflict,
one of Latin America's bloodiest. At the time, I worked at a torture treatment
center in Chicago where many Central Americans escaping brutal conflicts
throughout the region sought asylum. In Chicago, I would come to work with
political organizers, former guerrillas, trade unionists, journalists, university
students, and Indigenous leaders who were targeted for their efforts to oust a
U.S.-backed military dictatorship that brutalized their families and tore apart
their communities. Some were Indigenous teachers who dared to organized
adult literacy classes; others were community members who simply congre-
gated to pray at the local Catholic church. Many were targeted solely because
they are Indigenous—their ancestry held as a justification for their extinction.

In support groups, survivors shared how their families were disappeared in
broad daylight by military-trained death squads in unmarked vehicles and how
their children were killed in front of them. In immigration courtrooms, survivors were compelled to detail the gruesome torture techniques inflicted upon
their bodies and minds, techniques military officers learned in trainings at the
infamous U.S. School of the Americas (now named the Western Hemisphere
Institute for Security Cooperation). Survivors carried both ambivalence and
anger at seeking refuge in the United States, a country that had orchestrated
the assassination of democratically elected president Árbenz Guzmán in 1954,
spiraling Guatemala into a series of authoritarian regimes. In therapy sessions,
I interpreted for women as they recounted experiences of brutal gang rapes
and the emotional and social aftermath. In hospital waiting rooms, where I
accompanied survivors for treatment of the enduring physical consequences of
torture, they shared how state terror tore their families apart, disappeared loved
ones, displaced communities, and produced a culture of fear that has pervaded
everyday life for generations.

In my time working with Central American immigrant communities in Chicago and later in a community health center in Momostenango receiving refugees returning from Mexico, I learned the history of Guatemala—its colonial violence, internal displacements, and social suffering. I learned of the darkest dimensions of humanity, the depths of which continue to haunt me. I also witnessed how people organize and find hope amid the generations of traumas inflicted upon their families and communities. I learned the complex ways migration has figured and continues to figure in the lives of Maya people in Guatemala—as a response to violence, natural disasters, poverty, foreign destabilization, development promises, and environmental degradation; as a rite of passage; and as a cultural elaboration of care. Now twenty years later, I examine the insidious, intergenerational effects of this historical violence and its contemporary manifestations on their children and grandchildren—Leticia, Juan Gabriel, and Manuel—in "postconflict" Guatemala.

ACKNOWLEDGMENTS

I AM DEEPLY INDEBTED to the young people, parents, and community members who welcomed me and my children into their homes and their lives over the past seven years. I am incredibly privileged that you entrusted me with your stories and grateful for the wisdom you have imparted.

To Ruth Gomberg-Muñoz, Samantha Gottlieb, Diane Nititham, and Kristin Yarris, thank you for your thoughtful critiques on various drafts during the project's development. To Michele Statz, my astute and witty coeditor of *Youth Circulations,* thank you for your partnership and friendship over the years. A special thank you to Michelle McKinley and Susan Coutin for your endless guidance, enthusiasm, and support.

I am grateful for a thriving community of publicly engaged scholars, including Leisy Abrego, Elena Jackson Albarrán, Adam Avrushin, Deanna Barenboim, Erin Beck, Rebecca Berke Galemba, Deborah Boehm, Álvaro Caballeros, Heide Castañeda, Aurora Chang, Marisol Clark-Ibáñez, Cati Coe, Juan Dardón Sosa, Whitney Duncan, Christine El Ouardani, Marjorie Faulstich Orellana, Caitlin Fouratt, Patricia Foxen, Amelia Frank-Vitale, Christina Getrich, Judith Gibbons, Carol Girón, Claudia Gonzáles, Julia González Deras, Tobin Hansen, David Hernández, Joseph Heyman, Sarah Horton, Katherine Kaufka

Waltz, Jaymelee Kim, Nolan Kline, Losh Lainez, William Lopez, Jorge Daniel Lorenzana, Cynthia Lubin Langtiw, Stephanie Maher, Gabriela Maldonado, José Miranda Gómez, Briana Nichols, Mariela Nuñez-Janes, Kathleen Odell, Anita Ortiz-Maddali, Irene Palma Calderón, Ruth Piedrasanta, Alfredo Danilo Rivera, Sophia Rodriguez, Ursula Roldán Andrade, Kari Smalkoski, Aryah Somers, Lynn Stephen, Angela Steusse, Rachel Stryker, Miguel Ugalde, Fernando Us Alvarez, Maria Vidal de Haymes, Wendy Vogt, Joseph Wiltberger, Rosemary Yax, and Kris Zentgraf, among others. Each in your own way has shaped this manuscript. Special thanks to Lily House-Peters for assistance with data visualizations.

In addition, I am appreciative of opportunities to engage with practitioners, attorneys, social entrepreneurs, and activists dedicated to issues of migration and deportation in the United States and Guatemala. Special thanks to Walter Arreaga, Willy Barreno, Jenny Dale, Jhonathan Gómez, Mario González, Eduardo Jiménez, Adriana López Martínez, Wendy Lum, Ana Leticia Pirrir, John Slocum, and Tara Wagner. Special gratitude extends to Asociación Colectivo Vida Digna's Anna Aziza Grewe, Ana-Isabel Braconnier De Léon, Carlos Escalante Villagrán, Maria García Maldonado, Johana López Aguilón, Aida López Huinil, Wagner Ely López Huinil, Vinicio Ortiz Chete, Haydee Ramírez Méndez, Luis Pedro Reyes Escalante, Henning Sac Morales, and Maria Alejandra Vásquez Tizol for welcoming me and my children into your life's work. I am honored to walk with you.

I am deeply indebted to community members of Almolonga who generously shared their knowledge, experiences, and perspectives with our research team. Thank you to the Mayor Pedro Siquiná Yac and the municipal leaders of the Consejo Comunitario de Desarrollo who supported the survey. Special thanks to representatives of Núcleo Familiar Educativo para el Desarrollo in Almolonga and to Miguel Angel Nolascos for their collaboration with youth focus groups and workshops. The survey would not have been possible without the intellectual generosity, insights, and commitment of Giovanni Batz and Celeste Sánchez López. I could not have hoped for better collaborators. I was fortunate to work alongside an incredible interdisciplinary team of researchers who thoughtfully informed and compassionately undertook the community survey: Alejandro Chán Saquic, Catarina Chay Quiej, Sandra Chuc Norato, Angélica Mejía López, Amparo Monzón Alvarado, and Elizabeth Pérez Romero.

Each of you has taught me valuable lessons about the importance of compassion and dignity.

Several students provided invaluable research assistance throughout the course of the project, including Jose Aceves, Niki Albanez, Guadalupe Ayala Arroyo, Angelique Dayap, Yesenia Hernandez, Jose Iniguez, Sophia Lee, Laura Ochoa, Amber Reyes, Jina Shim, and Denina Steed.

This research was supported by the National Science Foundation (NSF, SES-1456889), jointly funded through the Law and Social Sciences Program and the Cultural Anthropology Program, and the American Council of Learned Societies. At NSF, I am thankful for the encouragement, guidance, and patience of Marjorie Zatz, Jon Gould, and Deborah Winslow. Pilot data collection was supported by a faculty seed grant at National Louis University, where I am grateful for the support of Terri Atienza, Shaunti Knauth, Lucille Morgan, Bradley Olson, Todd Price, Kamau Rashid, Wytress Richardson, Gale Stam, Stephen Thompson, and Judah Viola. At California State University, Long Beach (CSULB), I am appreciative for the collegiality of the Department of Human Development and the support of Wendy Lopez, Deborah Thien, Terie Bostic, and the staff of the CSULB Research Foundation.

Thank you to Michelle Lipinski of Stanford University Press who patiently and professionally shepherded this manuscript through publication. Special thanks to production editor Jessica Ling and copy editor Mary Carman Barbosa for their skillful direction in the final stages of publication. The manuscript benefited from three anonymous reviewers who modeled insightful, constructive critiques and recommendations. All mistakes and errors are my own. Portions of chapter five appear in Heidbrink, Lauren (2019), "Youth Negotiate Deportation" (in *Illegal Encounters: The Effects of Detention and Deportation on Young People*, edited by Deborah Boehm and Susan Terrio, NYU Press). Portions of chapter six appear in Heidbrink, Lauren (2019), "The Coercive Power of Debt: Migration and Deportation of Guatemalan Indigenous Youth" (*Journal of Latin American and Caribbean Anthropology* 24, no. 1, 263–81). They are reprinted with permission here.

Conducting long-term, international fieldwork with three children does not happen effortlessly. It necessitates a supportive and generous community that spans geography. In Chicago, a huge shout-out to the SOS Babysitting Co-op and the Odell-Booth and Cassel-Miller families for caring for my children, for feeding my family, and above all, for your friendship. In Guatemala, special thanks to Eliana Lara, Lindsey Horwitz, and Frederick and Lisa Wandke Anderson and your children for the hikes, meals, sleepovers, and conversations. To my travel wife Jennifer Richards, thanks to you, Ben, and Abby for spending your summer with us. I am deeply indebted to my parents Carol and Peter Heidbrink and my in-laws Cora and Mario Afable for caring for our family in my absences and for traversing international borders to bring the kids to Guatemala. Knowing that the children were basking in grandparents' rules allowed me to focus on my work with only modest guilt. My love and gratitude to my children Gabriela, Mateo, and Liliana, who are the best research assistants an anthropologist could ask for. Every day, you inspire me to engage with the world in new ways and to imagine a future filled with humor, kindness, and dignity. And to my partner Walter, whom I adore.

Royalties that I receive from the sale of this book will be donated to Indigenous organizations working with youth in the highlands of Guatemala.

ABBREVIATIONS

APP	Alliance for Prosperity Plan (Plan de la Alianza para la Prosperidad)
CA-4	Central America-4 Free Mobility Agreement
CAFTA-DR	Dominican Republic–Central America Free Trade Agreement
CAM	Central American Minors
CARSI	Central American Regional Security Initiative
CBP	U.S. Customs and Border Protection
CICIG	Comisión Internacional contra la Impunidad en Guatemala (International Commission against Impunity in Guatemala)
COCODE	Consejos Comunitarios de Desarrollo (Community Development Councils)
DACA	Deferred Action for Childhood Arrivals
DHS	U.S. Department of Homeland Security
ICE	U.S. Immigration and Customs Enforcement
IIRIRA	Illegal Immigration Reform and Immigrant Responsibility Act
INM	Instituto Nacional de Migración (National Migration Institute)
INS	U.S. Immigration and Naturalization Services (legacy)

IOM	International Organization for Migration
NGO	Nongovernmental organization
ORR	Office of Refugee Resettlement
PFS	Programa Frontera Sur (Southern Border Program)
PGN	Procuraduría General de la Nación (Office of the Inspector General)
SBS	Secretaría de Bienestar Social (Secretariat of Social Welfare)
TVPRA	Trafficking Victims Protection Reauthorization Act
UNHCR	United Nations High Commissioner for Refugees
UNICEF	United Nations International Children's Emergency Fund
URNG	Unidad Revolucionaria Nacional Guatemalteca (Guatemalan National Revolutionary Unit)
USAID	U.S. Agency for International Development

Migranthood

INTRODUCTION

IN 2014, the public was caught off guard by a "humanitarian crisis" when nearly 70,000 unaccompanied children arrived at the southern U.S. border from Honduras, El Salvador, and Guatemala. The U.S. federal government scrambled to respond by hurriedly opening temporary processing centers on military bases along the U.S.-Mexico border and readying dozens of facilities for unaccompanied minors and migrant families.[1] Juan Gabriel was one of these youths. Community members from his hometown of Sipacapa who denounced the violence inflicted by security forces protecting the Canadian Marlin mine were found beaten or were killed under seemingly mysterious circumstances. "The police harassed us when we spoke up," Juan Gabriel explained. "There was no way out, no way to be safe or get help." Recognizing few ways to escape the physical and environmental consequences of the mine, Juan Gabriel migrated to the United States with his twenty-eight-year-old cousin. Upon arrival, U.S. Customs and Border Protection (CBP) apprehended Juan Gabriel, separated him from his cousin, and classified him as an unaccompanied minor.

Most migrants like Juan Gabriel hoped to be granted asylum, which, like refugee status, protects those who have a reasonable fear of persecution in their home countries. But the Obama administration maintained that young

Central Americans were economic migrants, not refugees, and requested $3.7 billion in emergency appropriations and additional discretionary powers to ensure the "faster repatriation" of children to their countries of origin. This included implementing "rocket dockets" to expedite their processing and deportation.[2] Advocates decried that these rapid deportation procedures violated international human rights law and disregarded the specialized protections provided to unaccompanied children under the U.S. Trafficking Victims Protection Reauthorization Act (TVPRA) of 2008.[3] Denouncements of these expedited procedures continue today under the Donald Trump administration.

Attorneys were thrown into overdrive. Newly established rocket dockets for children and families forced lawyers to prepare legal petitions for asylum within two weeks, a process that previously took at least one year. If they were lucky enough to receive a visit from voluntary legal organizations while in detention, unaccompanied children were expected to share their traumatic experiences in their first meeting with a paralegal; parents in family detention facilities were expected to divulge the reasons for migration in the presence of their young children. A volunteer attorney, Sara, traveled from Chicago to the Artesia Family Residential Center located in rural New Mexico, a private, for-profit facility nearly three hours from the nearest major airport. Following her visits with women and children at Artesia, Sara shared:

> It is an impossible scenario. I have to interview a woman who has been gang-raped by police, forcing her to disclose every detail she can remember in order to quickly assemble a viable legal claim for asylum. But the facility won't let her leave her children in someone else's care, so we are in a tiny trailer with her two kids playing at her feet. She is bawling and doesn't want to talk about her experiences, not to mention in front of her children. It goes against every impulse I have as a human and as a mother, and it defies my training as a lawyer.

Attorneys and paralegals around the country traveled to often remote facilities along the U.S.-Mexico border where children and families were and continue to be held in what legal advocates call "family detention camps" and "baby jails." Sara's experiences interviewing women and children in these facilities reveal the brutality of immigration detention and the broader U.S. deportation regime that coerce migrants and their advocates to comply with convoluted, violent, bureaucratic processes and compel their advocates to contort migrants' experiences into increasingly narrow forms of legal relief.

Juan Gabriel was initially detained alongside adults for seventy-two hours in a U.S. Border Patrol *hielera* (icebox), a holding cell known among migrants for its frigid temperatures. He was later transferred to a converted military hangar in Texas that held thousands of unaccompanied minors. He never was asked about the reasons for his migration, nor his fears should he be returned. He never met with an attorney nor received an audience before an immigration judge. He was not transferred to the Office of Refugee Resettlement (ORR), which has maintained legal purview over the detention of unaccompanied minors since 2003. Instead, he was deported to Guatemala six weeks later.

Pundits and policymakers largely attributed the influx of young migrants to an increase in gang violence, child abuse, and deepening poverty in Honduras, El Salvador, and Guatemala. Others speculated that migrating children expected to receive *permiso* (permission) to enter the United States, spurring their arrival in such high numbers. Like the Obama administration, most policymakers dismissed and continue to dismiss children as migrants in search of economic opportunities, rather than view them as refugees fleeing violence and instability. If popular accounts of young migrants' motives are distorted, so too are the depictions of their character and behavior upon arrival in the United States. Conservative media outlets engaged in flagrant fearmongering, depicting young migrants as gangbangers, delinquents, and disease carriers who threatened the U.S. homeland.[4] Parents of young migrants did not fare any better. On both sides of the political divide, narratives of naive, undevoted, uneducated, and often predatory parents thrusting their children into the hands of violent smugglers seeped into public discourse and public policy.

These discourses are not new, and disturbingly, they have not dissipated over time.[5] In the United States, unaccompanied children have long been cast either as *victims* deserving of care and services or as unauthorized *outlaws* subject to state discipline via detention and deportation.[6] These characterizations have only deepened under the Trump administration. In 2018, claiming a "crisis at the U.S. border," then U.S. Attorney General Jeff Sessions enacted a "zero-tolerance" policy, which ramped up criminal prosecutions for the unauthorized entry of migrants while forcibly removing children from their undocumented parents. In effect, the Trump administration rendered over 4,200 children "unaccompanied." Under past administrations and contrary to U.S. law, CBP and Immigration and Customs Enforcement (ICE) have separated migrant children from their parents. The scale in 2018, however, was unprecedented, with nearly 2,500 children placed in the Tornillo detention camp in Texas, adding to the already 49,100 children held in ORR facilities throughout the United States. While accelerating and intensifying anti-immigrant policies, the Trump administration's approach to migrating children is consistent with a long line of U.S. administrations that have treated unaccompanied minors as threats requiring containment and removal.

Notably absent from both the 2014 and the 2018 "crises" were discussions of the role of U.S. policy in destabilizing Central America. U.S. interventions in Central American armed conflicts since the 1960s actively have undermined democratically elected presidents in a quest to suppress the spread of communism and to advance American business interests in the region. Not discussed were the ways unequal multinational trade agreements such as the Dominican Republic–Central America Free Trade Agreement (CAFTA-DR) have deepened social inequality, making everyday survival of families like Leticia's, Juan Gabriel's, and Manuel's increasingly precarious. Also dismissed were analyses of how multinational extractive industries have invaded Central America, displacing primarily Indigenous communities and contaminating the land of predominantly agrarian nations. Instead, U.S. policymakers continue to prioritize securitization policies and programs within the United States and increasingly through Mexico by means of walls, technology, and military might rather than meaningful and systemic investment in social and economic programs in Central America. This remains U.S. foreign policy strategy, despite recognized research that these approaches produce transnational organized crime, enhance government corruption, and as a consequence, create increasingly costly and perilous journeys for migrants.

Historically, U.S. refugee and asylum policies have systematically discriminated against Central Americans. Today, even with recognition from the U.S. courts of these discriminatory practices, petitions for asylum by Central Americans are rarely approved. Attempts to limit asylum petitions on the basis of forced gang conscription, domestic violence, or gender identity have only narrowed the few avenues for securing legal protections in the United States. In addition, decades-long delays in family reunification petitions for Central

Americans who lawfully reside in the United States merely decrease children's options for reuniting with their parents. While people are often reduced to simplified understandings of migranthood—or how migration is socially constructed, practiced, and experienced—there is minimal acknowledgment of the role of the United States in producing it. Although much of the responsibility lies with the U.S. government and its policies, Central American governments likewise are complicit in inflicting violence on their citizenry through corruption, racism, and marginalization of Indigenous peoples, and by denying the most basic rights vital to leading a dignified life. Taken together, the migration of young Central Americans should come as no surprise. It is a policy-made crisis long in the making.

UNACCOMPANIED BUT NOT ALONE

Under U.S. legal code, an unaccompanied minor is an individual under the age of eighteen who has no lawful immigration status in the United States and who is not in the company of a parent or legal guardian who can provide care and custody. The Central American and Mexican governments have adopted similar definitions for "*niños y niñas no acompañados*" (unaccompanied children). The term itself garners social panic, as a child crossing international borders *alone* shocks collective sensibilities and provokes moral outrage. It likewise unsettles culturally held notions about the proper place for children—on playgrounds, in schools, with family, and dependent upon adults to provide and care for them. A child crossing international borders, unaccompanied by an adult, marks a child as "out of place" and devoid of a "good" or "proper" childhood.

Just as childhood is socially constructed, society shapes the discourses about people who migrate and the meanings of migranthood. In the United States, discourses of migranthood presume people migrate primarily from "underdeveloped" countries to "advanced" economies or "more-developed" nations in search of a better life. Understood as an individual choice, migration is largely divorced from the structural and historical forces that spur it. For children in particular, migranthood is considered abnormal; their movement is held as a disruption to their development and as a loss of their childhood. Migranthood additionally exists at the lived interstices of global discourses on race, gender, class, and of global ideologies of childhood and parenthood that are created and re-created through social structures and institutions. Embedded in policy, practice, and everyday life, migranthood is so ubiquitous that it is rarely interrogated or challenged. Yet, discourses of migranthood circulating in the law, media, and humanitarian interventions fail to consider how young people assign meaning to their migranthood, or to their lives beyond their experiences of migration. That these meanings shift over time, space, and cultures is largely ignored. As this book traces, migranthood among Indigenous peoples in present-day Guatemala is shaped by a long and ongoing history of violence, displacement and marginalization that continues to influence the ways children are socialized into migration and their sense of self, belonging, and future aspirations. In other words, just like childhood, migranthood must be understood contextually in relation to the values, beliefs, behaviors and social norms within communities and nations.

Take, for example, the term "unaccompanied child." Despite depictions by the media and nongovernmental organizations (NGOs) of the tender age of migrants, 88 percent of unaccompanied children are over thirteen years old,[7] and the average age is fourteen and a half. In the social context of many communities in Central America, this age firmly situates young people either in or entering into adulthood. Among Indigenous communities in Guatemala, these are youths with substantial social and financial responsibilities and who are often starting their own families and establishing their households. At sixteen years old, Leticia cares for her siblings, tends to the family home, sells produce at the local market, and earns piecemeal by sewing buttons on school uniforms. Her unpaid care work and her paid labor are critical to her family's well-being. Her astute awareness of her family's social and financial precarity informs household decisions about how and under what conditions she would migrate. Philosopher Judith Butler defines *precarity* as "the politically induced condition in which certain populations suffer from failing social and economic networks . . . becoming differentially exposed to injury, violence, and death."[8] For Butler, precarity disproportionately impacts the marginalized, poor, and disenfranchised like Leticia and her family who are exposed to economic insecurity, structural and interpersonal violence, and displacement. Migrant youth are critical contributors to the survival of their multigenerational households—as caregivers, social brokers, financial providers, and migrants. Their experiences reveal the enduring effects of deportation not only on their sense of identity and belonging but also on the survival of their households amid politically induced precarity. In an international context, however, cultural understandings that young people are coproviders clash with U.S. policies and practices predicated on middle-class norms of children being dependent upon adults and childhood exclusively as a space of play and schooling.[9]

And many children classified as unaccompanied minors may not be unaccompanied at all. Of the children whom I have encountered, the vast majority were *accompanied* by customary care providers—extended family, family friends, or community members—or *entrusted* to "facilitators" (smugglers) throughout the duration of their journeys. Juan Gabriel traveled with his older cousin, Leticia migrated with two friends, and Manuel migrated with two paternal cousins and a well-regarded store owner in the community who served as his smuggler. Young people are neither alone nor shorn of kinship ties as the term "unaccompanied" suggests; they are important members of expanded social and familial networks that, in many instances, facilitate their migration and adaptation over time and geographic space. This does not discount the considerable vulnerabilities that young migrants confront on their dangerous journeys or their need for legal and social protections; rather, it serves as a reminder that unaccompanied children are rarely "on their own," "unattached," or "abandoned" by "bad parents." They are children, siblings, cousins, partners, friends, and community members. In contrast to simplified and often-universalized depictions of migrant children as either victims or delinquents, their migranthood is infused with social meaning and in relationship to others.

Public discourse and migration literature largely depict unaccompanied children as recent arrivals or "newcomers." However, as young people in this book attest, their experiences and trajectories are far more diverse. Some remain in the United States only temporarily, while others have resided outside of their countries of birth for over a decade and are beneficiaries of President Obama's 2012 executive order, Deferred Action for Childhood Arrivals (DACA). Thus, the juridical category of "unaccompanied child" masks considerable variations in young people's experiences of migration, settlement, detention, and forced return.[10]

The activism of DREAMers/DACAmented youth[11] has garnered considerable attention—namely through youths' enactment of cultural belonging and civic engagement amid deportability[12]—yet other immigrant-origin youth remain peripheral to these processes, largely owing to differences in legal status, age, and contexts of reception, social capital, educational trajectories,[13] and as I argue, Indigenous identity. Through "no fault of their own," DREAMers/

DACAmented youth are widely identified as "ideal victims," a term that criminologist Nils Christie defines as "a person or category of individuals who—when hit by crime—most readily are given the complete and legitimate status of being a victim."[14] Indeed, public opinion polls consistently demonstrate broad and growing support for DREAMers/DACAmented youth across the U.S. political spectrum. In contrast, undocumented, unaccompanied youth are distinguished from their counterparts raised in the United States, instead identified as threats or invaders of the homeland or as economic migrants—categories that are often reserved for adult migrants. This book accordingly considers the sociopolitical implications of expanding *some* young im/migrants' opportunities for legal and socioeconomic incorporation while neglecting or foreclosing those of others.

Since the influx of children from Central America to the United States in 2014, scholars have turned their attention to unaccompanied child migration.[15] Several researchers have analyzed institutions caring for children[16] and the legal systems that seek their removal.[17] Because immigration detention for unaccompanied youth in the United States is highly restrictive and, with a few exceptions,[18] nearly impossible for researchers to access, scholars often rely on NGOs and legal service providers to identify young migrants. As a consequence, the limited but growing scholarship on unaccompanied child migration tends to focus on youth who, following release, have viable legal claims such as asylum, as victims of trafficking (T-visas) or crime (U-visas), or as special immigrant juveniles (SIJ visas) who have been abused, abandoned, or neglected, and on young people who remain in countries of destination.[19] This has unwittingly reified the "unaccompanied child" as a category of analysis while simultaneously privileging those who arrive and seek legal status in the United States over those who never arrive, evade apprehension, or are removed from the country. By focusing on young people following their deportation from Mexico and the United States, experiences often overlooked or undervalued, *Migranthood* seeks to destabilize the category of "unaccompanied child" through young people's diverse and multifaceted experiences, trajectories, and outcomes.[20] This complexity and variation likewise illustrates how migranthood is not a fixed, singular, or even inevitable condition. Rather, laws, policies, and at times research work in tandem to construct, reinforce, and pathologize migration.

By negating this heterogeneity of experience, the category of unaccompanied child is inherently nation-state–centric. It reduces young people's experiences into a classification that is legible only to those in power—Border Patrol which apprehends them; lawyers who represent them; or policymakers who seek to protect or remove them—thereby rendering young people voiceless and agentless. The irony remains: even as they are recognized by state authorities as unaccompanied children, young people simultaneously are dismissed as economic actors rather than refugees, ignoring histories of inequality, violence, and discrimination that do not easily fit into the few forms of legal relief that immigration law has designated available to them. By interrogating the category of "unaccompanied child" with the diverse physical, psychological, relational, and existential experiences of young people on the move, we may begin to recognize that young people are social actors and that their complex lives and diverse perspectives matter beyond the migranthood ascribed to them. Or, as Leticia aptly synthesized, "I am more than a migrant. I am more than my migration."

A DISPROPORTIONATE IMPACT

The scale of child migration from Central America is difficult to assess, even more so of Indigenous youth. In 2003, the U.S. government began to centralize data on the numbers of unaccompanied children apprehended in the United States each year; Guatemalan authorities began to consistently record statistics on child migration only in 2008. The absence of statistics across the region is emblematic of the ways children historically have been overlooked in migration studies and public policy—either considered as miniature adults, folded into family migration statistics, or not counted at all. The limited data on child migration now available reveal that child migration from Central America is on the rise. From fiscal year 2010 to 2019, the number of primarily Central American and Mexican unaccompanied migrant children apprehended by the Border Patrol nearly quadrupled, increasing from 18,168 to 76,020 children.[21] (See Table 1.) By 2019, Guatemalans comprised 40 percent of all unaccompanied children apprehended in the United States.

There has been an even more exponential growth in the number of nuclear family units migrating from Central America to the United States, increasing from 15,056 individuals in families apprehended in 2013 to 473,682 in 2019.[22] While data that distinguish children from adults within these family units are not publicly available, CBP has indicated that, of the 75,802 individuals migrating as family units in 2017, 54 percent were minors.[23] Once again, Guatemalan families comprise 40 percent of all family units apprehended in the United States.[24] (See Table 2.)

Both the Obama and Trump administrations have claimed that the migration of Central Americans has slowed considerably since 2014. Indeed, the number of unaccompanied children apprehended at the U.S.-Mexico border plummeted by 58 percent in 2015 and again in 2017.[25] The Obama administration largely attributed the apparent decline to an influx of development aid to the Central American region through the Alliance for Prosperity Plan (APP), the centerpiece of U.S. foreign policy toward Central America, which claims to create conditions that would allow people to remain in their countries of origin. Believing the "humanitarian crisis at the border" had passed, by 2016, humanitarian organizations consolidated or closed their programs and international aid began to dry up. The media and the public likewise moved on. Alternatively, the Trump administration attributed the apparent 2017 decrease in child migration to enhanced border enforcement and Trump's virulent anti-immigrant rhetoric. Despite claims to the contrary, the numbers of children migrating have not fallen; in fact, they are rising. But children do not always arrive at the U.S. border.

With the initiation of the Programa Frontera Sur (PFS, Southern Border Program) in 2014, a U.S.-funded securitization effort to enhance Mexican immigration enforcement, the number of children deported from the United States decreased temporarily while the number of children interdicted in and deported from Mexico skyrocketed. Data from Mexico's Instituto Nacional de Migración (INM, National Migration Institute) reveal that the number of children (accompanied and unaccompanied) deported from Mexico rose from 5,966 in 2012 to 38,514 in 2016.[26] (See Table 3.) These statistics are indicative of larger trends in which deportations of individuals (adults and children alike) by Mexican authorities increased from 79,643 in 2012 to 181,163 at its peak in 2015—a 227 percent increase.[27] Like U.S. statistics, however, Mexican data have limitations. Both U.S. and Mexican data sets reflect only children apprehended by state authorities, not those who evaded apprehension or were released without official processing. Mexican authorities do not maintain statistics on family units. In spite of these limitations, when taken together, the

TABLE 1: Unaccompanied Children Encountered in the U.S., by Fiscal Year (2009–2019)*

Country	FY2009	FY2010	FY2011	FY2012	FY2013	FY2014	FY2015	FY2017	FY2018	FY2019
El Salvador	1,221	1,910	1,394	3,314	5,990	16,404	9,389	9,143	4,949	12,021
Guatemala	1,115	1,517	1,565	3,835	8,068	17,057	13,589	14,827	22,327	30,329
Honduras	968	1,017	974	2,997	6,747	18,244	5,409	7,784	10,913	20,398
Mexico	16,114	13,724	11,768	13,974	17,240	15,634	11,012	8,877	10,136	10,487
Other	—	454	366	361	788	1,292	636	915	1,711	2,785
Total	19,418	18,622	16,067	24,481	38,833	68,631	40,035	41,546	50,036	76,020

* https://www.cbp.gov/newsroom/stats/usbp-sw-border-apprehensions

TABLE 2: Individuals in Family Units Encountered in the U.S. by Fiscal Year (2013–2019)*

Country	FY2012	FY2013	FY2014	FY2015	FY2016	FY2017	FY2018	FY2019
El Salvador	636	1,883	14,883	10,872	27,114	24,122	13,669	58,897
Guatemala	340	996	12,006	12,813	23,067	24,657	50,401	185,233
Honduras	513	3,902	34,495	10,671	20,226	22,366	39,439	188,416
Mexico	8,844	7,356	5,639	4,276	3,481	2,217	2,261	6,004
Other	—	919	1,711	1,421	3,969	2, 397	1,142	35,132
Total	10,333	15,056	68,684	40,053	77,857	75,802	107,212	473,682

* https://www.cbp.gov/sites/default/files/assets/documents/2019-Mar/bp-total-monthly-family-units-sector
-fy13-fy18.pdf *and* https://www.cbp.gov/newsroom/stats/usbp-sw-border-apprehensions

total number of children apprehended in the United States and Mexico in 2018
surpasses 2014 "crisis" levels. With the Trump administration's 2019 efforts to
repeal specialized protections for unaccompanied minors under the 1996 Flores
Settlement Agreement and the 2008 bipartisan legislation of the TVPRA, the
number of deported children will continue to rise.[28]

This is not the first time the United States has enlisted mass deportation
as state policy. The first deportation law was enacted in the Alien Act of 1798,
which allowed for the removal of any undocumented person who was determined to be "dangerous." The 1882 Chinese Exclusion Act suspended the immigration of Chinese laborers for ten years and prohibited the naturalization
of Chinese in the United States, among other restrictive measures. The 1892
Act to Prohibit the Coming of Chinese Persons into the United States, also
known as the Geary Act, required Chinese immigrants to register with federal
authorities and secure a certificate of their right to be in the United States or
face imprisonment and deportation. In effect, the Geary Act invented the first
national system of mass deportation.

Historian Kelly Lytle Hernández traces how Operation Wetback of 1954
subsequently resulted in the mass deportation of nearly 300,000 Mexican nationals. In contrast to popular claims that this was the single largest deportation
campaign in U.S. history, Lytle Hernandez contends that Operation Wetback
was actually an attempt to crack down on agricultural employers who sought
to resist the Bracero Program, a bilateral agreement between the United States
and Mexico that from 1942 to 1964 allowed for nearly 4.6 million Mexicans to
work on short-term contracts. Employers resisted, preferring unregulated and
inexpensive labor over the labor protections and minimum wage stipulated by
the program. In South Texas, ranchers and farmers took up arms against the
Border Patrol when it came to apprehend undocumented workers. In its crackdown on employers rather than migrants, the Border Patrol undertook raids of
farms, restaurants, and Mexican communities in an effort to pressure ranchers
and farmers into compliance. By the summer of 1954, the Border Patrol and
South Texas employers entered into an agreement to lessen the number of immigration raids in exchange for watered-down protections for workers. Thus,
when the Trump administration bans individuals on the basis of nationality,
conducts large-scale raids, detains immigrants in tent camps, bypasses international refugee protections, and threatens to deport immigrants en masse,

TABLE 3: Children Returned from Mexico, by Calendar Year (2012–2018)*

Country	2012	2013	2014	2015	2016	2017	2018
El Salvador	1,280	1,703	4,885	7,838	9,759	2,622	2,503
Guatemala	2,393	3,012	7,973	19,437	16,715	9,258	12,191
Honduras	2,169	3,686	9,661	10,165	11,464	5,411	10,994
United States	60	37	153	239	167	254	95
Other	64	139	424	835	2,009	521	182
Total	5,966	8,577	23,096	38,514	40,114	18,066	25,965

* http://portales.segob.gob.mx/es/PoliticaMigratoria/Boletines_Estadisticos. Extranjeros presentados y devueltos: 3.2.8 (Eventos de retorno asistido de menores según continente, país de nacionalidad, grupos de edad, condición de viaje y sexo).

TABLE 4: Individuals Returned from Mexico, by Calendar Year (2012–2018)*

Country	2012	2013	2014	2015	2016	2017	2018
El Salvador	12,725	14,586	19,800	34,716	33,384	12,074	12,003
Guatemala	35,137	30,231	42,808	82,597	62,299	36,337	44,254
Honduras	29,166	33,079	41,661	57,823	53,857	31,249	51,562
United States	667	722	953	2,282	132	2,281	1618
Other	1,948	2,284	2,592	3,745	10,200	11,905	2,880
Total	79,643	80,902	107,814	181,163	159,872	93,846	112,317

* http://portales.segob.gob.mx/es/PoliticaMigratoria/Boletines_Estadisticos. Extranjeros presentados y devueltos: Table 3.2.2 (Eventos de extranjeros devueltos por la autoridad migratoria mexicana, según grupos de edad, sexo y condición de viaje).

it is building upon a robust architecture of immigration enforcement that is, according to Lytle Hernández, "one of the least constitutional and most racist realms of governance in U.S. law and life."[29] To date, analysis of this institutionalized racism, however, has largely overlooked discussions of indigeneity.

Although the countries of El Salvador, Guatemala, and Honduras are often homogenized, the levels of migration and deportation of children are not experienced uniformly across the region nor within individual countries. As borne out in the abovementioned statistics, Guatemalan minors are consistently the largest group of young people entering Mexico and the United States; they are also disproportionately deported in comparison to their Honduran and Salvadoran counterparts.[30] Over the last decade, the number of Guatemalan children deported from the United States and Mexico has increased ninefold. Racialized as Latinxs in the United States and homogenized by policymakers, the Indigenous identity of Guatemalan youth remains largely obscured in discussions of Central American migration.

According to Guatemala's Secretaría de Bienestar Social (SBS, Secretariat of Social Welfare), 95 percent of returned minors aged birth to seventeen years old are Indigenous—primarily Mam and K'iche' children from rural communities in the departments of Quetzaltenango, San Marcos, Quiché, Huehuetenango, and Totonicapán.[31] By 2017, 66 percent of children deported to Guatemala were boys and nearly 34 percent were girls, a considerable shift in gender composition from four years prior, when just 18 percent of deported children were female. A Freedom of Information Act to CBP regarding the communities of origin of unaccompanied children over the decade 2007–2017 reveals that Guatemalan migrant minors originate from primarily Indigenous communities in the highlands and along the Mexican-Guatemalan borderlands, where historically there are shared Indigenous identities with the Maya in Southern Mexico. (See Figure 1 and Appendix 1.) Internal reports from SBS shared with me indicate that over 86 percent of deported children designate that poverty and the search for employment are the primary reasons for unaccompanied migration, while an additional 12 percent seek family reunification in the United States and 2 percent pursue travel or work in Mexico.[32] As young people I spoke with confirm, poverty rates and pursuit of employment mask far more complex understandings of the reasons for migration among Indigenous communities.

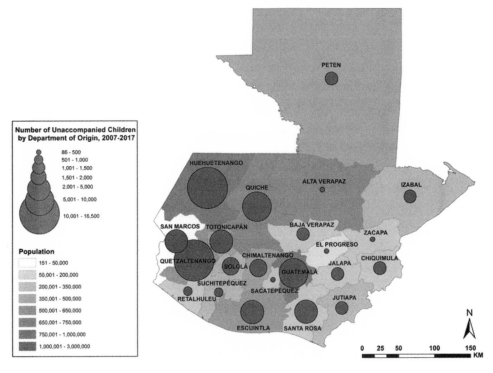

FIGURE 1. Unaccompanied Children Encountered in the U.S. by Guatemalan
Department of Origin, by Fiscal Year (2007–2017)

For the Maya of present-day Guatemala, migration is a survival strategy
rooted in intertwining histories of land ownership, violence, and debt. Migration in the region developed during the colonial era and escalated during the
armed conflict (1960–1996) that killed or disappeared over 200,000 people,
internally displaced one million people, and spurred over 200,000 people to
flee the country (with 46,000 registering with the U.N. High Commissioner
for Refugees in Mexico).[33] While migration in "postconflict" Guatemala is
largely characterized by labor migration to the Pacific coast of Guatemala, to
southern Mexico, and to the United States, legacies of colonialism and conflict
within Indigenous communities in the highlands of Guatemala continue to
shape collective imaginaries of migration as well as the capital resources available
to Indigenous families for daily survival.[34] As seasonal, regional, and transnational migrants, young people enlist migration as a collective and historically

rooted survival strategy that responds to their past experiences of violence and marginalization and to their present and future needs.

Discussions of indigeneity are critically important to understanding the ways colonial domination, neoliberal capitalism, and securitized approaches to migration management disproportionately impact Indigenous peoples over time. The erasure of indigeneity from discussions of migration is yet another form of racialized violence inflicted upon Indigenous communities, as it negates the discrimination and violence Indigenous people encounter in Central America as well as in zones of transit through Mexico, upon arrival in the United States, and following return. Discussions of the migration of Indigenous children are likewise critical to examining the relationship between international development that claims to create alternatives to migration which, as Juan Gabriel attests, is devastating Indigenous communities. Child migration—historically and in the contemporary moment—is an intergenerational necessity for the survival of Indigenous communities. By interrogating this migration, we likewise learn of the lasting and transnational reach of public policy—across geopolitical space and generations—on Indigenous peoples.

DEPORTATION AND THE SECURITY-DEVELOPMENT NEXUS

"Guatemala es país de origen, destino, tránsito y retorno" (Guatemala is a nation of origin, destination, transit, and return), explained the assistant director of the Casa del Migrante in Tecún Umán in 2015 as we sat in the courtyard of the shelter for transiting migrants. Three men leaned against the courtyard wall and two women sat on a blanket, sharing orange slices and attempting to hide in the limited shade of the July sun. With their backpacks and cellular phones, I initially mistook them for college-aged volunteers at the migrant shelter. "No, they are three Brazilians, a Colombian, and a Nicaraguan passing through. People from all over the world find themselves here in Guatemala. Some are coming; most are going; many are returned and trying again. People move in all directions. It's all connected; we're all connected," he reflected. The assistant director, a K'iche' man in his mid-forties, references *la cosmovisión del Pueblo Maya,* or Maya cosmovision, a system of values and beliefs in which the world, life, things, and time are interconnected. When these forces are in harmony, we experience true freedom, he later explained. This belief in interconnectivity

strongly influences my theoretical approach and methodological commitments to study child migration intergenerationally, relationally (to people, places, beliefs, and the environment), spatially, and conceptually.

Until recently, migration scholarship framed the process of migration as occurring in roughly three linear stages: premigration, involving the decision and preparations to move; migration, which is the physical movement of an individual from one place to another; and postmigration, which involves settlement in a new society.[35] Yet, as anthropologist Aiwha Ong reminds us, migration is a dynamic process, in which people circulate through time and space with great flexibility and uncertainty.[36] With the global expansion of detention and deportation as routine state practice, the linearity of premigration, migration, and postmigration settlement fails to reflect the multiplicity and variation of migration and the ways these circulations, and the policies that undergird them, are interconnected.

Take, for example, the postmigration stage. In their generative volume, *The Deportation Regime*, Nicholas De Genova and Nathalie Peutz productively expand state-based understandings of postmigration settlement by arguing that deportability—or the totalizing fear of deportation—is a "mode of being" shaping everyday movements.[37] Deportability creates a state of exception for unauthorized migrants in which abjectivity and illegality constrain the everyday lives of individuals in the postmigration stage.[38] From accessing health care[39] and public benefits for citizen children[40] to pursuing legal protections from community and intrafamilial violence, remediation from workplace abuses,[41] and school attendance,[42] fear of removal has a totalizing effect on the lives of adults and young people alike. To the extent that the literature focuses on children, it reveals how the state inflicts trauma upon U.S. citizen children of undocumented parents through community surveillance, immigration raids, and parental deportation.[43] Children may experience sudden parental removal and indeterminate absence as a trauma akin to premature parental death, with heightened symptomatology of nightmares, flashbacks, depression, anxiety, and at times, suicidality.[44] The loss of a care provider and/or head of household may additionally deepen poverty and result in homelessness in the short term and adversely impact a child's health and well-being over the long term. Given that nearly 16.6 million people live in mixed-status families in the United States, postmigration research is critically important to understanding the far-reaching consequences of state-inflicted trauma via deportation and forced familial separations.[45]

An emerging subset of literature attempts to expand the postdeportation stage of migration by examining the uncertainty and insecurity that deportation generates over time.[46] Focusing primarily on adults, scholars have documented how forced return may shift gender roles,[47] intergenerational relationships,[48] cultural modes of belonging,[49] and political engagement. Over time, tensions and divisions may emerge, communication may become stunted, and familial power dynamics may shift. Some families collapse under the stress of social stigma, loss of reputation, the social dimensions of trauma, and financial ruin. These studies underscore how the full force of the state inflicts violence upon individual migrants and how this state violence is experienced across borders.

Although in a new "era of mass deportations"[50] in which there is a generalized "normalcy of deportation,"[51] considerably less attention has been given to the outcomes of deportees *over time,* particularly to the experiences of young people who are subject to deportation. Indeed, among immigration attorneys representing unaccompanied children, deportation constitutes a "black hole where unaccompanied children easily fall through the cracks."[52] Yet, deportation is not an isolated event, nor does it mark the end of the story. For many youths, remigration—either of themselves or of a family member—becomes the only viable coping strategy to navigate the oppressive conditions resulting from deportation.[53] In other words, deportation is not a singular act or stage of migration along a linear trajectory, as postdeportation suggests; it is an ongoing, multidirectional process—one that begins with the reasons why a young person migrates and extends well beyond their physical return.[54] Examining the motivations for migration, the experiences of deportation, and the rationales for remigration as interrelated processes, instead of as a series of discrete, unidirectional stages, allows us to understand young people's ongoing mobility across social, economic, political, and geographic space. It likewise allows us to recognize the interconnected and scaled effects of deportation over time from the intimate and interpersonal to the communal, national, and regional to the global and structural.

The study of deportation and its long-term impacts reveals the consequences of an increasingly securitized approach to both migration management and development. Underpinning much of contemporary migration management strategies are claims that migration is a security issue, and in so doing, migration is pathologized—framed as harming individuals, particularly children;

damaging economies in countries of origin *and* destination; posing threats to public safety; and eroding social and cultural values. Within such framings, deterrence and containment present as logical responses. These logics are woven into public policy and institutional practices across nation-states. Since the presidency of Ronald Reagan, the United States has enlisted the Mexican state to thwart through-migration from countries to its south, expanding the U.S. deportation dragnet across geopolitical borders. Regional initiatives such as the Mérida Initiative (initiated in 2007), the Southern Border Program (Programa Frontera Sur, initiated in 2014), and the Alliance for Prosperity Plan (Plan de la Alianza para la Prosperidad, initiated in 2015), among others, each purport to enhance economic development, strengthen institutions, fight corruption, and create alternatives to migration.

To illustrate the increasingly securitized approaches to migration, we must look only to commonly utilized language among lawmakers, advocates, and even researchers—a "surge" of unaccompanied children from the "Northern Triangle"—to characterize the movement of Central American children and youth. In recent history, the U.S. military enlisted the term "surge" to characterize major deployments of military forces during both the Iraq War in 2007 under George W. Bush and the war in Afghanistan in 2009 and in 2016 and 2017 under the administrations of Barack Obama and Donald Trump, respectively. Enlisting the same terminology reduces the mobility of Central American youth to an allegedly sudden yet strategic movement of individuals from a U.S. military zone—the "Northern Triangle." This terminology strips children of the essential social and kinship ties necessary to move across vast distances and under dangerous conditions, negates their paid and unpaid care work enacted to support themselves and their families, and ignores the meanings they assign to their migration. Notably, young migrants do *not* describe their lives, social networks, home countries, or reasons for mobility with these terms. Nor should we.

As unaccompanied children garnered considerable public attention since 2014, so too they have become the objects of development discourse and humanitarian intervention. In examining the policies and practices designed for deported youth, *Migranthood* grapples with the relationship between securitization and development by tracing the experiences of Indigenous youth who are the subjects of these interventions. Analysis at the intersection of public discourse, policy analysis, institutional practices, and the experiences of young migrants sheds light on the intended and unintended, immediate and persistent, everyday and systemic impacts of securitized development on young migrants, their families, and their communities. As the narratives of Indigenous Guatemalan youth and their families illuminate, the continued privileging of security over social, political, and economic conditions spurs rather than deters migration not just today but also of future generations. In the process, these national, regional, and foreign policies exacerbate entrenched structural violence and deepen the everyday precarity families must navigate with ever-fewer resources available to them. By interrogating how violence is produced and practiced across borders alongside how young people navigate this violence, *Migranthood* seeks to complicate linear conceptualizations of migratory stages and to compel us to rethink our current understandings of why children are on the move.

ENTERING THE FIELD

In 2013, when I began research with young Guatemalans deported from the United States and Mexico, few people were familiar with the subject of unaccompanied children, and even fewer with what happens to them following return. My prior research (2006–2010) examined the contradictory conceptualizations of care between the U.S. Office of Refugee Resettlement; federally subcontracted, NGO-run facilities for unaccompanied minors; and young people themselves. I traced the ways that NGOs became part of the immigration industrial complex through everyday surveillance in facilities, restricting information, bureaucratizing care, and assessing the suitability of family relationships.[55] I routinely observed how the scarce resources available to unaccompanied children were directed to those identified as having prospects for legal status in the United States. For those whose experiences did not easily fit into the few forms of legal relief available to children—asylum, trafficking visas, special immigrant juvenile visas, or as victims of crime—and whose families were unable or unwilling to sponsor their children from federal custody, young people confronted prolonged detention and near-certain removal. Of these individuals, Guatemalans were and continue to be the largest group of young people deported from ORR facilities. In my hundreds of interviews with attorneys, social workers, and guardians ad litem across the United States during and since that research, few knew what happened to children following removal to countries of origin. Enlisting community and professional contacts from my previous work with the Guatemalan community in Chicago and in the highlands of Guatemala, I endeavored to find out.

I began spending several months per year in Guatemala City and in the departments of San Marcos, Quetzaltenango, Sololá, and Totonicapán, meeting with NGOs, government officials, activists, community groups, and young people and their families. A researcher in Guatemala is ubiquitous. Guatemalans are well-accustomed to foreign researchers studying cultural practices of Guatemala's twenty-three Maya and two non-Maya Indigenous groups and to forensic anthropologists exhuming mass graves to uncover the atrocities of the armed conflict and its aftermath. Proud of their efforts to welcome deportees, a representative from the Ministerio de Relaciones Exteriores (Ministry of Foreign Affairs) whom I interviewed invited me to observe how deportees arrived at Guatemala City's Air Force base. In 2013, only a handful of unaccompanied minors were returned by air on deportation flights from the United States to Guatemala City's military base or via commercial flights from northern Mexico to Guatemala's La Aurora international airport. One weekly bus returned from Mexico to the city of Quetzaltenango (known as Xela, the capital of the department of Quetzaltenango), with an average of forty-five unaccompanied children on board. By 2014, this would change dramatically. Once weekly buses began to arrive daily, sometimes three times per day, deporting children en masse from Mexico. Deportation flights from the United States and northern Mexico also arrived daily, sometimes multiple flights per day. From 2013 to 2015, I observed how deportees deplaned from seventeen different U.S. Department of Homeland Security (DHS) chartered flights, the orientation that adults and children received, and how Guatemalan authorities administratively processed them. The Ministry of Foreign Affairs and the Procuraduría General de la Nación (PGN, Office of the Inspector General) allowed me to interview staff involved in these procedures. My ongoing presence over multiple years allowed me to witness how Guatemalan institutions struggled to receive a growing number of deportees. These shifts likewise necessitated that I innovate research methods in response to a rapidly changing political and policy landscape.

Across several weeks each year, the Director of SBS allowed me to observe their two government facilities—one in Guatemala City and one in the department of Quetzaltenango—as facility staff interviewed and attended to unaccompanied children. I interacted with children, playing foosball and cards or drinking tea as they waited for their parents to arrive. I spent days sitting in the waiting areas of SBS facilities with parents as they anticipated emotional reunions, at times after prolonged separations. In meeting rooms, I also witnessed the discriminatory treatment parents and young people received by government officials who rebuked parents for "sending" their children into harm's way, blamed them for their poverty, and shamed adults and children alike as *"indios maleducados"* (bad-mannered Indians) and *"gente atrasada"* (backward people). My stomach churned at the dehumanizing, racist treatment they confronted and continue to confront in their everyday interactions with state officials and "helping" professionals.

In addition to the dozens of children and families I encountered at SBS facilities, fifty deported youths shared their experiences with me over three of my five years of fieldwork. I met eight of these young people in U.S. detention facilities or following release and deportation to Guatemala, twenty-nine in SBS facilities following deportation from the United States or Mexico, and thirteen through personal or professional contacts and snowball sampling. All of them had been deported as unaccompanied minors from the United States or Mexico, often multiple times. Based primarily in the departments of Quetzaltenango, San Marcos, Sololá, and Totonicapán from where the majority of young Guatemalan migrants originate, I conducted participant observations among these young people (fourteen girls and thirty-six boys) and their families during mealtimes, at family and community gatherings, and at school or work, typically for multiday visits and at least twice per year. Conversations were primarily conducted in Spanish with the occasional use of a Mam or K'iche' interpreter.

Given the unique and diverse experiences of youths, my research methods were necessarily responsive to their individualized contexts. Accordingly, the depth and length of my visits varied depending on the time of year and the household circumstances, as I was always cognizant not to overstay my welcome. Their experiences unfolded over time and in fits and starts. Through casual conversations with young people, their families, and peers, I slowly pieced together demographic data, family histories, migration journeys; learned of cultural values and social norms; and deciphered intergenerational dynamics that at the outset were not apparent or readily accessible to an outsider. Several deported youths originated from the same communities and at times the same immediate or extended families. This longitudinal ethnographic fieldwork allowed me to trace the ongoing and sometimes tumultuous reintegration of deported children over time.

That I traveled on buses throughout the western highlands, often with my three young children in tow, was intriguing to many; that my children are mixed-race, even more so. While physically and emotionally taxing to solo-parent while conducting fieldwork, I found that the presence of and curiosity about my children unexpectedly helped to establish rapport and ease with me as a mother, first, and as a foreign, white anthropologist, second. Visibly marked as a mother opened possibilities for me to speak with parents about their own childhoods, childrearing practices, aspirations for their children's futures, and their often heart-wrenching decisions about their child's migration. Given my children's young ages (two, five, and seven years old at the start of my fieldwork), parents of teenagers imparted their wisdom to me about the shifting needs and demands of children as they age, sometimes shaming me for my own parenting practices such as not dressing them warmly enough. As a woman and a mother, these conversations created an intimacy with parents that I might not have otherwise experienced. It likewise created opportunities to speak with women and girls about their gendered experiences of migration and return.

My children's energy levels spontaneously inspired the method of walking ethnography as an opportunity to engage with migrant youth. When I visited young people in their communities, they would guide me and my children around town, pointing out their places of work, schools, local markets, and hangouts. This walking ethnography allowed me to grasp how young people circulate through and embody space and how they engage in social life within their communities.[56] It also provoked discussions of experiences in specific locations that likely would not have surfaced in everyday conversations or in more sedentary interviews. The intimacy nurtured by these strolls allowed for a level of confidence and confidentiality that was not possible in a bustling family courtyard under the gaze or within earshot of inquisitive family members and neighbors.

Through this multisited research, I grew accustomed to the logistical and methodological challenges of working with a mobile population of youth—of the endless hours on buses traversing Guatemala's expansive highlands to visit with young people and their families; of the ways young people fall in and out of communication with me over time; and of the possibilities and limitations of maintaining contact via email, cellular phones, Skype, WhatsApp, or Facebook. On multiple occasions, young people were physically difficult to locate. I would arrive at their homes only to find out they were harvesting sugarcane in plantations along the Pacific coast, working on coffee groves in southern Mexico, or laboring as domestic workers in Guatemala City or in Tapachula, Mexico. Some were en route to the United States once again. During each period of fieldwork, I would return time and again to households, speaking with family members even when youths or their siblings may have (re)migrated. Methodologically, my relationships with grandparents, parents, siblings, and extended family members proved essential to examining continuity and change over time, even if unable to physically connect with a young migrant. Ethically, focusing on the household rather than exclusively on an individual child or youth also mitigated the appearance of privileging one sibling (who migrated) over another (who remained in the country of origin), realities that I would learn routinely transpire in households following a youth's return and within development initiatives and humanitarian interventions. In so doing, I trace the enduring consequences of migration and removal and the ways removal shapes intimate, familial relationships in gendered and often age-specific ways.

I also conducted in-depth interviews with 253 stakeholders working with young migrants in Guatemala, Southern Mexico, and the United States, including government officials, embassy personnel, migration authorities, reception center staff, community leaders, NGO workers, attorneys, and researchers. These interviews were conducted in either Spanish or English and spanned from forty-five minutes to three hours. Formal interviews with the U.S. Department of State and with international organizations such as United Nations International Children's Emergency Fund (UNICEF), U.S. Agency for International Development (USAID), and the International Organization for Migration (IOM) revealed a sharp contrast between international policy responses to child migration and the experiences described by young migrants and their families. By moving across these diverse spaces and places, I sought to highlight the contradictions between policy and practice and between young people and those who claim to speak on their behalf.

Then, the "humanitarian crisis" of 2014 ensued. In the United States, public debates roared, and federal authorities and NGOs scrambled to attend to the "surge" of unaccompanied children. So, too, Guatemalan officials with PGN and SBS struggled to receive an increasing volume of deported children and to respond to the media mayhem. News reporters hounded parents for interviews as they arrived at SBS facilities. Photographers shoved cameras in children's faces as they were reunified with family. Young people's photos were splashed across local newspapers, international news media, and on the nightly news. In the summer of 2014 as I left the SBS facility in Xela, I was accosted by a Guatemala City–based radio broadcaster seeking an interview with anyone with access to the facility. Thrusting a microphone in my face, he asked, "What did you see? Why are they leaving? Is it the violence or are their parents abusing them?" Startled by the frenetic litany of questions, I ineloquently mumbled, "It's more complicated than that" and invited him to talk over coffee the following day. He never called.

The frenzy compelled me once again to recalibrate my research methods. I continued to visit youths and their families, but I no longer felt it ethical to conduct observations and interviews at the airport and in government facilities under the heightened and incessant gaze of government bureaucrats, foreign officials, and the international media. While I still visited on occasion and interacted with staff, in 2015 I stopped observing regularly at the Guatemala City Air Force base and in SBS facilities receiving deported youths. Instead, my focus shifted to mixed-method, community-based research. Through partnerships with Indigenous organizations, teachers, and older youth, I engaged youth as ethnographers of their own lives by enlisting video and photo elicitation in a local community center, facilitating workshops on migration and identity with a local organization, and initiating a collaborative oral history project with a local librarian. Through these participatory methods, I encountered an additional eighty-three Mam and K'iche' youths who had returned or been returned to Guatemala, 54 percent of whom had migrated unaccompanied by a parent or guardian, but rarely alone; five were U.S. citizen children who accompanied their parents to Guatemala following parental deportation. These methodological shifts allowed me to refine key themes and dynamics across a more diverse group of young migrants and to examine the ways they made sense of heightened media, policy, and humanitarian attention to child migration, as well as the ways young people embody and, at times, actively resist migranthood.

By 2016, the numbers of Guatemalan youth reaching the United States began to decline. The media moved on to the next "crisis," and development programs began to close. Yet the numbers of children deported from Mexico continued to rise, primarily due to increased funding from the Alliance for Prosperity Plan (APP), which supported enhanced immigration enforcement throughout Mexico. Until that time, my research had focused on government policies and practices and the experiences of individual young people and their families across multiple communities and government sites. Given the multi-sited nature of my research, I struggled to grasp the scale and enduring effects of deportation on communities. Part of the reason for the limited knowledge on these community-level impacts is at once methodological and logistical. Rarely are large groups deported at the same time to a single location. Methodologically, the dispersal of deportees often across vast geographic distances presents unique challenges to researchers tracing the scalar impacts of deportation on communities. The very feelings of isolation and stigma that a deportee endures—as one of only a few people deported to a single community—illustrate the logistical challenges and considerable financial costs of working with deportees across vast distances. There has been some important scholarship on the political and economic impacts of Mexican hometown associations that illustrates how migrant remittances (financial transfers sent by individuals abroad) collectively invest in public works, in community events, and during crises; however, the community-level impacts of deportation beyond the loss of financial remittances remain underexamined.[57] In Guatemala, there has been one mass deportation of migrants to San José Calderas in the department of Chimaltenango following a 2008 workplace raid at the Agriprocessors meatpacking plant in Postville, Iowa. It was the most expensive ($6 million) and largest raid in U.S. history to that date, in which 900 heavily armed federal agents stormed the plant and apprehended 389 undocumented workers, 293 of whom were from Guatemala and 160 of whom were returned to San José Calderas. Initially, the community organized, developing a collective of deportees called Asociación Por Mejoramiento de Deportados Guatemaltecos (Association for the Improvement of Guatemalan Deportees). Over time, however, these ties wore threadbare and many of the deportees have remigrated.

In an effort to grapple with these challenges, I approached the mayor, the municipal council, the Community Development Council (Consejo

Comunitario de Desarrollo, COCODE), and key religious leaders of a peri-urban town in the department of Quetzaltenango called Almolonga to explore the desirability and feasibility of conducting a household survey. Guatemalan authorities hold Almolonga as an alternative to migration due to its thriving, globalized, agrarian-based economy, yet as community leaders identified, the out-migration of youth persists. Along with an interdisciplinary team of six Guatemalan and two Guatemalan-American research assistants, we conducted a household survey of 148 households in Almolonga on a wide array of indicators, including education, health, food security, employment, financial debt, and migration. What emerged was a rich and complex exploration of how the Indigenous communities enlist migration as an intergenerational survival strategy to navigate marginalization and precarity. So, too, the survey reveals important localized critiques of development and migranthood.

Taken together, these mixed methods uncovered the multidimensional experiences of young people and the impacts of migration and deportation on individuals, households and communities. This multisited study—in court rooms, government facilities, and communities across Guatemala, Mexico, and the United States—proved essential to understanding the physical, conceptual, and technological geographies that youth negotiate as well as the social isolation they experience at various moments prior to, during, or following (re)migration and deportation. These diverse methodological approaches likewise compel anthropologists to consider how our methods not only must respond to the needs of the communities where we work but also might inform policymakers who urgently need rigorous and contextualized data.

ENSUING CHAPTERS

In order to understand the impacts of securitized development on migration from Indigenous communities, we must first understand how Indigenous youth conceive of their migration. Chapter one enlists multisited, transnational ethnography to examine how children are socialized into migranthood as a means of household well-being and betterment through diverse forms of migration, including seasonal, regional, rural-to-urban, and increasingly, transnational. In tracing how young people as social agents, caregivers, and migrants enlist social agency through diverse forms of mobility, we see how the contemporary migration of Indigenous youth is a cultural elaboration of care.

Chapter two examines the consequential disconnect between the ways young people assign meaning to migranthood and the ways those in power assign meaning to it. Utilizing the method of multimedia elicitation, young people dissect public discourses about young migrants, identifying the ways these discourses infantilize young people, criminalize their parents, and patholo-gize migration. In dissecting the campaign and its many pitfalls, young people widen the frame of reference by alternatively interpreting the reasons for and consequences of migration and deportation.

Despite media headlines claiming that child migration is the crisis du jour, chapter three argues that the influx of young migrants in 2014 and 2018 con-stituted policy-made crises. I situate the *testimonio* of Liseth, a Mam woman who was a refugee in Mexico as a child in the 1980s, alongside key historical and contemporary policy initiatives to illustrate how colonialism, armed con-flict, the proliferation of plantations, and extractive industries have displaced Indigenous peoples across generations and contribute to the contemporary migration of young people in "postconflict" Guatemala.

Chapter four analyzes how discourses about migranthood seep into govern-ment interventions and institutional practice and how young people experience them. Analyzing official development narratives *about* youth alongside narra-tives *by* youth reveals the disconnect between the imagined and lived experi-ences of young people and their families.

Chapter five examines how young people variously experience removal following deportation—as children of deported parents or *madres y padres deportadxs*; as *llegadxs* (arrivals), U.S. citizen children who accompany their parents to Guatemala following removal; and as *retornadxs* (returnees), unac-companied minors who are deported. Focusing on how young people negotiate returns across legal categories and longitudinally highlights how deportation is a process, one with rippling effects on individuals and families over time and space. It likewise reveals the everyday meanings of migranthood and how those meanings shift.

Chapter six grapples with the community-level impacts of securitization and development in the highland town of Almolonga. Enlisting a household survey, this chapter examines local critiques of development and migranthood and ex-plores how community members alternatively navigate precarity through the growing use of credit and debt, often with detrimental effects across generations.

The book concludes with the perspectives of young people on *el derecho a no migrar* (the right to not migrate), which challenge assumptions that development creates alternatives to migration. Moving beyond critique, young people endeavor to imagine and to create *el buen vivir,* a movement rooted in a revalorization and resignification of Indigenous cosmovision in the contemporary moment.

CHAPTER I

YOUTH AS AGENTS, CAREGIVERS, AND MIGRANTS

DOMINGO SQUINTED at the menu hanging overhead, debating between the *tacos de carnitas* and the *torta de longaniza*. "It's a tough decision," I echoed. We stepped to the counter for lunch at a taquería in La Villita on Chicago's southwest side—*"Seis tacos de carnitas, por favor,"* I ordered for us. Seeking reprieve from the scorching August heat, we found a table near the solitary oscillating fan. We sipped *aguas de Jamaica* (hibiscus water) as we processed our recent meeting with a paralegal from a legal aid organization who we hoped would represent Domingo at his upcoming removal proceedings. I met Domingo's older sister in 2013 in an SBS facility when she was deported from Mexico to San Marcos, Guatemala. A year later, she sent a WhatsApp message asking me to help her fourteen-year-old brother who was recently released from an Office of Refugee Resettlement (ORR) facility for unaccompanied minors in Texas. Domingo arrived in Chicago where he was living with a distant family friend, Rosalía, who had agreed to sponsor him from detention. With limited support to enroll in school or to secure legal representation, Domingo was struggling. Rosalía, a single mother of three children, worked full time at a gas station. She could not afford to take the time off from work to find Domingo an attorney, even less so to pay the $5,000 fee. Domingo explained, "I don't want to be a burden. I do what I can. She's helping me with a place to sleep and gives me a little money." In turn, Domingo helped out around the house, cleaned, took Rosalía's kids to one of the few public parks in La Villita, and remained at home with them so she could pick up overnight shifts at a nearby diner.

Earlier, the paralegal Liz had invited us to sit at an oval table in a cramped conference room. We carefully maneuvered between an oversized cardboard box exploding with Styrofoam cups and paper plates and a half-dozen black plastic bags filled with secondhand clothes waiting to be sorted. As we sat down in two mismatched rolling chairs, Liz turned to a clean page on her yellow steno pad. A multipage intake questionnaire lay on the table, but she never turned the pages. Liz had it memorized. In what amounted to a forty-five minute interview, she asked a litany of questions in Spanish to assess Domingo's options to remain lawfully in the United States, stopping to rephrase questions only when it was clear that Domingo, as a nonnative Spanish speaker, did not understand. She began:

PARALEGAL: In Guatemala, did the gangs harass, target, threaten, or assault you?

DOMINGO: They make everyone pay a tax. They harassed me every so often, but they didn't beat me up, if that's what you mean, no.

P: Were you ever harassed, targeted, threatened, or assaulted because you are Maya Mam?

D: All the time.

P: By whom?

D: Store owners, teachers, police, the government . . . you name it.

P: Do you have a religion? And, were you able to practice your religion freely in Guatemala?

D: Evangelical. I went to a church nearby my house.

P: Have you ever been physically hurt or hit by your parents?

D: My parents? They hit me when I did something wrong.

P: Has anyone ever physically abused you?

D: No.

P: Has anyone ever sexually abused you?

D: No.

P: Since arriving in the U.S., have you ever been forced to work without pay?

    D: No.

    P: Since arriving in the U.S., have you ever been forced to have sexual contact
        with anyone against your will?

    D: No.

    P: Have you been victim of a crime here in the United States?

    D: I was robbed last month. They took some money and my bus pass.

Taking a breath of resignation, Liz concluded by asking, "So tell me one more
time, in your own words, why did you migrate to the United States?" Domingo
replied unequivocally, "To help my family . . . to better our circumstances."

"She's not going to take my case, is she?" Domingo later asked me, as he
slurped the last drops of his juice. "Isn't what I suffered enough? She didn't
ask me about the trip. I mean, I experienced some bad things, but that's
not enough, is it? It's not enough that I'm a good person, trying to help my
family and make something of myself." Indeed, the supervising attorney
whom I have known for over a decade called me the next week declining
to represent Domingo. She explained, "Most Guatemalan kids come here
for economic reasons. They come because they want to earn better wages
and seek a better life. Very few come for school or even out of fear from
the gangs. There may be a few cases a year of abuse or neglect, but largely
they come because mom and dad can't provide the life they want or because
they want to get ahead."

Domingo's encounters with immigration attorneys are not unique. Under
immigration law, there are few avenues through which economic migrants
might remain lawfully in the United States beyond obtaining a specialty work
visa typically reserved for high-skilled workers. That Domingo regularly was
taxed by local gangs for safe passage to and from school or that he systematically was discriminated against for being Maya Mam was insufficient grounds
to remain in the United States. To qualify for asylum, he had to be targeted
on account of his race, religion, nationality, membership of a particular social
group, or political opinion. Alternatively, he could be eligible for specialized
visas as a victim of trafficking, of crime in the United States, or of abuse, abandonment, or neglect. Domingo's experiences did not fit easily into these narrow
categories. Instead, he and most Indigenous Guatemalans, even children, are
perceived as individual economic actors in pursuit of personal financial gain
and material self-interests.

What the forty-five minute interview failed to grasp, and what immigration law is ineffectual in reflecting, are the complex and historical meanings that underlie seemingly innocuous phrases like "to help my family" and "to better our circumstances." In contrast to juridical categories and popular discourses of migranthood, Indigenous youth like Domingo have long enlisted migration—internal, seasonal, regional, and increasingly transnational—as a form of inter-generational caregiving. Young people enlist their paid labor, unpaid care work, and mobility to ensure the survival of their multigenerational households amid marginality and precarity in Guatemala. As this chapter argues, migranthood is at once relational and contextual, developing as a social value and economic necessity among Maya families in Guatemala. Put another way, youth mobility is a *cultural elaboration of care,* one rooted in long-standing displacements of Indigenous communities by colonial authorities, dictatorship, genocide, and foreign intervention that continue to destabilize the region.

"*Está listo su orden*" (Your order is ready), the woman yelled from behind the counter. We were no longer hungry.

MIGRATION AS CARE

In contexts of globalization, migration and care are intimately linked. Feminist scholar Rhacel Salazar Parreñas examines the transnational transfer of caregiving and reproductive labor by women in the Philippines who travel to serve as caregivers for children and the elderly in the global North.[1] She details how Filipina migrants leave their children in the care of poorer women in the Philippines, who in turn entrust their children to the progressively lower-waged or unpaid care of family members. Parreñas argues that there is an "international division of reproductive labor" in which poorer women in the Philippines provide reproductive labor to "wealthier women in receiving nations."[2] Sociologist Arlie Hochschild synthesized this growing phenomenon of women migrating transnationally to perform care and socially reproductive labor with the concept of "global care chains."[3] Scholars have continued to refine this concept through analyses of how these migration dynamics are additionally racialized, gendered, and classed.[4] Others have identified how the physical absence of wives and mothers, in turn, shapes the reproductive labor of men and challenges traditional notions of masculinity and the performance of fatherhood.[5] Across these varied contexts, the concept of global care chains productively underscores the interconnected social and transnational kinship networks in which migrants and their labor are embedded.

Primarily focused on women and only recently on men, however, this literature predominantly depicts children as either left behind in the global South or as privileged beneficiaries of caregiving in the global North.[6] In part, this stems both from failing to fully recognize children as social actors and from the increasing transnational relationships among families across borders. This chapter examines how young people like Domingo are also agents of transnational caregiving as their paid labor and unpaid care work circulate through geographic and virtual spaces and across generations. From very young ages, Indigenous children in Guatemala are contributors to household economies by such means as domestic labor, childcare, work in family businesses, and piecemeal tasks such as sewing or bundling spices, often with minimal financial compensation, if any. Even children as young as six or seven years old contribute to family farms or businesses and participate in seasonal migration to the Pacific coast and southern Mexico as well as rural-to-urban migration. Across generations, these experiences develop young people's knowledge, cultivate their work ethic, and hone specialized skills that become essential upon entering the paid labor force as teenagers. To understand the contemporary movements of Indigenous youth and social constructions of migranthood, we must situate their mobility within a genealogy of forced displacement and oppression from colonialism, plantation labor, foreign intervention, and armed conflict to the present-day erosion of collective and familial subsistence farming.

"Social agency" is a social-scientific term referring to the actions and choices individuals make consciously and subconsciously. Agency is shaped by upbringing, cultural beliefs and norms, and social status, among other factors.[7] For many Indigenous youths, their early experiences establish cultural norms and social expectations of obligation and belonging within expansive kinship networks, expectations that span generations and geography. Social agency is not exclusively individualized and self-determined but also may assume historical and collective dimensions. The social agency of young people is nestled within interdependent social networks and, in contexts of migration, involves a series of choices made within historical and contemporary constraints. Anthropologist Nicholas Van Hear argues that migration decisions are best conceptualized along an axis of choice in which individuals may move in multiple directions, with varying degrees of choice and compulsion that, at times, are difficult to disentangle.[8] In other words, the social agency of migrant youth defies simplified typologies of migration as voluntary (economic) and involuntary (forced).

Seemingly new patterns of migration among Central American children suggest that youth are engaged in familial survival strategies that are increasingly transnational and youth-led. Among Indigenous families, young people enact care and belonging through the decision to migrate, their financial contributions to family, and through their unpaid care work. They shape household bonds and mediate conflict by providing emotional and social support to family members adapting to new cultural, social, and economic contexts.[9] This does not ignore or negate the poverty, violence or abuse that may spur some young people to migrate; instead, it recognizes that youth as social actors and values the cultural, social, and kinship networks in which they are embedded. Subsequent chapters turn to the complex and multiple geographies of violence and insecurity that underpin migratory decisions. Here, I focus on the meanings young people assign to their physical and social mobility, rather than how those in power assign meaning to it. I seek to move beyond reified tropes of young people as simple victims or migrant typologies (such as refugee, economic migrant, or unaccompanied child) to recognize young people as social agents in their own right and, importantly, to learn what they *do* with their agency.

TODOS SOMOS MIGRANTES: SEASONAL MIGRATION

In the summer of 2013, I visited Don Balam, a former colleague and Maya spiritual guide in Momostenango. As we walked through town from the central plaza to his home on the outskirts, we met Juan Diego and his son Alfredo who were returning home from working in the fields. Juan Diego invited us into his home for *atol de elote*. Sitting on the only available white plastic chairs, Don Balam and I sipped the sweet corn-and-milk drink as Alfredo crouched nearby, drawing circles with a stick in the dirt. "*Todos somos migrantes*" (We are all migrants), he explained. Alfredo had been participating in migration to the Pacific coast since the age of nine. Now, at age seventeen, he expounded, "My father and uncles went with their father when they were little, but they harvested corn back then. It's just what we do. Now, it's sugarcane; it's hard work.

I probably wasn't much help when I was younger, but I tried here and there. I helped clean up after them in the fields and brought them lunch. Now, I am old enough and can keep pace."

Juan Diego explained how he and his brother (Alfredo's uncle) came of age in the 1970s and 1980s harvesting corn on small familial plots and more frequently working on corporate-owned sugar plantations. He described how Maya youth of the highlands often migrate from very early ages along historical seasonal patterns to the Pacific coast of Guatemala to harvest coffee, sugarcane, and corn.[10] These patterns have a violent genealogy. During the Spanish colonial period, Maya people were forcibly relocated to serve as slaves. The colonial authorities compelled Indigenous people to migrate in order to provide a range of compulsory labor, including *servicio personal,* labor provided in the form of a tribute or encomienda for the benefit of Spaniards; *servicio ordinario,* a form of cheap labor; and *congregación,* the forcible resettlement of people to facilitate exploitation of their labor.[11] Through forced labor on plantations and extreme violence, the Spanish minority asserted its dominance over Indigenous peoples until independence in 1821, with slavery being abolished two years later in 1823.

Freedom from forced labor for Indigenous people was short lived. The ladino (those with a mix of Spanish and Indigenous heritages) elite took power following the withdrawal of the Spaniards and maintained a monopoly on land rights. They established a system of plantations that benefited from an inexpensive, Indigenous labor force and stripped Indigenous peoples of their land. President Justo Rufino Barrios (1873–1885) created new institutions to monitor land use and implemented a series of land reform programs that required landowners to claim individual legal titles to their land.[12] These bureaucratic reforms were contrary to Maya cultural traditions of communal cultivation and ownership. Juan Diego described how his ancestors had previously farmed communally, and when they failed to secure the newly required individual land titles, the government reclassified their land as "unclaimed" and redistributed the plots primarily to the ladino elite.[13] Unaware of the land reform program and in the absence of eviction by the government, many Indigenous farmers like Juan Diego's great-grandparents continued to cultivate the land, not recognizing until decades later that they had lost all legal rights to property.

As anthropologist Patricia Foxen describes in her ethnography of K'iche' transnational migration, President Barrios's land reforms sought to stimulate coffee as the leading export, while providing "cheap seasonal agricultural labor on large coastal *haciendas* (estates or plantations). These laws targeted Mayas whose 'duty' it was to work on plantations[14] [and] included the legislation of *mandamiento* [forced labor requiring each Indian community to supply a speci-fied amount of labor each year] and *habilitación* [debt servitude]."[15] During this time, laborers were saddled with substantial financial debts that they passed on to their children. A multigenerational system of debt peonage emerged in which many migrated to the Pacific coast to labor as *colonos* (permanent workers) or as *jornaleros* (day laborers or seasonal workers)—migration patterns still in ef-fect over 140 years later. The labor of *jornaleros* became "the property of cof-fee, sugar, and cotton *latifundistas* (plantation owners), many of whom rented out to Indians in the highlands in exchange for plantation labor."[16] Barrios's policies not only displaced thousands of Indigenous farmers but also initiated the erosion of the traditional system of communal land ownership honored by Indigenous communities at the time.

By the early twentieth century, enterprising German immigrants and ladi-nos began to capitalize on the land seizures of the 1870s. Once again, newly established coffee plantations benefited from the inexpensive manual labor of Indigenous peoples who had previously occupied and cultivated the land. While Indigenous Guatemalans like Juan Diego's family had worked as seasonal migrants along the Pacific coast since the nineteenth century, the 1950s saw increased regional migration of Guatemalan laborers into Mexico as the con-solidation of large tracts of land into the hands of the elite limited the capacity for survival of Indigenous communities in rural Guatemala.[17] By 1979, over two-thirds of Guatemala's population resided in rural areas, yet approximately 54 percent of land plots were too small to support subsistence farming.[18] This trend has only continued.

Now, as Alfredo astutely identified and Juan Diego historicized, there have been notable shifts in Guatemalan agriculture. Since the early 2000s, major land rushes among sugarcane and African palm producers increasingly have driven subsistence corn farmers out of work in an attempt to satiate U.S. and European demands for biofuel. Some small farmers have sold their land due to failed crops and the associated financial debt (see chapter six); others are coerced into selling their land when neighboring plantations cut off their water supply or when access to public roads becomes deliberately restricted. Juan Diego clarified, "The buses stop, so there is no way to get to the land. *La renta* [charged to the bus drivers] gets too high." Here, Juan Diego references *la renta*, a daily fee imposed by gangs, narcotraffickers, and private security of multinational corporations on bus drivers to ensure safe passage. These concurrent strategies choke off access to land and coerce landowners to sell their properties, most commonly for mining speculation. "Others are threatened or beaten," Alfredo chimed in.

There are few protections for small landowners and even fewer for laborers like Alfredo and Juan Diego against harassment and coercion by elite landowners and multinational corporations. In response to a public call for protections of the lands of small farmers, a 2013 rural development law sought to promote enhanced access to land, employment, and labor protections. However, it was met with fierce opposition by large landholders and private businesses and quickly was rejected by the Guatemalan congress. Without state intervention or legal protections, wage-labor migration continues unabated. Indeed, the seasonal migration has become more of an individual or family strategy rather than a collective enterprise as in previous generations.[19] As a family strategy, young people—girls and boys—participate through their labor in the fields or through their everyday activities of shopping, cooking, and cleaning, as Alfredo described of his childhood.

HEMOS HECHO DESDE SIEMPRE:
REGIONAL MIGRATION

Plantations in southern Mexico likewise rely upon the labor of Indigenous Guatemalans. Ignacio, sixteen years old and recently deported from Mexico, explained that his family began working seasonally in Chiapas, Mexico: "In Mexico, it costs more to get there, but the wages are better, and we make a bit more in the exchange rate from pesos to quetzales." At nine years old, Ignacio began accompanying his uncles and cousins to southern Mexico. Massaging his palm with his thumb, he described his first trip to Mexico:

> At first, it was an adventure, a way to escape school. I remember sleeping on the floor at the camp and tending the chickens with another boy, Manuel. We

fed them every morning and cleaned up the living barracks—washed, swept, made beds. Occasionally, a man would tell us to sort seeds. We were paid by the number of kilos we could sort. I remember my fingers hurt, but I didn't stop because I wanted to contribute. They bled and cramped up at first. They hurt for days. Still do, but I got used to it. Manuel and I would race to see who could sort the most; we made a game of it, so we wouldn't be so bored. Now [at age sixteen], my fingers are too fat, so I pick grapes.

Youth as young as six or seven years old describe migrating to labor camps principally in Chiapas, Oaxaca, and Veracruz in southern Mexico. Initially, children may accompany their parents, extended family, or fellow community members as helpers on coffee plantations. The labor of children in particular is enlisted in tasks requiring fine motor skills, such as picking coffee, cleaning crops, and classifying and packing exotic plants.[20] National statistics indicate that approximately 13 percent of migration to Mexico is attributed to youth aged fifteen to eighteen years old; because official statistics do not count children under fourteen years old, the data likely underestimate the scale of child labor migration.[21] For Ignacio, migration to Mexico was a means by which he and his family responded to their immediate needs, while minimizing the assumption of large debts and avoiding the risks associated with migration to more distant locations.

Young people describe learning the bus routes and safe crossing points over time, and developing relationships with foremen who might later hire them. Upon reaching sixteen years old, Guatemalan youth legally can travel alone with documentation indicating parental permission to work. Frequently, however, these documents are neither provided nor requested. Many youths say they continue to migrate, joining siblings, cousins, and peers, in order to support their families and to plan for their own marriages, parenthood, and households. For those like Ignacio willing to brave the increasingly dangerous journey further north, grape harvesting in central Mexico promises better wages and relatively less taxing physical labor. Regional migrants may confront the cartels and gangs that troll migratory routes and charge a tax for passage and may likewise encounter enhanced immigration enforcement in Mexico. In 2016, immigration officers detained Ignacio and his uncle at Siglo XXI, Mexico's largest detention facility located in Tapachula, Chiapas. Initially surprised,

Ignacio later reflected, *"Hemos hecho desde siempre. ¿Por qué estoy aquí?"* (We have always done this. Why am I here [being detained]?) He described how he was detained alongside several farmers with muddied sandals and machetes who immigration authorities apprehended as they worked their own lands along the Guatemala-Mexico border.

UN EQUILIBRIO: INTERNAL MIGRATION

Indigenous youth sequentially or concurrently may participate in other contemporary patterns of rural-to-urban migration. As poverty deepens in the highlands, Indigenous youth may travel to Guatemala City temporarily, semipermanently, or permanently to participate in the growing private security industry, serving as guards for private homes and businesses of the elite. Young people also labor in the informal sector, shining shoes, washing and guarding cars, and/or selling wares on the roadside or *chicle* (gum) in the marketplace. I encountered a few very young children (ages six to nine), mostly boys, who made the trip to Guatemala City alone; more frequently, thirteen- to seventeen-year-olds travel by themselves and negotiate labor agreements as *ayudantes* (assistants) in small shops or on buses. When physically capable, boys participate in the construction industry in Guatemala City, which offers higher wages but few labor protections. Girls also migrate to Guatemala City, at times to work as waitresses or assistants in restaurants and shops, provide childcare, or more commonly, serve as domestic laborers or caregivers for the elderly in middle-class households.

When she was thirteen years old, Maria Clara traveled to Guatemala City from the K'akchiquel community of San Marcos La Laguna in the department of Sololá. She recalled, "My mother didn't support me leaving but I think my father understood why I left." She sipped her hot chocolate as I tried to catch a glimpse of my children who were climbing in an indoor play place at a café in Guatemala City where we were meeting. Maria Clara, now seventeen years old, explained her reasons for moving to Guatemala City. "I wanted to have my own money and to be more independent. I didn't want to stay in San Marcos [La Laguna] for the rest of my life; I wanted to see something and to help my family." Her older brother also left the family home in 2012 without his parents' blessings, migrating to the United States where I would eventually meet him at a facility for unaccompanied minors in Chicago. The small envelope with $300 and two photographs that I was hand delivering to Maria Clara from her brother was testament to this aspiration. Maria Clara laughed as she thumbed through the photographs of her brother, hair slicked back, standing next to a yellow corvette with black racing stripes. Another photograph showed her brother with the nighttime lights of the Chicago skyline illuminated behind him. "He's seeing something for sure. I can't imagine," she chuckled.

Maria Clara described that her cousin had secured her a position as a domestic worker in the middle-class home of an engineer and his family in Guatemala City's Zona 12, where she cleaned, cooked, and tended to their three children six days per week. "It's not so bad. It could be worse like the girls who get trapped into selling themselves in [Mexico's southern city of] Tapachula. At least my *patrona* [employer] is not cruel and I get one day off to myself." In Guatemala, there are no standard legal protections providing for minimum wage nor for an eight-hour work day. In spite of her sixteen-hour days and minimal pay, Maria Clara felt fortunate as the labor conditions of other Indigenous youth who migrate to Guatemala City are often far more abusive and exploitative.

"I try to establish *un equilibrio* [a balance]," she explained regarding her efforts to send money home to her parents and still afford an occasional luxury item, such as floral soaps and lotions, a new blouse, earrings, or magazines. At first glance, it would appear that Maria Clara is attempting to juggle the economic needs of and social obligations to her family with her own desire to enjoy material goods that are often restricted to the middle and upper classes, but this *equilibrio* defies neoliberal understandings of migranthood as simple economic migration. Here, Maria Clara is invoking the K'akchiquel concept of balance. As anthropologist Edward Fischer explains, contrary to notions of balance as a seesaw in which quantities (goods, time, and the like) are distributed in oppositional relation to a center point, balance is understood as centeredness.[22] That is, feeling grounded physically and metaphysically or in harmony between humans and the cosmos. For Maria Clara, the meaning she assigns to her obligations are firmly rooted in cultural values and beliefs that intimately bind her to family, community, and indeed the universe.

These multiple and often interrelated migratory trajectories—seasonal, regional, and internal—are not uniquely a contemporary phenomenon nor mutually exclusive. Over time, a culture of migration has developed as a means of survival and as a social value.[23] It is deeply ingrained in Maya youths' formative experiences. For Alfredo, seasonal migration is "just what we do" because *"todos somos migrantes"* (we are all migrants). For Ignacio, regional migration is an activity; *"hemos hecho desde siempre"* (we have always done this). For Maria Clara, family members who migrated to the United States and to Guatemala City facilitated her internal migration and her ongoing contributions to family, while enabling her to nurture a material and cosmic *equilibrio* in her life. Alfredo, Ignacio, and Maria Clara understand their migranthood as interwoven with their personal desires, social obligations, and cultural values, and it enables their contributions through their paid labor and unpaid care work. For others, these contributions take the form of transnational migration.

UN ACTO DE AMOR

As with seasonal, regional, and internal migration, young people's caregiving roles and social obligations shape the decision to migrate internationally. Some youths migrate seasonally or regionally for years before undertaking more distant transnational migration. For Maribel, transnational migration marked the first time she would leave her village of Ixchiguan in the department of San Marcos. As we strolled through Ixchiguan's Saturday market, Maribel explained that at the age of thirteen, she volunteered to migrate in support of her family. Her father had died in a bus accident three years prior, and her mother was facing complications from untreated diabetes. With an older brother already living outside of Atlanta, Maribel was the eldest child remaining in Ixchiguan.

She described both her motivations for and apprehensions about migration, explaining, "I know it will be hard, but I must go. I am preparing myself—my body, my mind. We don't have the conditions for survival here. My family needs me. *Me toca migrar.* [It's my turn to migrate.]" Maribel and her family were well aware of the dangers of irregular migration—including extreme weather, riding the freight trains through Mexico, gangs, police corruption, and sexual violence. Her younger brother, whom I had met one year prior in an SBS facility for unaccompanied minors deported from Mexico to Xela, had shared the gruesome details with Maribel and me in the family's courtyard. Yet Maribel's commitment to her family remained her most salient motivation for migration, a decision that her mother openly grieved but reluctantly supported as the only alternative for familial survival. Maribel's younger brother, whom I had come to Ixchiguan to visit, had just left for the United States; Maribel hoped to meet him *"al otro lado"* (on the other side).

Maribel's neighbor, fourteen-year-old Bernardo, had also recently left Ixchiguan. Bernardo's parents initially forbade his migration, citing their reliance on his wages. Sitting at their kitchen table, his father Armando described the deliberations of their son's desire to migrate: "I told [my son] that we didn't have the money to support him going to the United States. He managed to gather together funds from his uncle in Maryland, sold his motorcycle, borrowed from friends—all to pay the coyote. I worry about him. Every day I worry, but I know he is resourceful and hardworking. He will survive." Showing me a picture of his son standing in front of a grocery store in Los Angeles, Armando said, "*Él será alguien. Soy orgulloso. Fíjate, migración es un acto de amor.*" (He will be someone. I am proud. Look, migration is an act of love.)

With his parents' tacit support, Bernardo was able to draw on his peer and familial connections to secure the necessary funding to ensure a modestly safer passage to the United States through the contracting of a *pollero de confianza* (trusted smuggler) well known in Ixchiguan. Without familial support and social capital, Bernardo might not have had the financial resources to undertake irregular migration, yet as a resourceful, hardworking, and determined young man, he gathered piecemeal the necessary funds and incurred considerable financial debt to migrate transnationally. For many, migration bolsters young people's important position within kinship, communal, and ethnic networks—networks that offer emotional and financial support over time and space. Now, as a migrant in the United States, Bernardo is a source of pride for his family. For his father, this migration is the embodiment of Bernardo's love for and commitment to his family.

In my interviews, many young migrants described the conditions prompting migration in terms of high rates of unemployment, scarce arable land, mounting familial debt, limited employment and education opportunities, and family emergencies (such as accidents, illness, and death). Alongside these structural causes, migration mediates and is mediated by social relationships and cultural values. Young people shared their desire to contribute to familial survival and sustenance of future generations. Amid the extreme poverty and structural violence, young people and their families are left with few viable options to meet everyday household needs while remaining in Guatemala. In a cultural context that values and depends upon their contributions to households and communities, Indigenous youth enlist migration—be it seasonal, regional, internal, or transnational—as a historically rooted strategy to navigate growing poverty and instability in Guatemala.

REMESAS TIENEN ROSTRO . . . TIENEN RACISMO

In contexts of regional and seasonal migration, analyses of household survival—both by families themselves and by researchers—generally ignore young people's paid and unpaid contributions. Within transnational migration, however, financial contributions in the form of remittances are assigned considerable significance. In traditional development discourse, remittances are generally understood as financial contributions made by adult, economic migrants in the global North to sustain households in the global South. In Guatemala, many actors have a stake in the growing flow of remittances: banks, money transfer companies, states, communities, NGOs, multinational corporations, churches, and beneficiaries themselves, not to mention those engaged in the movement (extrajudicial or state sanctioned) of people and goods across borders. The World Bank reported that $9.49 billion was remitted in 2018 alone, 12.1 percent of Guatemala's annual gross domestic product.[24] Because of the sizable financial contribution made by the estimated 1.5 million Guatemalans working abroad, migrants are seen as, in the words of former President Óscar Berger, national "heroes and heroines of Guatemala."[25] While institutions such as the World Bank monitor the growth of remittances as an indicator of development, research has found that remittances among Maya families in the highlands of Guatemala have not been a development panacea.[26]

Discussions of remittances are predicated on a limited understanding of them as exclusively financial transfers of money from adults to families in countries of origin. However, for Indigenous migrant youth in the United States, their economic contributions to the household assume additional layers of meaning. *"Remesas tienen rostro"* (Remittances have a face), explained Carlos. At age fifteen he harvested pecans in Georgia, dividing one-third of his monthly income between his pregnant young wife Jacqueline in Maryland and his family in Cajolá. Carlos and Jacqueline, whom I met in 2012 in an ORR facility for unaccompanied minors outside of El Paso, Texas, had migrated with the hopes of earning money to purchase land in anticipation of starting their own family. Sitting in their family's courtyard in Cajolá three years later, Carlos's mother detailed how she utilized Carlos's monthly remittances. "We pay for food and school fees first. We save a little for land. If there is a little that remains, we buy the children clothes."

Carlos's family relies upon his monthly remittances, albeit modest, for their everyday life and the education of his younger siblings, a contribution that brings Carlos pride. As we drank coffee at a local diner in northern Georgia, Carlos remarked, "It feels good. My family has worked hard. Now, it's my turn." For Carlos, remittances are relational and socially meaningful. Through his transnational migration, he feels better equipped to contribute financially to his family, and as a result, gains personal satisfaction and pride. His remittances have direct material impacts on his family, making possible the investment in a *tortillería* (tortilla shop) and a *tienda* (small store) adjacent to the family home as well as greater social standing from being modestly upwardly mobile. His contributions are not anonymized financial transfers; they are infused with care and commitment to his family. They have a face.

In the wake of the 2016 U.S. presidential election, many families began to brace for mass deportations, a campaign promise of then candidate Donald Trump. With considerable anxiety about the safety of loved ones living undocumented in the United States, families began to make difficult decisions about how to reallocate already limited economic resources. Prior to the elections, Valentina's monthly remittances from Georgia covered her thirteen-year-old daughter Lucía's private school fees in San Marcos. Overtaxed and underfunded, Guatemala's public schools often lack the most basic resources such as textbooks, bathrooms, blackboards, and qualified teachers. As such, families like Lucía's prioritize the use of remittances to enroll their children in a growing number of urban private schools that purport higher quality of instructors and specialized accommodations. Following the election of Donald Trump, however, Valentina's life in Georgia became exceedingly precarious. Fearful of a raid at the meatpacking plant where she worked, according to her daughter Lucía, Valentina stopped going to work. Anxious about encountering openly racist attacks emboldened by Trump's xenophobic rhetoric, she rarely left her apartment to purchase groceries or to attend church. "She was really worried, and we were worried for her," Lucía explained of her mother's situation. Compelled by her newly restricted income, the family made the difficult decision to withdraw Lucía from private school. Valentina's parents with whom Lucía lived in San

Marcos began to send reverse remittances—the equivalent of Lucía's monthly tuition payments—to Valentina in Georgia to sustain her until, they hoped, the anti-immigrant climate in the United States would lessen.

Given that 16.6 percent of Guatemalans live in the United States, Lucía's family was not alone. These concerns were widespread. Several families reported sending money, from $100 to $500 per month, to the United States when their migrant family members initially arrived and needed financial support to pay for rent, transportation, and food while they sought employment. Lucía's grandfather shared that, during the 2008 financial crisis, he sent several money transfers of short-term loans to Valentina when she was unemployed, in an effort to delay her premature return to Guatemala. "We had invested so much, and she suffered to get to the other side. I didn't want her or anyone else to have to take that journey again," he rationalized. Following the 2016 presidential elections, families described how they sold land, consolidated households, deferred starting new businesses, or chose not to invest in additional harvests, all in an effort to keep income liquid and accessible as they braced for the economic fallout of lost income resulting from the detention and deportation of a loved one. Wary of the heightened anti-immigrant rhetoric of Donald Trump, Lucía's uncle observed, *"Remesas tienen racismo"* (Remittances have racism).

Lucía told me, "My mom went to the United States for me, to support my education. Although I'm not in school right now, I hope it will pass, and I'll return next term when she can be safe in Georgia." Lucía's emotional support of and her grandparents' reverse remittances to her mother demonstrate that remittances can be multidirectional, dynamic, and nonmaterial. Particularly in periods of crisis or adversity, regardless of direction, remittances enable the sustenance of transnational households over time.

For Maya youth and their families, remittances are total social events—dynamic, multidirectional, and multilayered—rooted in contemporary phenomena but also in a historical context of loss of land and displacement that has given rise to a culture of migration among young people. Don Balam from Momostenango shared with me, "With remittances, we can create spaces that have excluded us. We are in a better position to follow our journey, to organize in solidarity with others both here and there [in the United States], and to restore the rightful order of our land." For Don Balam, remittances are perceived as a vehicle through which communities may right past wrongs and might purchase and redistribute pilfered land. Thus, remittances link the present to the past but also to the future.[27] The varied financial, social, and historical meanings of remittances attest to the need to understand migration and corresponding remittances beyond singularly economic terms. By contextualizing and historicizing migranthood and the social networks that facilitate youth mobility, we begin to understand its meaning for young people and their families.

OVERLOOKED AND UNDERVALUED

In addition to social and financial remittances, Indigenous migrant youth contribute their unpaid care work to the survival of their households. Rather than reinforcing a bright-line distinction between paid labor and unpaid care work, sociologist Nicola Yeates suggests that care "covers a range of activities to promote and maintain the personal health and welfare of people."[28] For Indigenous youth, either in the United States or following their deportation to Guatemala, their care work consists of cooking, cleaning, shopping, childcare, elder care, maintenance, and tending animals. Young people shape household bonds and mediate conflict by providing critical emotional and social support to family members adapting to new cultural, social, and economic contexts.[29] Their care work is vital to the maintenance of a household over time and across geopolitical distance.

Ramona, a thirteen-year-old from a Mam community in the department of Quetzaltenango, emigrated to Louisiana, where she cared for her young niece and nephew while her elder sister worked as a waitress and her brother-in-law as a carpenter. Following her deportation to Guatemala, Ramona explained:

> My sister and brother-in-law are working hard for us. They are doing their best to support our family and they helped to get me [to the United States]. I just did my part, helping however I could—making tortillas, preparing lunches, washing clothes, watching the kids. They were teaching me English and helped me with my homework when I got frustrated. I really missed my family and friends. I did my best there. It wasn't always easy there, but it isn't easy here in Guatemala either.

Ramona identified her contributions as caring for her niece and nephew as well as supporting the household through everyday domestic chores. While Ramona acknowledged the loneliness and homesickness that accompanied her migration, she also recognized the benefits of living in a multilingual and supportive household.

At age fifteen, Aura cleaned houses alongside her twenty-five-year-old aunt Hilda in Chicago, together saving money to finance her younger brother's migration in two years' time. As we exited the bus heading to the Museum of Science and Industry on the city's south side, Aura described to me, "Hilda helped me to travel here. She provides me a place to live and found me this work. She is patient and kind. She says she remembers what it was like when she first arrived, and I really see how she cares for my parents by supporting me. I trust that I, too, can contribute to my family and to those that come after me." Consistent with Maya cosmovision that holds that all things and actions transmit positive and negative potential, Aura recognized that her care work maintained the potential to meaningfully impact herself and others. Aura did not view her own actions and interests in a vacuum. Rather, her care work was a form of interlocking responsibility to Hilda, her family, and her community for their financial, emotional, material, and spiritual support.

While care work is often gendered, with girls providing considerable emotional and domestic labor, young boys also are critical caregivers to their families in their home countries and elsewhere. At sixteen years old, Marvin joined his father in Oregon after six years of separation. While his mother Gisela and younger siblings remained in Guatemala, Marvin and his father worked as migrant farmworkers up and down the West Coast, remitting money each month to pay school fees and gradually to build their family home. Gisela described:

> I worry about [my husband]—he doesn't tell me what life is like there. He sounds tired and his health is not good. I'm so glad Marvin is with his father, so he can cheer him up when he is missing us. And, Marvin tells me how life over there is. He helps me to know that we will be together again. It is just a matter of a couple of more years apart.

Marvin provided emotional support and feelings of connectedness to his father following a prolonged separation. He also offered assurances to his mother in Guatemala with updates on his father's health, a source of anxiety for Gisela. Through his presence over the past year in Oregon, Marvin facilitated familial sentiments of belonging in multiple sites, despite their geographic separation.

As members of transnational households, many young people maintain their sense of kinship and belonging in spite of geographic distance. Upon arrival in the United States, many young migrants describe remaining intricately connected to communities of origin through phone and WhatsApp calls, text messages, social media, emails, letters, and remittances and by sending such material goods as clothing, shoes, and technology such as radios, tablets, cellular phones, and computers. In addition, young migrants report sending money for special events such as patron saint festivals; ceremonies; holidays; life events such as marriages, births, and deaths; and special fundraising initiatives, such as the construction of a soccer field or playground or specific infrastructure improvements to local parks, roads, or churches. Thus, for most young migrants, physical absence does not signify that they are devalued members of families and communities; rather, they demonstrate their ongoing interconnectedness to familial, cultural, and social networks that facilitate their migration, settlement, and at times, return. Examining the paid and unpaid care work of young people considers both the material and immaterial ways in which they contribute to household well-being over geographic space and the ways families may express their cultural and social valuation of young people's labor, which is "often overlooked and undervalued."[30]

CARE ACROSS GENERATIONS

In the context of the migration of Indigenous youth, examining migration through the lens of care allows us to consider the material and affective contributions of young people and how the intensity and direction of care and caregiving shift over time. Anthropologist Kristin Yarris explores the ways Nicaraguan grandmothers care for their grandchildren when mothers migrate, tracing how moral and cultural values are brokered and regenerated by grandmothers.[31] In contrast to migration literature that predominantly focuses on the labor of migrants, Yarris opens up critical avenues to understand how care is embedded in diverse familial, social, political, and often gendered dynamics and how care moves across generations. So, too, Indigenous children in Guatemala circulate care. A young girl may be the recipient of her mother's or grandmother's care, but as she enters early adolescence, her assumption of household responsibility and caregiving grows. The needs of parents and children are under constant negotiation; transnational migration as a rite of passage for many youths demarcates a pivotal shift in the obligation for and distribution of care across the generations, in which a parent's investment of financial and social capital in their child's migration becomes an investment in the household's future well-being.

Tracing the ways that care circulates in and through households reveals that migranthood is relational. Young people participate in transnational caregiving across borders and generations and, over time, the migration of Indigenous youth has become a cultural elaboration of care. Analyzing the unpaid care work of young people alongside their paid labor signifies that physical absence or separation does not necessarily indicate a lack of emotional connection or belonging between youth and their families; to the contrary, among Indigenous communities, how a family decides who migrates may be an expression of trust, love, and investment rather than of abuse, neglect, or abandonment as is often depicted. By examining young people as recipients of caregiving and as caregivers themselves, and the ways care circulates, we might likewise conceptualize mobility more broadly, including the social and economic mobility that may facilitate or result from migration. In this way, we might learn the multiple and varied ways that children—as people and as socially constructed categories—move across geopolitical borders, through culturally defined stages of life, and across spaces designed to shape their experiences of growing up.

CHAPTER 2

WIDENING THE FRAME

DURING THE SUMMER OF 2014, headlines of every major news outlet covered the seemingly surprising arrival of tens of thousands of young migrants: "Children at the Border" *(New York Times);* "More Youths Crossing U.S.-Mexico Border Alone" *(LA Times);* "Desperation, Hope and Children on the Border" *(CNN);* "Obama Calls Wave of Children Across U.S.-Mexican Border 'Urgent Humanitarian Situation'" *(Washington Post).* I boarded a plane, returning to Guatemala for a second summer of research at the height of this influx of Central American children arriving unaccompanied in the United States.

As I waited in the customs queue in Mexico City's international airport, a pseudodocumentary played overhead on a loop on large flat-screen television. Dressed in a red hoodie and faded jeans, a young girl's shoulders shivered, her head bent. Her face was concealed from the camera's gaze. She wept as she recounted her rape, which had occurred on a clandestine route along the U.S.-Mexico border. A uniformed Mexican immigration officer sat by her side consoling her. I glanced around in disbelief. The other travelers in line seemed oblivious to the irony that this film, an effort to deter irregular migration, played at an official checkpoint in an international airport to an audience with their passports and costly airline tickets in hand. Tax dollars not well spent, I dismissed. When I landed two hours later in Guatemala City's La Aurora airport, the same film played on a loop on televisions throughout the terminal.

Transferring to a bus station in Zona 3, I began the four-hour pilgrimage west to Xela, a town in the western highlands that would serve as my base for fieldwork that summer. An impressive marimba rendition of Celine Dion's song "Power of Love" blared on the bus's radio as we pulled out of the station. I settled into my seat, longing for my favorite empanada vendor, Mario, to board the bus outside of Mixico, a suburb notorious for some of the most gruesome homicides routinely showcased by the national newspaper *Prensa Libre*. Not even thirty minutes later while staring out the window, I spotted a newly pasted billboard featuring an image of a menacing man's face with a notorious "M" (for the gang Mara Salvatrucha, or MS-13) tattooed on his cheek. The billboard cautioned, "*El coyote no quiere a su hijo.*" (The smuggler does not care about your child.) I immediately thought of Juana from San Francisco el Alto, whose father had been a smuggler for nearly a decade; he loves his child. And, since when did the gangs secure a monopoly on human smuggling? Besides, is a coyote supposed to love your child? More public funds wasted on misdirected warnings.

In the weeks that followed, I would discover that the videos, billboards, public service announcements (PSAs), and even songs on the radio were all elements of the stunningly expansive Dangers Awareness Campaign, which later was renamed the Know the Facts Campaign. The multimillion-dollar initiative was the brainchild of the U.S. Customs and Border Protection; CBP hired a Washington, DC–based advertising firm to develop radio spots, billboards, and television, magazine, and newspaper advertisements warning parents of would-be migrants of the dangers of migration through Mexico. CBP reached out to Central American governments, faith-based organizations, NGOs, and the news media to circulate over 6,500 PSAs broadcast in Spanish throughout the region and in U.S. cities with large Central American communities.[1] Humanitarian organizations such as UNICEF and Save the Children provided corollary programs to complement CBP's message: "Do not send your children to the United States. The route is dangerous."

The Know the Facts campaign and its Dangers Awareness predecessor were intended to convince would-be migrants that the dangers of the trip were high, and the likelihood of arrival was low. The campaign was directed specifically toward the families of young Central Americans with the messages of "The journey is too dangerous"; "Children will not get legal papers if they make it"; and "They are the future—let's protect them."[2] The campaign reductively framed child migrants as ill-informed of the dangers of migration and their parents as naively entrusting their children to criminal smugglers who did not have their best interests at heart. Considerably less altruistic, the U.S. Department of Homeland Security (DHS) simultaneously expanded its detention of families and children, as then DHS Secretary Jeh Johnson said, to send a message "to those who are . . . contemplating coming here illegally [that] we will send you back . . . People in Central America should see and will see that if they make this journey and spend several thousand dollars to do that, we will send them back and they will have wasted their money."[3] Dubious of the efficacy of these efforts to dissuade Central American migration, I wondered, how did young people digest these messages? What frames of reference did they draw upon when viewing the advertisements and PSAs? And, did the campaigns impact their opinions about or, more importantly, their decisions whether to migrate? And so I asked. Analyzing these discourses alongside young people in Guatemala—the target audience of the campaigns and government initiatives—allows us to explore the histories, feelings, and experiences that youth draw from to understand the discourses about migranthood and ultimately to evaluate the efficacy of policy responses to child migration.

CONSTRUCTING AND DECONSTRUCTING DISCOURSES

With the support of Estela, a high school teacher whom I met through a fellow professor from the Universidad de San Carlos, we convened a small, mixed-gender group (six boys and five girls) of eleven Mam youths, aged fourteen to seventeen years old, to discuss the campaigns. Enlisting multimedia elicitation, we explored several examples—radio spots, videos, images, and songs—asking young people to analyze and reflect upon the messages of the campaign. What were the most salient assertions that emerged about child migrants, their families, and their communities? How did the campaign resonate with or diverge from their knowledge and experiences of migration?

Prior to our meeting, I knew five of the young participants—Alexa, Andrea, Francisco, Gustavo, and Mateo—having met them either in U.S. facilities for unaccompanied minors prior to deportation, upon removal in Guatemalan government facilities, or through community contacts. Each either had attempted to migrate or was the sibling of a young migrant. The remaining six participants—Arturo, Carolina, Fernando, Giovanni, Liliana, and Sandra—were identified by Estela through an after-school program she ran at a community center in San Juan Ostuncalco. Because most of this small group of young people already knew each other from the community, there was some preexisting social ease among them. Given that recounting experiences of migration and deportation—either one's own or a family member's—can be potentially traumatizing, group conversation allowed the youths to decide on their own terms whether and how much to disclose about their personal experiences. To my surprise, the process provoked three hours of conversation and debate as the group shared at-times divergent interpretations of a single image, song, or video. Estela and I aimed to intervene as little as possible, allowing the youths to direct the discussion. I was grateful to observe the conversation that unfolded.

As a research method, visual elicitation—or photo elicitation, as it is commonly termed—utilizes photographs, videos, paintings, or advertisements to evoke observations, feelings, and memories in participants. While one-on-one interviews may elicit similar insights, visual elicitation facilitates developing rapport with participants and allows researchers to better grasp people's social worlds and perspectives. Multimedia elicitation likewise creates opportunities to open up additional dimensions of experience and memory that interviews may fail to uncover. Playing music and showing videos in addition to photographs revealed the various ways youth consume media and allowed us to pay attention to visual appearance, tone, and music in addition to the content of the messages. Sandra tapped her foot to a *cumbia* detailing the hazards of migration; Mateo rolled his eyes as a woman with heavy makeup equated migration with death; Alexa grimaced as the announcer told her to search for the "Guatemalan dream."

Examining the ways these media and the broader campaigns connected to and diverged from their lived experiences created opportunities for young people to critically assess how outsiders imagine and produce discourses about their lives. As young people waded through the multiple assertions of these campaigns, they assessed the credibility, persuasiveness, and legitimacy of the messages based on sociocultural values, personal experiences, and the experiences of their families and peers. With few prompts from Estela or me, they analyzed the content, form, structure, and patterned messages of these campaigns, revealing how discourses produce meaning about and are understood by young people. For youth in particular, this proved powerful as they are typically objects of and not participants in discussions about policies and programs designed for them. In contrast, this participatory process was premised upon the recognition that young people are *experts by experience*. They possess a wealth of local knowledge, skills, and capacities to contribute their insights and analysis. They merely lack the opportunity to do so. Explicitly acknowledging young people's expertise and eliciting their insights created opportunities for them to widen the frame of analysis with their knowledge and, in so doing, dismantled the discourses about them. When given the opportunity, they generated counter-narratives about migranthood.

For analytical clarity, I individually detail the discourses youth identified as they unfolded in our conversations with full recognition that they are co-constituted and mutually reinforced. Alongside excerpts from our conversations, I provide details from the local and transnational archive that young people draw upon to demonstrate how these discourses replicate long-standing violence and entrenched racism toward Central Americans in Mexico and the United States generally and Indigenous peoples in Guatemala specifically. Young people identified several salient discourses in campaigns, including assumptions about the reasons why young people migrate, how they decide to migrate, and the roles of their parents in the process. Young people highlighted critical absences in the media campaign, gaps that ignore the structural factors—such as security, development, employment, education, and health care—that shape their everyday lives and that pathologize their Indigenous identity.

CONDITIONS OF MIGRATION
"It's got a catchy beat," Sandra observed.

"La Bestia del sur le llaman. Al maldito tren de la muerte" (They call her the Beast from the South, this wretched train of death), Liliana crooned the refrain.

"Es pura mierda" (It's all bullshit), Mateo chimed in. "It's not like we don't know the risks. We know them already."

We sat in plastic chairs in a two-room community center off the central plaza in San Juan Ostuncalco listening to a cumbia song commissioned and produced by CBP that played across twenty-one radio stations in Central America in the summer of 2014. Named after the iconic La Bestia (the Beast), the freight train running through Mexico upon which many migrants journey, the song warns:

Colgados en sus vagones	Hanging on the railcars
De la serpiente de acero	Of this iron beast
Van migrantes como reses	Migrants go as cattle
En camino al matadero,	To the slaughterhouse
Por la ruta del infierno	Taking hell's route
Entre humos de dolores.	Within a cloud of pain.
Este trueno que estremece	This shuddering thunder
No conoce de favores	Does not know about favors
Lleva tres seises tatuados	It wears three sixes tattooed
En sus ruedas y su frente.	On her wheels and her head.
Feudo mara salvatrucha,	Mara Salvatrucha feud,
La quincena de coyotes.	Coyotes' payday.
Un mortero que machaca,	A crushing mortar,
Un machete que desgaja.	A slicing machete.
La Bestia del sur le llaman	They call her the Beast from the South
Al maldito tren de la muerte.	This wretched train of death,
Con el diablo en la caldera,	With the devil in the boiler
Pita, ruge y se retuerce.	Whistles, roars, twists and turns.

Hovered around a long card table, as we ate *pan dulce* (sweet bread) and sipped *aguas* (sodas), I asked young people about the risks of migration. They shared:

ANDREA: Extortion. Kidnapping. Rape. Assassinations. You run the risk of losing your life during the trip.

ARTURO: My dad said crossing into the United States used to be the hardest part, but it seems like you have to endure so much before you even arrive.

GIOVANNI: Just yesterday, two bodies returned. They drowned while crossing the Río Bravo.

MATEO: The police shake you down, take your money and your bag. And if it isn't the police, it is the gangs who are hopped up on drugs and throw you off the train just for fun. It's brutal.

ALEXA: Women are raped. My cousin got an anti-Mexico shot [birth control] before she left and cut her hair to look like a boy. She didn't want to get pregnant.

GUSTAVO: Nature can get you . . . the snakes or coyotes, the desert, the sun or cold. My cousin told me that the desert is fatal—that even if you are hot, you shouldn't take off your shirt . . . that you will never have enough water to satisfy you.

LILIANA: Mexico is a *matadero* [slaughterhouse] and a cemetery for us as Central Americans. We've faced such bad treatment there for so long.

FERNANDO: For us, Mexico is the Bermuda Triangle. People are disappeared, and you never hear from them again.

Our conversation quickly revealed that the risks of irregular migration are well known to youth—whether from cartels, gangs, police, or other migrants who prey on migrants as they pass through Mexico, usually en route to the United States. Almost all of the young people sitting around the table had personal experiences through parents, cousins, siblings, or peers who had migrated or attempted to migrate. Andrea, Mateo, and Francisco themselves had migrated and were deported. This familiarity with migration is not unique to this group of young people, as nearly 1.7 million Guatemalans—roughly 10 percent of the country's population—were deported from the United States and Mexico between 2012 and 2018.

Young people pointedly identified Mexico as a zone of transit that is particularly dangerous. As Arturo astutely posited, "My dad said crossing into the United States used to be the hardest part." Indeed, securitized responses to migration have intensified within zones of transit since the time when his father migrated in the 1990s. As scholars have documented, until recently, would-be migrants could cross relatively easily from Guatemala into Mexico, but once inside Mexico they now confront violence from multiple angles and from diverse state and nonstate actors.[4]

"They rape you or threaten to rape your kids," Alexa explained. She detailed how women must hide and contort their gender as a form of protection from all manner of actors:

Women must wear baggy men's clothes and cut their hair really short or dye
it darker. Wearing a baseball cap helps. Some women tape their chest, so you
can't see that they are feminine. And, wearing different shoes. That's a total
giveaway . . . if your feet are small and you are wearing tennis shoes, they can
tell . . . We have to remain silent, so they can't tell we are women from our
voices . . . If you can, it's just better to pay more to be safe.

As I looked around the table, almost everyone nodded their heads in knowing agreement. Estimates on the prevalence of sexual violence along migratory
routes are difficult to trace. Recent reports approximate that 80 percent of
women and girls experience sexual violence while transiting through Mexico.[5]
Strikingly, in 2014, only six cases of rape of migrants were reported officially
to Mexican authorities, leaving perpetrators with extensive impunity. Activists
contend that these low rates are emblematic of the Mexican state's efforts to
stifle denouncements of human rights abuses of transit migrants. Since that
time, Mexican officials have failed to disclose the number of sexual assaults
reported by migrants.

Alexa described the availability of birth control injections that last three
months, injections youth colloquially call "anti-Mexico shots." Women and
girls access injections at local pharmacies, midwifery offices, or some private
hospitals, she explained. "It costs but better than having to provide for a *coy-
otito* [baby smuggler] . . . But the shots don't protect us from disease. I heard
about a girl who got AIDS when she was raped."

In spite of the availability, there is considerable stigma associated with birth
control, particularly among young, unmarried women in the highlands of Guatemala. "It's not something you want people to know about because they think
you are a prostitute. People think you have to be a *cuerpomátic* [to reach the
United States]," Andrea explained, using a slang word combining *cuerpo*, or
body in Spanish, with Credomatic, a credit card company well known throughout Central America. In this view, sex is a form of currency for women to secure
protection from smugglers or authorities, rather than as a trauma inflicted upon
women and girls. The girls in our discussion particularly were attuned to the
gendered risks of migration that bring rape, pregnancy, sexually transmitted
infections, and accusations of promiscuity. They identified ways women and
girls prepare themselves psychologically and physically for the probability of
rape as they framed sexual violence as a "cost" of migration. Notably, there was

little recognition—in neither the campaign nor our discussion—that boys and men are also subject to sexual violence, a reality largely ignored in research, in public discourse, and in communities.[6]

CRIMINALIZATION OF SMUGGLING

For several of the young people participating in the discussion, the song's conflation of the Mara Salvatrucha gang with coyotes as monopolizing smuggling routes proved erroneous. They identified more diverse and complex relationships between migrants and smugglers. Gustavo offered this explanation:

> My cousin's smuggler was his boss at a local carpentry shop. My cousin worked for him for three years. The gang started coming for him to pay a tax and my cousin got tired of it. He couldn't make any money; the tax was too high, so he had to leave. His boss charged him 20,000 quetzales [2,630 USD] just for his costs, no profit or nothing. He took cars and buses all the way north.

Andrea shared, "My sister hired a *pollero* [smuggler] who was a member of the COCODE. She paid extra for someone trusted because for women you never know what will happen."

Like the Guatemala City billboard of the MS-13 gang member who "does not love your child," coyotes are typically portrayed as shadowy criminals who exploit the most desperate for profit. Indeed, cartels and gangs that historically focused on the smuggling of drugs and guns are now in the business of human smuggling. "Mom and pop" smugglers once able to transport people from Guatemala now are challenged to navigate limited access to the transportation routes that are heavily policed by immigration enforcement and/or controlled by the Mexican cartels. The cost of irregular migration from Guatemala to the United States has spiked accordingly from $1,000 in the 1990s to $12,500 in 2019.[7] But this shift did not develop by happenstance; it is a reaction to an increasingly militarized response to migration management since the 1990s and early 2000s, as discussed in the next chapter. Yet relationships with longtime facilitators of migration remain, and in most instances, are preferred by young people and their families because they are trusted individuals in the community and maintain a well-known track record. As Arturo, Gustavo, and Andrea described, trusted smugglers may be family members, community leaders, local police, or employers, who for financial profit, personal connection, or other motivations facilitate the movement of people across international borders. While some smugglers forge alliances with drug cartels and gangs, the reductive depictions of smugglers as good or bad actors fail to resonate with these and other young Guatemalans I encountered.

These rudimentary depictions also prove counterproductive to public policy in Guatemala. For example, in 2015 at the insistence of the United States, the Guatemalan Congress passed a series of "anticoyote laws" to extend prison sentences for convicted smugglers from six to eight years, and upwards of thirteen years for smuggling children and pregnant women; to criminalize additional forms of assistance such as falsifying documents, providing employment, or aiding in the passage of migrants; and to enact fines of up to $50,000 for smugglers.[8] Analogous proposals were made in Honduras and El Salvador. Failure to implement these provisions would result in curtailed development aid, USAID contended. In the first few months of its implementation in Guatemala, I met four parents who were confronting significant fines and three parents who were detained as "smugglers" when their children arrived unaccompanied in the United States.

Parallel policies emerged in the United States. In February of 2017, then DHS Secretary John Kelly signed a memo promising to penalize anyone who paid smugglers to bring a child across the border.[9] In it, "parents and family members" are explicitly identified as subject to prosecution if they have paid to have their children brought into the United States. It was contrastingly characterized by immigration advocates as the "cruel and morally outrageous" rounding up of parents and by ICE officials as a "humanitarian effort" to target human smugglers.[10] Arrests in the United States began in earnest in late 2017. Some parents or relatives who sponsored unaccompanied children from federal custody faced criminal smuggling-related charges and prison time; others were placed in deportation proceedings along with their children.[11] Rather than target criminal smugglers, migrants and their families in the United States and Central America have become more perniciously ensnared in the growing global enforcement dragnet, attesting to the ways smugglers and smuggling are grossly misunderstood.[12] In other words, the categorization of smuggling as a criminal activity allows the state to deter, punish, and ultimately justify securitized responses to irregular migration, when in many instances, families seek out trusted individuals to create opportunities for children along the safest available routes.

These media campaigns and corresponding policies extend beyond criminalizing smugglers, or even parents, in an effort to deter migration. They criminalize migration itself. Rather than invest in social programs or economic development in the region, the PSAs and corresponding policies attempt to scare, intimidate, and coerce would-be migrants and their families from undertaking a journey. In so doing, this campaign and corresponding policies remain focused on the idea that young migrants and their families are singularly responsible for migratory decisions, rather than the underlying conditions that make remaining in Guatemala untenable or even dangerous. The irony remains that the approach of the PSAs and antismuggling legislation contributes to the same securitized approaches to migration management that both created the very economic, political, and social precarity spurring migration from Guatemala and produced the increasingly deadly terrain through Mexico—an irony that is likewise perverse. Thus, the power of political rhetoric is interconnected with how discourses are created, institutionalized, practiced, and reinforced.

"MEXICO IS A CEMETERY": THEN AND NOW

Initial discussions of the roles and relationships of smugglers to transnational migration eventually segued into an animated discussion of "La Bestia." "Besides," Arturo explained, "the song talks about the gangs, right? 'Mara Salvatrucha feud, Coyotes' payday.' But if you go with a smuggler, it isn't on the train, at least not if you have some *pisto* [cash]. If you've got *pisto*, you go another route. The train is for when you have no help."

Carolina described the difficulty climbing atop the train, especially for those traveling with young children. "My aunt said that they had to pay the conductor to stop the train, so she could get on and off with my [two-year-old] cousin; it is worth the extra money."

Francisco, who had been quiet until this point in the conversation, agreed. "It's hard to get on but harder to stay on and worse to get off." He shared that he had attempted to migrate to the United States via the freight train, only to be apprehended twice by Mexican immigration officials.

> I felt like I was going to die because the train twists and turns. I had to watch out for low branches that surprise you. It's hard to hold on; the train is old and noisy, and I didn't know when it will shift or jump. The devil really is in the boiler. It was scary, but I also felt so alive . . . I didn't expect that.

Alexa echoed, "You see on the news so many stories of people who lose their arms or legs. Or, even about those *bandilleros* [gang members] who are all drugged up, and they just throw people off. I'm glad our *compañero* [companion] is still alive."

La Bestia increasingly has become a target for enforcement efforts in Mexico. In 2014 at the U.S. and Mexican government's behest, private train companies ran the beleaguered trains at enhanced speed, at times derailing with fatal consequences; companies were pressured to hire private security forces to patrol the trains, forces that, according to migrants, harass and throw them from moving trains. In 2016, the Mexican government reclaimed from the Ferrocarriles Chiapas-Mayab Rail Company one of the four rail lines running north and shut down the trains, detouring migrants by foot to more remote and hazardous routes. As with government efforts to obstruct migrants from denouncing sexual violence, the Mexican state created bureaucratic barriers to reporting other types of abuse to Mexican authorities and threatened victims with jail and heavy fines for unlawfully residing, even if momentarily, in Mexico. Activists contend that Mexico is in direct violation of non-refoulement provisions in its Law on Refugees, which was revised in 2011 to create a more humane response to the presence of unaccompanied minors in transit.

It is important to note that the song "La Bestia" is not the Border Patrol's first foray into enlisting advertising tactics to discourage undocumented migration. In 1998, it developed the Border Safety Initiative, which created "*migra corridos*" in the style of Mexican folk ballads to convey the tragic and deadly consequences of border crossing. By playing these on radio stations alongside popular music, the Border Patrol sought to subversively influence public opinion. That the Border Patrol enlisted a genre rooted in Mexican oral history is noteworthy. Corridos typically narrate timely political and popular issues, celebrating heroic achievements or deeds. As Chicana and Chicano Studies scholar María Herrera-Sobek explains, since its inception in the mid-nineteenth century, the corrido has been a genre centered in the clash of cultures between Mexicans and Anglos along the U.S.-Mexico border.[13] The content of corridos, she writes, "frequently encompassed a political purpose, since they tended to be subversive as well as informative, providing historical narratives for the community who lacked the venues of established newspapers or printing presses."[14] U.S. immigration enforcement appropriated a traditional Mexican genre in order to captivate and mislead the audience, all in an effort to simultaneously exclude Mexicans and Central Americans from the United States. Now, the Border Patrol has turned to *cumbias.*

With the implementation of Programa Frontera Sur (Southern Border Program) in 2014, which I discuss in greater length in chapter three, traditional migratory routes have all but shut down. In July of 2014, Mexican President Enrique Peña Nieto dispatched over three hundred immigration agents to southern Mexico and began routine raids of La Bestia in an effort to deter migration. Under the guise of humanitarianism, Peña Nieto claimed, "The government will continue to evaluate the strategies and redouble its efforts in these areas, with the objective of guaranteeing the human rights and security of migrants moving through our country."[15] On the ground, this translated into an increased number of checkpoints, primarily in the southern states of Chiapas, Oaxaca, Veracruz, and Tabasco, to block undocumented migration. The violence along border corridors and the state's militarized response to irregular migration exemplify how the U.S. and Mexican states collude to compel migrants along specific, deadly routes that amplify rather than mitigate their vulnerability.

This collusion is not without precedence. Central Americans historically have confronted a toxic blend of immigration enforcement and long-standing xenophobia particularly acute for Indigenous peoples. That Liliana identified Mexico as a cemetery for Central Americans is particularly poignant, alluding to Guatemala's genocide and the nearly two hundred thousand primarily Indigenous Guatemalans who sought protection in Mexico during Guatemala's thirty-six year armed conflict. Some youths throughout my research had limited knowledge of the intricacies of the conflict in Guatemala or of the personal and collective traumas their parents and grandparents endured. Yet, Liliana explained, "The memories live in me." Young people draw from this collective history of suffering, even if not fully grasped or directly experienced, as they situate discourses about contemporary Indigenous migration. Liliana's evocation of this historical narrative about the persecution of Indigenous Guatemalans in Mexico, that "[w]e've faced such bad treatment there for so long," illustrates the discursive power of these historical injustices that become reinscribed in the present day.

For Liliana, the song "La Bestia" erroneously relies on an indiscriminate characterization of Mexico as violent rather than the specific and historical experiences of Indigenous Guatemalans in Mexico or the Mexican state's complicity in historical and emerging forms of violence toward Central Americans. For Fernando, "Mexico is the Bermuda Triangle" in which "[p]eople are disappeared." In using "disappeared" for the over seventy thousand Central American migrants gone missing in Mexico in the last decade, Fernando links the contemporary disappearance of migrants to state-orchestrated disappearances during Latin America's wars in the 1970s and 1980s in which authoritarian regimes "disappeared" or kidnapped and killed hundreds of thousands of people throughout the region. In Guatemala, the Commission for Historical Clarification documented that the military disappeared forty-five thousand Guatemalans, many of whom continue to be unaccounted for since the end of the armed conflict.

Through young people's analyses, we see how Central Americans are victims not just of one, but of multiple borders that transcend time and national territory. Youth are well aware that border violence and death are not geographically constrained to the U.S.-Mexico borderlands. As literary scholar Maritza Cárdenas argues, La Bestia itself has become emblematic of a shared trauma of Central American migrants, a known reality that dehumanizes migrants while simultaneously offering promise of a different future.[16] "You have to endure so much before you even arrive," as Arturo observed. Or, as Francisco dryly joked, *"Bienvenido a México. ¡Escoja la manera de morir!"* (Welcome to Mexico. Choose what way to die!)

For those who are able to reach the U.S.-Mexico borderlands, the journey is not over, and the ensuing crossing may prove deadly as migrant deaths continue to rise. Scholars have demonstrated how the U.S. policy Prevention Through Deterrence implemented in 1994 effectively sealed Mexico's borders with California and Texas, funneling migrants through Arizona's Sonora desert and leading to a greater number of deaths. According to the Colibrí Center for Human Rights, from 1990 to 1999, the average number of migrant deaths in southern Arizona was 12 per year. From 2000 to 2017, the average number of deaths increased to 157 per year. From 1998 to 2017, along the U.S.-Mexico border overall, the U.S. Border Patrol recovered the remains of more than 7,216 migrants, a number that underrepresents the actual number of deaths in the border region, where physical remains decompose in the desert heat or are consumed by animals.[17]

The number of disappearances of migrants suggest a much higher death toll. Movimiento Mesoamericano Migrante reports between 70,000 and 120,000 migrants have been disappeared in Mexico between 2006 and 2016.[18] Elaborating on Achille Mbembé's concept, anthropologist Jason de León argues that U.S. policymakers have engaged in *necropolitics,* or the social and political power to dictate how some people live and how some die, in which the state enlists the desert as an instrument of migration regulation and an instrument of death.[19] Migration scholars in Europe similarly document how European countries passively enlist the Mediterranean Sea to manage and deter (through death) migrants from entering Europe.[20] In this way, policymakers around the world attempt to wash their hands through the erasures of bodies from the landscape, leaving nature to physically disappear migrants. Notably, these policies are not passive state actions, rather they are deliberate and strategic approaches to the increasing number of people on the move worldwide.[21]

Much of the Dangers Awareness and Know the Facts campaigns is centered on the assumption that the contemporary risks of migration remain obscured from the general public. In eliciting the experiences and analyses of young people, it is readily apparent that youth have intimate and profound experiences with migration. Giovanni's recounting of two bodies repatriated to his community the day prior speaks to the normalcy with which young people encounter the hazards and consequences of migration. Throughout our conversations, several young people referenced the 2010 San Fernando massacre, the most notorious of large-scale violence against Central American migrants in which the Zetas (a criminal group founded by defectors from the Mexican special forces) executed seventy-two migrants from Central and South America and buried them in a shallow grave in Tamaulipas, Mexico. Young people are aware of the dangers of migration; they know the facts.

Arguably, the campaign was not intended just to publicize the dangers of migration. It likewise proffered that migratory trajectories assume a predictable form—violence, and then death. In contrast to discourses that depict young migrants as uneducated about the risks of migration and that these risks are unavoidable, young people identified variations in experiences, migratory trajectories, and meanings of migration. They also identified critical gaps in the migratory narrative represented in "La Bestia." In their analysis, youth discursively linked the dangers of migration to historical experiences of repression of Indigenous Guatemalans by Mexican authorities during the armed conflict. For young people, the song and the broader campaign fail to acknowledge the role of the U.S. and Mexican states—whether by direct action, collusion, or negligence—in creating this instability and violence that have manufactured an increasingly deadly terrain for Central Americans. Ultimately, youth as *experts by experience* conducted a more nuanced, holistic, and historicized analysis of child migration, calling into question reductive and monolithic depictions of migranthood.

INNOCENCE AND LOVE

A light-skinned woman with long chestnut hair stood against a blurred gray backdrop. Her pearl drop earrings framed her dramatically made-up eyes and rose-colored lipstick. Anitza, as the advertisement calls her, was dressed in a scoop-necked, form-fitting white blouse with fringed sleeves. "She looks like a *[tele]novela* star," Carolina offered. In the bottom-right corner of the screen, a faint figure of a child wearing a baseball cap stared across the horizon. As we huddled around my computer, debating the age of the child, I turned up the volume and played the public service announcement once again. Anitza warned:

> Esa inocencia y ese amor que usted miran a la mirada de sus hijos todos los días podría perderse en segundos cuando ellos están solos en el desierto. No mandan a sus hijos a los Estados Unidos. [Un locutor] Busquemos el sueño guatemalteco. Dejarlos ir, es dejarlos morir.

> That innocence and that love you see in your children's eyes every day could be lost in seconds when they are alone in the desert. Don't send your children to the United States. [A male announcer] Let's find the Guatemalan dream. Letting them go is letting them die.

At the video's end, uncontrollable laughter ensued. "Is this for real?" Mateo cackled. *"Dejarlos ir, es dejarlos morir,"* Gustavo parroted in a melodramatically booming voice.

LH: This doesn't speak to you? Why do you laugh?

MATEO: Man, where to start?

LILIANA: So much. There are so many places [to start]. The voice . . . it's so dramatic.

ALEXA: *¡Qué fufurufa!* [How stuck-up!] Just look at her . . . she doesn't look like us or dress like us.

CAROLINA: *¡Cabal!* [So right!]

FRANCISCO: Bet she doesn't speak Mam, either.

ARTURO: I'd bet she's never been to the desert; she'd be darker if she had.

MATEO: She's more *güera* [light-skinned] than you! No offense.

LH: None taken.

CAROLINA: So, let me get this straight, she doesn't look like me, dress like me, speak my language . . . and she still wants to tell *me* what *not* to do? *¡Púchica!* (Oh my gosh!)

Their critiques in rapid succession surprised me; Estela chuckled. From observations in classrooms and interviews with teachers and school administrators, I have observed how the Guatemalan public education system professes compliance to dominant narratives—to copy and memorize, to recite information verbatim, and to conform, often at the expense of questioning authority or valuing one's own identity, language, and history. During our planning sessions, I confessed my concerns to Estela. Would young people simply tell me what they thought I wanted to hear? That they so readily and vividly critiqued this PSA spoke not to my acumen as an anthropologist but instead to the opportunities Estela cultivated for young people to critically analyze the world around them, and in turn, the degree to which the narratives outright ignore these youths' realities.

As young people quickly pointed out, the PSAs broadcast in Spanish fail to reflect that 95 percent of child migrants from Guatemala are Indigenous, principally from the areas bordering Mexico. As Francisco knowingly intimated, "Bet she doesn't speak Mam, either." Why did advertisements directly targeting young Guatemalan migrants fail to recognize or outright ignore that child migration from Guatemala primarily and disproportionately impacts Indigenous communities? That Anitza (and the eleven other public service announcements in this series) was notably *not* Indigenous, did not dress in *traje* (traditional dress), nor speak any of Guatemala's twenty-one Maya and two non-Maya (Xinca and Garifuna) Amerindian languages reveals larger exclusions of indigeneity in discussions of migration from Guatemala. Young people also spoke to the intersecting racial and class divide between ladinos such as Anitza and Indigenous people in Guatemala. That she is light-skinned and considered snobbish links her race to her perceived elitist appearance and behavior. Anitza, they conjectured, had never visited the desert, which undermined her claims to knowledge and authority on the perils of migration. As Carolina summarized, this woman and by extension the campaign's producers do not share in race, class, language, age, appearance, or experience, yet still lecture them and more specifically their parents about the dangers of transnational migration. The blatant hypocrisy in the PSA reveals the disconnect of how young people and their migranthood are imagined by those in power and, in contrast, how youth understand their own lives and futures.

It is important to recall that we met in San Juan Ostuncalco, a town of roughly fifty thousand inhabitants in the department of Quetzaltenango whose residents largely benefit from public amenities such as electricity and have access to consumer items such as televisions and radios in stores around the central park, in the town's market, and in Xela, Guatemala's second-largest city an hour bus ride away. In many communities where I conducted research, however, families lack the financial resources to procure a television and reliable electricity with which to view the PSA. In many communities in the highlands, Spanish is not the primary language. Thus, even the delivery modality, not just the message's content, misses the mark for many Indigenous communities impacted by child migration.

> LH: What do you think about the phrase: "That innocence and that love that you see in your children's eyes every day"?
>
> CAROLINA: Sure, I understand it. Parents love their children, but I don't think they believe we remain innocent forever. I mean, maybe when we were babies, but not now.
>
> GIOVANNI: I have a friend who left [migrated] because his mom's new boyfriend didn't treat him well. My friend wasn't his son, and he didn't want him around; another mouth to feed.
>
> MATEO: My mom thinks I'm *malcriado* [spoiled]!
>
> LILIANA: Why do youth have to be innocent? What if we do something wrong or bad? Is it only okay to migrate then?
>
> ALEXA: It's not as if our parents stop loving us when we leave. Though it's true that you do see a lot of terrible things so maybe we do lose our innocence during the journey. But I'd hope my mother wouldn't love me any less.
>
> MATEO: We see a lot of difficult things even without leaving San Juan.

Young people quickly recognized that the depictions of childhood—filled with innocence, love, and protection—apply unevenly and shift over time. Carolina questioned the temporality of the claim that children are innocent—"maybe when we were babies"—but that a parent's love or concern is not necessarily limited to chronological age, as Alexa contended. A disconnect between young people's perspectives and those of the advertisements is seen in the visual and rhetorical depictions of migrants as *"niños y niñas"* (boys and girls), belying the fact that the average age of unaccompanied migrants from Guatemala is fourteen and a half. Many young Guatemalans at the age of thirteen or fourteen do not view themselves as dependent children, rather they speak of contributing to their families, pursuing education, starting careers, and beginning their own families.

Arturo added, "It makes me think of the other video we watched . . . that children shouldn't be doing 'adult' things." Arturo was referencing another PSA we reviewed that had claimed: *"No podemos permitir que los niños dejen de ser niños por hacer algo que no les corresponde."* (We cannot allow children to stop being children by doing something that doesn't suit them.) Indeed, in Guatemala, depictions of childhood filled with consumer goods and toys and free of "adult" responsibilities routinely circulate in the media. The PSA, as young people described it, is rooted in a romanticized ideal of childhood—a space characterized by play and innocence, by the absence of responsibility and "adult" knowledge, and by minimal physical and emotional maturity, unlike Giovanni's friend, who experienced feelings of being unwanted by his parents. What happens if one's homelife does not echo these oversimplified narratives of childhood? What if parental care and family affection, typically depicted within nuclear families, looks different or is not present at all? Or, as Mateo jokes, what if he is *malcriado*? As young people insightfully critiqued, the PSAs presume that childhood is both universally experienced and static.

What scholars of childhood studies readily recognize and what these youths identified is that childhood is a cultural construction; that is, childhood varies across time, location, gender, ethnicity, and class.[22] Young people quickly deconstructed the oversimplifications that undergird the campaign's intended intervention. The youths sitting around the table notably did not live idealized childhoods according to U.S. or Guatemalan middle-class social norms. Carolina, Alexa, and Liliana described waking early each day to prepare food for the family; Mateo, Giovanni, and Arturo each assisted with an array of household chores before school. Those who attended school returned home to tend animals, care for younger siblings or aging grandparents, clean, wash clothes, or work in the fields. Alexa sewed school uniform shirts for sale at a local store

while her eleven-year-old sister sewed zippers, sold piecemeal for three quetzales (forty U.S. cents) to a tailor a few towns over. Francisco no longer attended
school; he migrated seasonally to the coast to work on sugar plantations, and
when in San Juan, he farmed with his father and elder siblings. None of the
youths described their lives as free from financial concerns or "adult" responsibilities. Rather, they spoke of these tasks and responsibilities as social obligations to their families.

"My parents do not care for me less because I earn money from sewing;
they are grateful to me for the little I contribute, and I am grateful to them
for bringing me into this work and caring for me. It is all a part of the circle
that connects me to them and us to others," Alexa explained. Her sage insights
do not discount the material deprivation that young people and their families
must navigate; they do, however, recognize the reciprocal social, emotional,
and financial contributions of young people as social actors, caregivers, and
migrants (see chapter one).

PATHOLOGIZING PARENTS

A girl dressed in faded jeans and a red tee-shirt, perhaps seven or eight years
old, sat huddled on the ground, knees drawn to her chest. Hand to her face,
she wiped away an invisible tear. A highly coiffed woman named Maria Luisa
stands in the foreground, pointing sternly at viewing parents. She lectured:

> Si quieres más oportunidades para tus hijos, no los envíes en un camino inci-
> erto y peligroso. Con la migración infantil no encontrarán mejores oportuni-
> dades de vida. De hecho, pueden encontrar la muerte. Recuerde que como
> padres nuestro deber es proteger. [Un locator] Busquemos el sueño guate-
> malteco. Dejarlos ir es dejarlos morir.

> If you want more opportunities for your children, do not send them down an
> uncertain and dangerous road. With child migration, they will not find better
> life opportunities. In fact, they can find death. Remember that as parents, our
> duty is to protect. [A male announcer] Let's find the Guatemalan dream. Let-
> ting them go is letting them die.

Looking around the table, I asked, "Do you think your parents would send
you to the United States?"

Without hesitation, Mateo replied with his usual levity, "I don't think the post office could take a package my size!" The ridiculousness, even bravado, of his suggestion matched the responses of some youths, who appeared simultaneously bewildered and increasingly suspect of the messages delivered in the campaigns.

> FRANCISCO: My parents didn't *send* my brother. He wanted to go. We all wanted him to go, I mean, we didn't *want* him to, but we needed him to and he seemed okay with it.
>
> LILIANA: "Don't send your children to the United States." She acts like we have nothing to say [about it]. I don't want to migrate if I don't have to, and my parents wouldn't force me.
>
> ALEXA: I don't know. I kind of agree that when someone migrates, you have to prepare yourself for the worst. When my cousin went to El Norte [the United States], my aunt cried and cried because she feared she would never see her again. You do have to be prepared.
>
> FRANCISCO: Yeah, you never know if you will ever hear from them again, but it's not like my parents wanted to *kill* my brother. It's not their fault if something terrible were to happen. They may feel that they are responsible so maybe the ad is just trying to make them feel guilty.
>
> MATEO: I don't know about you all, but I want to hear more about this Guatemalan dream. *¡Que chilero!* [How cool!]

Just as young people identified that adults are presumed responsible for children—and children thereby dependent upon adults—so, too, they recognized how parents are held as culpable for a young person's migration. The advertisements, they argued, framed migranthood explicitly as a corruption of a child's innate innocence and implicitly as a lapse in parental love and dedication. Put another way, children who are victims of parental or adult malfeasance migrate. Yet, in these youths' experiences, parents did not force their children to migrate unwillingly or unknowingly to the United States. For Mateo, the absurdity of a parent sending him against his will was as far-fetched as being sent to the United States via Guatemala's now defunct national postal service.

Liliana contested that these portrayals of parents simultaneously overshadowed young people's social agency in contexts of migration. "[L]ike we have nothing to say" echoes the position of the child as inferior or somehow exclusively

dependent and stands in marked contrast to the integral roles children often assume in familial decision-making processes, as well as to the decisions they make
as interdependent social actors.[23] After over three hours of conversation, it was
clear young people had a great deal to say about their lives, their communities,
and migration. They described how their families recognize that migration is
highly susceptible to failure and is undertaken at great cost. The three youths
who had attempted to migrate—Francisco, Mateo, and Andrea—viewed the
decision to migrate as a gesture of their parents' trust in them to provide for their
families, as a collective investment in their future, or as a long-held promise to
reunite in the United States. In contrast to popular depictions of unaccompanied children in the United States and Central America as unattached, youth
are not migrating "on their own." Rather, they tap into complex social networks
to facilitate transnational migration. By ignoring the social and financial capital
necessary to facilitate movement and settlement of young people, discourses of
migranthood simultaneously reduce child migration as a symptom of parents'
lack of knowledge and ignore the diverse contexts in which young people may
choose migration with or without familial support.

These campaigns were not alone in their pathologization of migrants' parents; they were accompanied by UNICEF's simultaneously developed parenting
classes intended to "educate" parents on the hazards associated with migration.
Rolled out in 2014 and 2015, the course curriculum presumed that young
people passively acquiesce to parental decision-making and that parents were
also ignorant of the dangers of migration. The antismuggling laws in Guatemala
and the United States similarly reduce the multifaceted conditions that spur
child migration to ones of parental ignorance and culpability. Emerging from
differing cultural constructions of childhood, outside assessments of parental
fitness and modes of caregiving become markers of "unenlightened parents"
or "backward cultures." This narrative derives from cultural constructions of
childhood and parenthood that significantly are not shared by young people
and their families.[24]

EL SUEÑO GUATEMALTECO

Each public service announcement in this series ends with a male announcer's
booming voice commanding the audience: *"Busquemos el sueño guatemalteco.
Dejarlos ir es dejarlos morir."* (Let's find the Guatemalan dream. Letting them

go is letting them die.) I asked young people a series of questions explicitly about *el sueño guatemalteco*—What do you think about the Guatemalan dream? What is it, and is it attainable?

ARTURO: If a family struggles to eat and the government doesn't provide work, what can we or our parents do? If there is a need, we work.

ALEXA: It's better to be on our own land, the land of eternal spring, than in the United States without family and without a career we can work toward. It's better that I study and move forward in our country, but when there isn't opportunity to work or to survive here, what choice do I really have?

FRANCISCO: The government should really offer free education, stable jobs, and security. Maybe then there would be a possibility of a Guatemalan dream. Right now, with this corrupt government, I truly don't see it.

FERNANDO: When I was younger, I wanted to grow up to be a gringo [non–Latin American]. That was my dream.

CAROLINA: Please explain it to me how to fulfill my dream. I just don't see where to begin. Is it to have a big home, two Mercedes, the latest phone, and stylish clothes? Can I wear my *traje* and speak Mam and still achieve the dream? That is not *el buen vivir* [Indigenous conceptualization of good living].

GUSTAVO: What if it's not safe to work here? No matter my education, my career, my wages, it isn't relevant if I can't be safe in my community or go to church or school or play soccer. It's their fantasy, not my reality.

MATEO: Maybe it's all a conspiracy.

ESTELA: A conspiracy?

MATEO: . . . to have us think there is a dream so that we work, and work and work, and the elite keep benefiting from us.

ALEXA: I dream of *el derecho a no migrar* [the right to not migrate].

Countering the illusive American dream with a call to develop the Guatemalan dream did not resonate with young people's everyday experiences of under-resourced schools, high unemployment, and financial instability in San Juan Ostuncalco. For Francisco, migration is not evidence of a failure of personal or collective imagination or even a lack of knowledge of the risks of migration, as these public policies suggest. Even for those able to secure an education and pursue a career, as Gustavo and Mateo argued, there is a shortage of employment opportunities for young professionals. Young people both in and beyond this gathering attributed a lack of livable wages and dignified work to the government's failure to create economic opportunities due to pervasive corruption, social inequality, and systemic racism. Gustavo and Mateo similarly were critical of the manipulation of their labor in the financial interests of the elite, a well-documented trend of the state privileging corporate interests over its citizenry. They squarely placed responsibility on the political leadership in Guatemala that repeatedly has failed to establish livable and dignified conditions for Indigenous communities and to secure public safety.

As Carolina intimated, the notion of a "Guatemalan dream" suggested in these advertisements is further reliant on a capitalist notion of success exemplified through conspicuous consumption and, notably, a suspension of outward markers of one's indigeneity. Fernando's childhood dream to become a gringo is a painful reminder that in Guatemala, valuation is bound up in notions of class, race, indigeneity, and migranthood. In contrast, Carolina expressed that wearing her *traje* and speaking Mam should not be the antithesis of success. Quite the contrary, she suggests her dream lies in aspiring for *el buen vivir*—a visionary Indigenous movement rooted in the valorization of Indigenous ways of knowing and the advancement of a collective well-being. In other words, *el buen vivir* is placed above individual material needs and wants and instead focuses on the *equilibrio* (harmony or balance) of the community, which, broadly conceived, includes people, nature, the spirits, and the Earth. For these Maya Mam youths, this balance is essential in enacting the right to not migrate.

RESISTANCE

If these messages about child migration and migranthood are so transparently false to the people for whom they are designed to reach, these campaigns cannot be effective in responding to the concerns or needs of Indigenous communities. Even while false, however, these discourses matter. They matter because they dehumanize migrants, homogenize the multiplicity and complexity of their experiences, render individuals and communities invisible, and reinforce inequality and injustices. They powerfully shape and are shaped by state and foreign policies, and they become embedded in institutional and social practice. Taken as naturalized and generally accepted knowledge, discourses not only are made material in bodies, spaces, and objects but likewise are internalized.[25] For the young people with whom I work, these discourses influence the social and emotional lives of young people and their families, affecting the ways they value and devalue migranthood and how they enact *belonging* in everyday life.

Discourses are not produced just by those in power but can be a form of resistance to domination by those with structurally less power.[26] As experts in their own lives, experiences, and communities, young people deconstructed narratives by enlisting their knowledge and expertise. They fluidly catalogued the risks of migration, at times sharing the personal experiences of friends, family members, and even themselves as migrants. They corrected misinformation and assumptions about how and why people migrate and in so doing deconstructed narratives that they and their parents are "uneducated" or "ill-informed." They defied narratives that romanticize childhood and negate their social agency, pushing back against discourses and institutional practices that resign them to simple victims of adult malfeasance and negate their contributions to household decisions. They widened the frame with counternarratives that adeptly situate contemporary migratory violence within an archive of racism toward Indigenous people in Guatemala and xenophobia toward Central Americans in Mexico and the United States.

CHAPTER 3

THE MAKING OF A CRISIS

THE INFLUX OF CENTRAL AMERICAN migrants to the United States has reignited long-standing debates contesting whether they are refugees or economic migrants. Media headlines and policymakers attribute the influx in recent years either to an increase in cartel and gang violence forcing refugees to flee horrific violence or to deepening poverty in El Salvador, Guatemala, and Honduras spurring families to better their life circumstances through economic migration. Explanations on both sides of the forced-versus-voluntary dichotomy largely ignore myriad historical and contextual factors that spur contemporary migration. As scholars have long documented and as youths' own analysis attest, such factors include the legacies of colonialism, enduring impacts of prolonged armed conflicts, the emergence of transnational gangs, and exploitative multinational economic agreements. And, while the rise in the numbers of children and families migrating from Central America is indeed alarming, it should come with little surprise; it is a policy crisis long in the making.

In discussion of Central American migration, the news media and advocacy communications alike portray migrants as victims of organized crime and unscrupulous state actors who inflict gruesome and often spectacular acts of violence, such as kidnapping, rape, disappearances, and murder. These narratives center on varied forms of interpersonal violence within families, between gangs and the youths they aim to conscript, or between corrupt officials and their unsuspecting victims. These often partial accounts paint entire nations, and indeed the region, as vicious and ungovernable. These narratives serve a purpose. They grab attention and provoke outrage and empathy. For the more cynical, they sell newspapers and garner donations. As anthropologist Laura Nader warns, they also risk humiliating and stigmatizing those with structurally less power.[1] Yet these spectacular forms of violence exist alongside far more mundane and no less impactful structural violence. As an anthropologist, I am not interested in contributing to a pornography of violence that highlights only the most egregious and visible forms of violence inflicted upon child victims. Instead, this chapter examines how this violence is produced and reproduced within policies and institutions and how it, in turn, results in more recognizable forms of violence.[2]

In particular, I examine the interplay between the principle strategies of the United States for curbing migration from the region through the securitization of migration management and development aid. Conventional wisdom suggests that people migrate from contexts of less employment and economic opportunity to contexts of greater employment and higher standards of living. In this view, people migrate from "less developed" countries in the global South to "more developed" countries in the global North. Yet scholars contend that development is not the panacea for migration.[3] Sociologist Doug Massey argues that over the short term, economic development actually increases migration through transformation of "rural, agrarian societies of small-scale institutions, stable social structures, and limited markets into urbanized, industrial societies dominated by large bureaucratic institutions, fluid social organizations, and strong, integrated markets."[4] So, too, scholars have documented how economic development in a context of rapid globalization shifts social and cultural values that might likewise lead to migration.[5] By the late 1990s and early 2000s, the relationship between economic development and migration took a distressing turn. Securitization has become discursively and institutionally integrated into development initiatives as a way to respond to the real and perceived existential threats of drugs, crime, terrorism, and migration—even of children.[6] While U.S. securitization previously centered on combatting communism in the region, the security-development nexus now reflects a growing concern for

fragile or failed states where underdevelopment is deemed potentially dangerous, principally in relationship to potential wars, terrorism, and the movement
of refugees and migrants.

This security-development nexus drives U.S. responses to migration management along its borders, in zones of transit in Mexico, and within policies
and institutions in Central America. To illustrate this nexus and its impact on
children, I dissect three contemporary policies that emerged in direct response to
Central American child migration—the Programa Frontera Sur (PFS, Southern
Border Program), a migration management program in Mexico; the Central
American Minors (CAM) program, which the U.S. Department of State established as an administrative process for youth confronting violence to travel
lawfully from Central America to the United States, avoiding the dangerous
journey through Mexico; and the Alliance for Prosperity Plan (APP), the centerpiece of U.S. foreign policy toward Central America. I examine how specific
policies and development initiatives across Guatemala, Mexico, and the United
States privilege short-term securitized migration management over long-term
social programs informed by the specific economic, social, and cultural dynamics in the region. In contrast to claims that development yields greater regional
security, I argue that these policies produce rather than alleviate the very structural violence young people and their families flee.

CARSICKNESS: THE MAKING OF A FRIENDSHIP

I first met Liseth, a thirty-five-year-old Mam woman, in 2014 at a series of public
workshops and events on child migration funded by USAID and coordinated
by the International Organization for Migration (IOM) in the department of
San Marcos. The Coordinator of IOM-Guatemala invited me to attend these
events to witness their new community initiatives in action. As a consultant,
Liseth helped coordinate the events with the Mam community in San Marcos.
In the early hours of Friday morning, we departed in an IOM pickup truck from
downtown San Marcos for Sibinal, a community along the Guatemala-Mexico
border. On our drive, Liseth and I became fast friends, identifying mutual ac-
quaintances, sharing tequila-infused home remedies for Liseth's oncoming cold,
and belting out Maná's "Rayando el sol" that played on the truck's radio, much
to the mortification of my children nestled in seats behind us. When two of
my children became carsick on San Marcos's winding mountain roads, Liseth

patiently helped care for them, massaging a pressure point on my six-year-old son's wrist to relieve his nausea while I held a plastic bag for my peakish three-year-old daughter. My eldest, then eight years old, blissfully slumbered beside her. Over the next two days of activities throughout San Marcos, I learned piecemeal of Liseth's flight from Guatemala in the late 1980s, her childhood in informal refugee settlements in Mexico, the impediments to her reintegration into community life in Guatemala, and her education and activism on behalf of young people now being deported from the United States and Mexico. As Liseth shared her life story, I was struck by its uncanny parallels with many of the stories young migrants had shared with me.

After nearly two years of friendship and several visits to her family home, I asked Liseth to participate in an oral history interview, or *testimonio,* as she more aptly came to term it. A *testimonio* is a method of recording and preserving a first-person, reflexive account with the conscious purpose of bearing witness to historical events. It is distinctively and intentionally political, designed to raise consciousness about past wrongs.[7] According to Brazilian educator Paulo Freire, *testimonio* is simultaneously a means of liberation from oppression and an act of solidarity endeavoring to speak for justice against crimes against humanity.[8] *Testimonio* as a method ensured that Liseth could offer her own insights and assessments of extraordinary historical events of her childhood while living as a refugee in Mexico. Over several weeks of meeting, Liseth recounted the following transcribed narrative, which she generously agreed to share here. Liseth's experiences of migration and return serve to contextualize contemporary child migration as a historically rooted strategy in the face of uncertainty and violence inflicted upon Indigenous communities. Her *testimonio* likewise illustrates how securitization and development policies are part of the ongoing approach to migration in the past, in the present, and if we do not radically shift course, in the future.

There were two people who had been killed, their bodies left on the side of road. No one touched them for days out of fear that it would bring attention and reprisals. Eventually, a bus driver couldn't stand it anymore, so he put the two bodies on his bus and transported them back to the community. He knew them, you see; they were his cousins. I was coming home from school with my brother. We boarded the bus not realizing that the bodies filled the aisles. I knew the situation was growing more intense, but it is different to see death up close . . . to see bullet holes in flesh, to see their bodies bloated from the rain, to smell the stench. I was six. My brother was twelve.

My family needed to leave. We thought we'd only be gone for a week. At the time, I had no idea we would be gone that long. I don't exactly know all of the reasons why we left at that particular moment, but we left with nothing, really, and walked awhile and then took buses closer to the border and then walked some more into Chiapas. We didn't tell anyone . . . not our family nor our neighbors. We just left. I felt like I understood why we were leaving, but at the time, I didn't understand the impact it would have on my life.

We arrived in Mexico and lived in a clandestine community with other refugees from Guatemala. There were no services and no organizations to help us. Eventually we moved to live in an area run by Catholic nuns. We thought it would be better than being in an area without support, but we were wrong. The way they treated us, like dirty Indians, as if our lives didn't matter beyond the free labor we provided to them. They gave us nothing and treated us so poorly. I don't remember a lot from that time, but I do remember feeling like they were wolves in sheep's clothing. It's hard to remember a place that inspires you to forget.

I eventually was able to go to school. My brother wasn't able to—I don't think he was interested anyway. He worked with my parents in the fields, and I found a purpose in school. My head was always in books. In some ways, it was easier for me because I was in school and I got an education while he had to work and shoulder a lot of the responsibilities with my parents. What I initially thought would be one or two weeks became eight years.

When we finally decided to return to Huehuetenango, it was scary. Just as we had left, we returned—with nothing. We returned to our home, but it wasn't ours anymore. Other people lived there now. It was complicated. We didn't know anyone. We didn't have anything that said the house or the land underneath was ours, no titles or legal certifications. It was our community's land anyway, not really ours. We cultivated it together. When we returned, it was just our word that our families had lived there for centuries. I think my parents decided that it just seemed too risky to try to force our way back. You see, the people living there were displaced too. They had also fled from the department of Quiché. I felt really disoriented. I had spent so long trying to remember this place only to find that it was no longer. I learned to forget the past so that I could survive the present.

When I returned to Guatemala, I found the doors closed. How many years of my life I lost! I tried to enroll in school but MINEDUC (Ministerio de Educación; Ministry of Education) wouldn't recognize my education in Mexico and, honestly, I was sin papeles (without documents) in Mexico when we were there. In Guatemala, I couldn't enroll in school. We tried and tried, so many offices, so many forms but never the right ones. My parents were desperate. Here we were, returning "home" but without papers. We were refugees once again but this time in our own country, on the lands of our ancestors. It was all a great deception for me—to not be wanted by my own country. It was an extremely difficult time for my family— to find work, me trying to go to school. At the time, I was upset and angry. I loved school. I still do. But I was stuck. The return was likely easier for my brother, or at least I thought, because he didn't have to manage accessing all of these institutions and paperwork; but now I see the consequences for him . . . he's lost, restless. He still can't sit long enough to be a husband or a father.

Eventually, my family and I returned to southern Mexico, leaving once again. After a year, we were able to get my paperwork in order in Mexico. The irony, right? I somehow got Mexican identification papers . . . to this day, I'm not sure how but I think my father made some arrangements [rubbing her fingers together to insinuate a bribe]. We returned to Guatemala once again, but by this time I had already lost three years of school and the teachers would not let me join the other kids my age. I was devastated. I survived by assuming my Mexican identity and hiding my Guatemalan identity, which is both a fiction and a reality at the same time. I entered school as a Chiapaneca [from Chiapas, Mexico], speaking Mam. I acted as if I was Mexican for a long time; it was just easier than having to explain why we left and where I was for all those years. I acted as if I were an immigrant here in my own country because this is what it felt like in this place. But I also didn't feel welcome in Mexico either.

It took nine years, but I finally made it back to school and eventually to university. I survived all of the taunting and torment and racism in university. I was determined to complete my studies no matter the ridicule. I still feel as if I don't have a home, anywhere on earth. I feel like a feather in a windstorm—each gust blows me in a new direction; I cannot land no matter how hard I try. It has taken its toll, but I turn inward and to my culture to find strength and connection. My nahual *[energy or spirit] is I'x [Jaguar], after all. I'x is a feminine energy, a spirit*

that seeks to protect Mother Earth. I'x is known for her passion, bravery, and com-
mitment. With her energies, I can confront difficulties that enter my path.

Now, I'm here. My hope comes and goes in my life, but I keep learning and
fighting. I am finding purpose in helping young people who are returned to Guate-
mala. I see me in them and them in me. Like me, they are returning to a country
that does not treat us well, to a place that shames us for who we are and what we've
experienced, to a place that doesn't value our culture or our identity . . . and to a
government that impedes us. Como Maya, hemos sufrido tanto. *[As Maya, we*
have suffered so much.] . . .

My hope for them? My hope is for them, just like me, to rediscover Maya cos-
movision, the Maya calendar and its accordance with the vigesimal, and to learn
about the ways we are connected to everything and everyone. Just like I did, they,
too, can find the strength in the past, to live in the present, and to imagine a future
that connects all of us.

HEMOS SUFRIDO TANTO

Liseth's deployment of the common phrase, *hemos sufrido tanto* compresses
centuries of abuse, violence, discrimination, and exploitation by the Spanish
colonial authority, the Catholic and evangelical churches, ladinos, the military
dictatorship, the U.S. Central Intelligence Agency (CIA), and contemporary
neoliberal policies.[9] Accomplished historians and anthropologists have provided
insightful scholarship on the impacts of colonialism, the plantation labor system
in the late nineteenth and early twentieth centuries, and the armed conflict on
Maya communities in the Americas.[10] Rather than replicate this well-established
body of literature, I provide an admittedly brief overview of Guatemala's armed
conflict before delving into how U.S. immigration policy and contemporary
securitization of aid create and institutionalize violence.

In response to the historic erosion of Indigenous land ownership discussed
in chapter one, democratically elected Guatemalan president Jacobo Árbenz
Guzmán (1951–1954) passed an agrarian reform act in 1952 known as Decree
900 that sought to expropriate uncultivated land from estates of over 223 acres
and to redistribute it to five hundred thousand landless, primarily Indigenous
campesinos (farmers).[11] This reappropriation of land impacted nearly 400,000
acres owned by U.S.-based United Fruit Company (UFC). In retaliation, the

UFC sought assistance from U.S. President Dwight D. Eisenhower and the CIA to overthrow the democratically elected Árbenz administration under the guise of a regional threat of communism.[12] Installing Carlos Castillo Armas as Guatemala's president, the United States began to consolidate private interests under a conservative military regime, laying the groundwork for Guatemala's brutal armed conflict that spanned from 1960 to 1996. In the 1980s, in an effort to counteract communities where the growing guerilla movement, Unidad Revolucionaria Nacional Guatemalteca (URNG, Guatemalan National Revolutionary Unity), had won favor, military dictator Efraín Ríos Montt awarded land parcels to influential Indigenous families in order to win their support.[13] The control and distribution of previously confiscated land titles was a potent means to further fragment Indigenous communities.[14] Such was the case for Liseth and her family. Their land was confiscated by authorities under Ríos Montt, only to then be abandoned when violence intensified. When Liseth and her family returned from Mexico, they found their land occupied and themselves with little means for reclaiming ownership.

As Liseth described, Indigenous Guatemalans were targeted and abused for seeking refuge in Mexico. Beginning in the late 1970s and into the early 1980s, during the height of the conflict, nearly two hundred thousand primarily Indigenous Guatemalans sought safety in southern Mexico. Approximately forty-six thousand people were housed either in United Nations High Commissioner for Refugees (UNHCR) refugee camps or in confined settlements, as Liseth described. During this period, the Comisión Mexicana de Ayuda a Refugiados (COMAR, Mexican Commission for Refugee Aid) merged with Mexican immigration enforcement to control the movements of Guatemalans in Mexico, restricting refugees to settlements that Guatemalans referred to as "concentration camps" for their deplorable conditions. COMAR regulated the movements of Guatemalan refugees, requiring special written permission to leave the camps and regularly threatening them with deportation to Guatemala, even at the height of the genocide. The Mexican government constrained the entry of medical and humanitarian aid, even harassing its own citizens and members of religious communities who sought to provide assistance to Guatemalan refugees. The Mexican government refused to register Mexican-born Guatemalans, who by virtue of birthright citizenship were Mexican citizens—an act that, as Liseth showed, has lasting consequences for school enrollment and land ownership. The government required all residents of Chiapas—many of whom share Maya heritage with Indigenous Guatemalan refugees—to carry their birth certificates. When stopped, they were asked a series of questions to "test" their national-ity—from the figures on the Mexican flag to demanding they sing the Mexi-can national anthem to quizzing their Spanish using Mexican colloquialisms. Scholars have documented that the systematic repression of Central Americans in Mexico during the armed conflict was a concerted effort backed by the U.S. Department of State to create such inhospitable conditions that refugees would return willingly to Guatemala.[15] Notably, these tactics—limiting circulation, denying rights to citizenship, harassing those seeking to aid refugees, and test-ing of cultural knowledge to ensure belonging—continue as tactics of policing contemporary Indigenous migration through Mexico.

The U.S. response was no better. As part of its foreign policy, the Reagan administration actively thwarted Guatemalans and Salvadorans from securing political asylum. In fiscal year 1984 at the height of violence under Ríos Montt, Immigration and Naturalization Services (INS; forerunner of today's Department of Homeland Security, DHS) statistics reveal that only 1 percent of Guatemalans was approved for asylum, in contrast to a 30 percent national average for all nation-alities.[16] Salvadorans, who were also in the midst of a civil war, encountered analo-gous government obstructions, with only 3 percent of asylum petitions approved. With robust documentation of such egregious, state-orchestrated disparities, in 1985 a coalition of churches, legal service providers, and human rights organi-zations including the American Civil Liberties Union filed a lawsuit against the federal government citing discrimination against Guatemalans and Salvadorans in political asylum proceedings in violation of the Refugee Act of 1980, which estab-lished uniform criteria for asylum eligibility. After years of litigation, the *American Baptist Churches (ABC) v. Thornburgh*[17] settlement agreement of 1991 recognized the discriminatory practices of the U.S. Citizenship and Immigration Services, the Executive Office of Immigration Review, and the U.S. Department of State and secured stays of deportation and de novo adjudication for many Guatemalan and Salvadoran migrants who were previously denied asylum.[18]

With the passing of the 1996 Illegal Immigration Reform and Immigrant Responsibility Act (IIRIRA) in the United States, the suspension of deporta-tion, or "hardship relief" was severely curtailed, leaving many undocumented immigrants in even more tenuous positions. Prior to IIRIRA, suspension of deportation could be granted for an individual who had been physically present in the United States for seven years, who had a "good moral character," and whose deportation would result in "extreme hardship" to the applicant or the applicant's U.S. citizen or permanent resident spouse, child, or parent. IIRIRA established stricter standards, including ten years of continuous presence and "exceptional and extremely unusual hardship" to a permanent resident of a citizen spouse, child, or parent.[19] It eliminated factors including prospective hardship on the applicant and disqualified almost all of those with criminal convictions. Under IIRIRA, hundreds of thousands of long-term residents who had resided in the United States before its implementation would have lost the possibility of remaining. To remedy this potential violation of the ABC settlement agreement, the U.S. Congress passed the 1997 Nicaraguan Adjustment and Central American Relief Act (NACARA)[20] establishing specialized procedures to secure legal permanent residency for some unauthorized migrants from Nicaragua, Guatemala, El Salvador, Cuba, and some countries of the former Soviet bloc who as de facto refugees had been categorically denied legal status in the 1980s and 1990s in the United States. Under NACARA, 200,000 Salvadorans, 150,000 Nicaraguans, 50,000 Guatemalans, and 5,000 Cubans were permitted to apply for hardship relief under policies prior to IIRIRA and to have their cases adjudicated by an asylum officer in lieu of an immigration judge, a move that expedited their legal petitions which otherwise would have dragged on for years. As legal permanent residents in the United States, many Guatemalans petitioned for family members, thereby establishing a steady flow of regularized Guatemalan immigrants to the United States. Since the 1970s, nearly twelve million Guatemalans have migrated both lawfully and irregularly to the United States and Canada, and they continue to serve as a compelling influence, particularly for young Guatemalans seeking to reunify with family members abroad.[21]

Through Liseth's retrospective reflections, we see the imperative to understand the current migration of young people—as well as the public discourses, legal violence,[22] and institutional responses—within broader legacies of colonialism, armed conflict, and foreign intervention in and beyond Guatemala. Decades of military repression and genocide were not instantaneously remedied with the signing of the 1996 Peace Accords that ceremoniously ended the conflict. For Liseth's family and many others who fled Guatemala, the Peace Accords signified the possibility of return, yet in practice, they continued to confront systematic discrimination as Indigenous people. In her home country, Liseth was compelled to conceal her Guatemalan identity and to accentuate her Mexican identity, albeit fictive, in order to navigate the institutional and legal obstacles confronting refugees returning to Guatemala. The state's historic hostility toward Indigenous migrants returning to Guatemala parallels many of the obstacles confronting people returning or returned to Guatemala today. While the armed conflict that led to Liseth's flight officially ended in 1996, its violent traces persist in postwar Guatemala with, as Liseth reminds us, enduring social and emotional impacts on young people's sense of belonging over time and the ways they conceptualize and experience "home."

WAR BY ANOTHER NAME

Migration from postconflict Guatemala is often attributed to visible forms of violence from gangs, cartels, and corrupt police. Indeed, Guatemala has one of the highest violent crime rates in Central America. In 2017, Guatemala's Policía Nacional Civil (PNC, National Civil Police) registered 4,409 homicides, resulting in a homicide rate of 6.1 per 100,000 inhabitants. This represents an important though modest decrease from the 4,778 homicides recorded in 2015. Criminologists point to the free circulation of narcotrafficking activities and gang-related violence as a primary reason for high rates of violent crime.[23] However, gangs are not native to Central America; scholars have meticulously documented the ways U.S. deportation policies created transnational criminal gangs in Central America through the deportation of nearly 129,000 gang members to the region starting in the early 2000s.[24] Met with few economic opportunities and limited social networks, and often after prolonged stays in the United States, criminal gangs took hold in Central America and flourished in the movement of cocaine and opiates from South America to a demanding public in the United States. In contemporary Guatemala, violent crime is aggravated further by an abundance of weapons (nearly 60 percent of the population possess firearms) held over from the armed conflict and with no official means of regulating ownership. Homicides and gang violence, however, are not the leading causes of migration, as pundits contend. Most of Guatemala's homicides are concentrated along the Honduran border and in the southeast of the country,[25] not in the regions from where the majority of people migrate—San Marcos, Huehuetenango, Totonicapán, Quiché, and Quetzaltenango—which experience lower rates of violent crime.

I spoke with Dionisio, a former URNG guerilla and now a human rights attorney in Guatemala City, about the sources of violence in postconflict Guatemala. Dionisio took out a well-worn envelope filled with tobacco from the front pocket of his army-green jacket, and slowly rolled a cigarette. Licking the paper, he explained:

> How can we talk about "postwar" when this has been going on for centuries? When current conditions of violence and overt hostility continue unabated? The *militares* (military personnel) who tried to exterminate us have not been brought to justice. They walk down the street with impunity. They occupy the Palacio Verde [former presidential palace]. Indigenous communities are still not full participants in society. We are still forced from our lands. The state does not represent or even recognize us. In fact, the state seeks to exterminate us, sometimes in visible but often in invisible ways. It is still war, just by another name.

The 1996 Peace Accords intended to usher in the transition to a multicultural democracy, yet as Dionisio identified, historical tensions and inequalities do not disappear overnight, nor in the two decades since the war's end. In many ways, postconflict reconstruction has reinforced strategies of oppression and social control that emerged during colonialism and the armed conflict, which continue in insidious and at times less recognizable forms of structural violence.

"Structural violence" refers to the historically and socially produced ways that social structures systematically inflict harm on individuals.[26] Medical anthropologist Paul Farmer explains:

> The arrangements are structural because they are embedded in the political and economic organization of our social world; they are violent because they cause injury to people . . . neither culture nor pure individual will be at fault; rather, historically given (and often economically driven) processes and forces conspire to constrain individual agency. Structural violence is visited upon all those whose social status denies them access to the fruits of scientific and social progress.[27]

In Guatemala, structural violence is ordinary and mundane. It manifests as everyday discrimination against Indigenous peoples, including through poor schooling; lack of investment in roads, electricity, and potable water; marginalization from the labor market; and corruption and impunity at all levels. Structural violence may also cause illness and even death due to failing to treat

preventable diseases, lack of medication, and the environmental contamination resulting from extractive industries. As anthropologists have documented
in contexts of migrant labor, over time these cumulative harms compromise
the quality of life or even shorten lives.[28] Structural violence encapsulates various forms of social and institutional deficiencies that have dire material consequences on people's lives, even if not immediately visible.

In postconflict Guatemala, structural violence reinforces existing social inequalities that are presumed as the seemingly inevitable social norm. Consider
the experiences of the youths cited in chapter one. In his interview with the
immigration paralegal in Chicago, Domingo described experiencing harassment and discrimination "all the time [from] store owners, teachers, police, the
government . . . you name it." Unable to survive, Alfredo, Ignacio, and Maria
Clara were compelled to migrate to the Pacific coast, Mexico, and Guatemala
City, respectively, to support their families through their paid labor and unpaid
care work. Their experiences of poverty and economic deprivation are borne
out in national statistics, with 59.3 percent of the population living in poverty
and 23.4 percent living in extreme poverty. It is important to note, however,
that Indigenous Guatemalans represent roughly 60 percent of the population
but make up 80 percent of the country's poor.

As scholars have cautioned, however, institutions do not act, people do.[29]
The term "structural violence" runs the risk of reifying institutions or policies
rather than implicating the individuals who make up the institutions or formu-
late public policies. Indeed, as Dionisio highlighted, direct violence and structural violence are not mutually exclusive in Guatemala, rather they reinforce
long-standing inequalities. The very *militares* who orchestrated the Guatemalan
genocide have not been brought to justice and now govern with impunity, de-
vising new ways to marginalize Indigenous communities from the nation. For
Dionisio, the visible and often invisible ways that the state seeks to exterminate
Indigenous people illustrates long-standing racism toward and oppression of
Indigenous communities in Guatemala.

Development is often cited as the silver bullet, critical to remedying structural inequities and creating alternatives to migration. Yet lopsided free trade
agreements such as the Dominican Republic–Central America Free Trade
Agreement (CAFTA-DR) have only deepened social inequality throughout the region.[30] Modeled after the North American Free Trade Agreement,

CAFTA-DR sought to liberalize trade and institutionalize neoliberal structural adjustment programs of the International Monetary Fund and World Bank. Establishing conditions conducive to foreign investment, CAFTA-DR focused primarily on police training, anticorruption initiatives, and developing a pliable workforce through free trade zones to meet international private-sector demands.

CAFTA-DR brought a boon in extractive megaprojects to Guatemala, such as multinational mining, hydroelectric plants, logging, petroleum extraction, and African-palm production, but has not delivered on development promises. Rather, they have destroyed economic resources and led to environmental degradation of Indigenous lands.[31] Take mining, for example. Mining profits are increasing at a rate of 10 percent annually, yet these profits are not distributed to communities that bear the brunt of the environmental consequences of diverted groundwater near mines and contaminated water supplies. Near multinational mines in San Marcos where I research, community members report increased rates of asthma, infant mortality, and cancer and a lower life expectancy in comparison to the national average.[32] In spite of assurances to resolve mining conflicts that adversely impact Indigenous communities, the government continues to issue speculative mining permits without holding legally obligatory *consultas comunitarias* (community consultations).

In general, *consultas comunitarias* are community gatherings held prior to decision-making in which Indigenous peoples are consulted on projects (investments, public decisions, and the like) that may affect them. In Maya ancestral practice, communities make decisions, not individuals. As such, external territorial or cultural entities cannot make decisions that impact the integrity and livelihood of Indigenous communities. *Consultas comunitarias* offer an avenue through which communities are informed prior to decision-making and allow for consensus building free of coercion and misinformation. For Indigenous communities that maintain limited access to resources and political power, these community forums are an essential step in respecting the autonomy of Indigenous communities in regard to their development. Although recognized under national and international laws, in practice, when *consultas comunitarias* are held (and often they are not), the perspectives of participants and their autonomy over Indigenous territories are often ignored. At times, community members are threatened if they voice dissent.

Hydroelectric development is perhaps the most illustrative of the egregiously unequal impacts of development on Indigenous communities in Guatemala. The proliferation of hydroelectric plants not only has displaced people from their lands but also has failed to benefit the communities most affected. Approximately 3,500 communities remain without electricity, the majority of which are located in the departments of Baja Verapaz, Alta Verapaz, and Quiché, which ironically are home to the Chixoy river that generates one-third of the country's electrical power. Similar patterns characterize the recently booming palm oil industry, for which there have been few *consultas comunitarias*. The palm oil industry inflicts violence on Indigenous peoples through land consolidation, contamination of water sources, devastation of fish and wildlife, and notoriously horrendous labor conditions. Meanwhile, the profits are monopolized by eight families who control all of Guatemala's processing plants and who produce 98 percent of the country's palm oil.[33] Anthropologist Giovanni Batz traces how Maya Ixil communities aptly label these primarily European and American industries as the *fourth invasion*—of megaprojects such as mining, hydroelectric projects, and African oil palm cultivation—following the three previous invasions: Spanish colonialism (1524–1821), the plantation economy (nineteenth century), and the armed conflict (1960–1996).[34] As Batz and others have documented, the extractive industries continue to displace farmers while taxing and depleting the land.[35] Serving the interests of large multinational firms in Guatemala such as agribusiness, mining, and energy firms, CAFTA-DR has resulted in considerable hardship for small farmers,[36] failed to implement enhanced labor protections,[37] and in turn, produced rather than deterred migration.

Natural disasters, including earthquakes, heavy rainstorms and drought, are also on the rise as a result of climate change, impacting agricultural production and the need to migrate for survival.[38] Among families in the departments of San Marcos and Quetzaltenango where I conduct research, this depletion or "loss of habitat"[39] spurs the migration of young people not only to meet the everyday needs of food and employment, but also to provide for the health-care needs of family members or to seek health care for themselves. Sociologist Saskia Sassen maintains, "These, then, are not the migrants in search of a better life who hope to send money and perhaps return to the family left behind. These are people in search of bare life, with no home to return to."[40] In such a context, deportation to communities ravaged by extractive industries under the guise of "development" compounds the precarity of youth who return to devastated communities.

Powerful social movements have emerged among Indigenous peoples in Guatemala, coalescing around disputes resulting from corporate land grabs, preservation of natural resources, the imposition of megaprojects, and the protection of workers' rights. With limited political representation of Indigenous communities, as Dionisio lamented, mass protest has become one of the most effective strategies to thwart multinational exploitation. Social movements have framed these megaprojects as a perpetuation of long-standing patterns of the state's racist violence and of foreign intervention, demanding systemic changes to counter the Guatemalan state's failure to recognize Indigenous identity and self-determination.[41] In response, the state has partnered with the private sector to systematically repress social resistance through coordinated violence, assassinations of environmental and Indigenous leaders, imprisonment of political activists, and forced displacement from communal lands.[42] As with the U.S. and Guatemalan protection of the private interests of the United Fruit Company during the armed conflict, securitization continues as part and parcel of private-sector interests.

Met with tightly coordinated state and private-sector repression, social movements have diversified the ways in which they resist, ranging from open uprisings, national marches, and petitions in national and international courts to everyday subversions such as road blockades and work slowdowns. They also have found allies within the United Nations International Commission against Impunity in Guatemala (CICIG, Comisión Internacional contra la Impunidad en Guatemala). In 2015, CICIG prosecutors brought corruption charges against President Otto Pérez Molina and Vice President Roxana Baldetti, along with over one dozen members of their cabinet who were caught pilfering public coffers. The public response included months of nationwide, intersectional protests under the banner #RenunciaYa (Step Down). Folding to public and international pressure, Pérez Molina and Baldetti eventually resigned. In 2017, Baldetti was found guilty; in 2019, Pérez Molina still awaits trial. Meanwhile, the subsequent president, Jimmy Morales, who ran under the campaign slogan *"Ni corrupto ni ladrón"* (Neither corrupt nor a thief), faced a CICIG corruption investigation. In 2018, Morales refused to renew CICIG's mandate in Guatemala and revoked the visas of its members in defiance of an order from Guatemala's Constitutional Court. The Trump administration remained largely silent in the face of widespread corruption and Morales's efforts to close CICIG, with Secretary of State Mike Pompeo simply stating, "Our relationship with Guatemala is important. We greatly appreciate Guatemala's efforts in counternarcotics and security." In September of 2019 and in spite of broad public support, CICIG closed its doors.

Rather than acknowledge how corruption undermines democracy in Central America and how U.S. interventions produce violence, the U.S. government continues to deploy securitization—through immigration enforcement and development aid to corrupt administrations—to suppress the entry and settlement of Central Americans, just as during the armed conflict. While Donald Trump has escalated the anti-immigrant rhetoric in the United States, there is remarkable and troubling continuity across U.S. Democratic and Republican administrations since President Harry Truman. In the past three decades, the United States has increasingly externalized its borders by mobilizing the Mexican state to manage and contain the through-migration of Central Americans, most explicitly through the Southern Border Program. We see this in Liseth's *testimonio* about events in the 1980s and 1990s and in Indigenous youths' experiences today. The securitized migration management has compounded structural violence in Guatemala, resulting in, as Dionisio termed it, war by another name.

LA OTRA FRONTERA

In 2014 the United States pressured Mexico "to stem the tide" of Central American migration through the Comprehensive Plan for the Southern Border, more commonly called Programa Frontera Sur. Since 2011, the U.S. Department of State has allocated more than $130 million from the Mérida Initiative, an initiative primarily intended to combat drug trafficking and to enhance Mexican border security along its 714-mile border with Guatemala and Belize. According to a research report commissioned by the U.S. Congress:

> As of February 2016, the State Department had delivered $20 million of assistance for Mexico's southern border region, mostly in the form of nonintrusive inspection equipment, mobile kiosks, canine teams, and training in immigration enforcement. Additional funding will support a biometric system, a secure communications network for Mexican agencies in the southern border region, and other new projects.[43]

Since that time, funding has continued with an additional $139 million in FY 2016 and $129 million in FY 2017. Programa Frontera Sur has created a more fluid circulation of data between the United States, Mexico, and Central America. This includes Mexican authorities collecting and sharing biometric data of migrants in Mexico, including fingerprints and ocular scans, in an effort to alert U.S. authorities to migrants en route. The Trump administration likewise shares these biometric data and any criminal histories of deportees with Central American authorities, granting Central American governments access to detailed records held in the U.S. Department of Justice National Crime Information Center.[44] For those deported to Central America, this practice has adverse consequences because it emboldens enforcement's propensity to redetain, track, and further criminalize returnees over time and often without access to justice. These policies and practices exacerbate already inhospitable conditions and social marginalization for deportees in Central America. The parallels with 1980s and early 1990s-era conditions that led to development of transnational gangs are uncanny.

Quickly assembled in response to the influx of unaccompanied children and families migrating to the United States, Programa Frontera Sur builds upon a longer pattern of programs designed to heighten security in southern Mexico, to foil trafficking in drugs and persons, and to thwart migration through and to Mexico.[45] Programa Frontera Sur claims to serve as "a mechanism . . . to strengthen the presence of [government] officials in the area and to coordinate actions with Central American countries in order to overcome common challenges to security and development, and to advance with the establishment of a more modern, efficient, prosperous and secure border."[46] It calls upon Mexican-Guatemalan border states of Campeche, Chiapas, Quintana Roo, and Tabasco "to work together to bring about effective actions to guarantee an adequate flow of people to the interior of national territory."[47]

Programa Frontera Sur expands the funding, technology, and training of Mexican and Central American police and the military to restore law and order and to thwart the irregular movement of goods and people across Mexico's southernmost border.[48] The program established "security belts," a multitier system of security that began along the Mexico-Guatemala border with eleven existing border patrol stations and moved northward to implement a belt across Chiapas, and thirdly in Oaxaca.[49] By August of 2014, Mexico's

Instituto Nacional de Migración (INM, National Institute of Migration) established over one hundred mobile highway checkpoints and roadblocks.[50] The
Mexican military, federal police, and state and local police joined INM officers
in conducting raids in search of undocumented migrants in Mexico. Immigration detention facilities began to expand and multiply, the result of well-worn
strategies of immigration enforcement in the United States. As a consequence,
Central American migrants face added dangers in traversing Mexico. In 2017,
the director of Casa de Migrante in Tecún Umán explained to me, "In the past
five years, we've seen increased brutality of Mexican authorities against migrants.
They are ruthless and corrupt . . . really they are no different than the Zetas
though perhaps not as well organized or resourced."

In response to rapidly deteriorating conditions for migrants in Mexico,
the nonprofit sectors of the United States and Central America pressured the
U.S. Department of State to implement the Central American Minors (CAM)
Refugee/Parole program. Initiated in 2014, the CAM program sought to create
safe alternatives to irregular migration of young people who are confronting
violence and whose parents are lawfully in the United States by establishing an
administrative process for youth to secure legal protections while still in their
respective countries of origin of El Salvador, Guatemala, and Honduras. In July
of 2016, the program expanded to include the biological parent or qualifying
care provider of an eligible child. While an important step in creating legal
alternatives to irregular migration, the process remained beleaguered, under-
utilized, and convoluted. It often took close to one year to adjudicate most petitions, in part due to administrative requirements for documentation and DNA
tests. Maynor, an immigration attorney in Guatemala City, explained to me,

> These cumbersome bureaucratic processes leave children who are confront-
> ing imminent violence with very little protection and with many, often insur-
> mountable, obstacles. Children who apply are taking a substantial risk by mak-
> ing their claims known to the very people they are fleeing but without any of
> the protections of living in a different country with some modicum of safety.

A modest 1,465 individuals were granted parole under the CAM program since
2014. A mere 31 children originated from Guatemala.[51]

In January of 2017 one of President Donald Trump's many executive or-
ders halted all refugee admissions for 120 days, which included suspending

the CAM program; in August, the Acting Secretary of Homeland Security Elaine Duke terminated the CAM program, leaving roughly 2,700 applicants conditionally granted parole but unable to travel to the United States. A Washington, DC–based attorney whom I interviewed regarding her consultation with the U.S. Department of State to devise the program reflected, "The CAM program was a token effort to appease critics and became quickly mired in bureaucratic red tape that failed to recognize the hardship the program created or the urgency of the conditions spurring migration. Now it's defunct, and we've literally abandoned children when they have put themselves and their families in harm's way." Two years later, following a series of lawsuits, DHS entered into an agreement with the plaintiffs to process the 2,700 applications that were conditionally approved prior to the termination of the program.

Central Americans are not alone in confronting the multiple and varied risks of migration through Mexico and the southern-shifting effects of Programa Frontera Sur. As American borders and ports of entry become increasingly difficult to cross, migrants from around the globe have joined Central Americans on migratory routes through Mexican border zones. In 2017 in Mexico, for example, 14,528 individuals filed for refugee status from twenty-two countries, including Cameroon, Congo, Cuba, Haiti, Israel, Russia, Somalia, and Venezuela, among others.[52] In turn, as Mexico becomes progressively perilous to traverse, migrants are seeking refugee status in Central America. An attorney with Casa de Migrante, a migrant shelter in Guatemala City, shared with me:

> Now there are people from all over, even Somalia, Pakistan, Nepal, China, Cuba, primarily, who come through here and Mexico. In 2016, there were only 128 asylum applicants in the whole of the country, primarily Salvadoran and some Venezuelan. Very few remain, most are passing through Guatemala and so government authorities have done very little to establish effective asylum procedures. Instead, they think if they ignore them, the problem will go away.

While refugee claims in Guatemala remain modest, neighboring Costa Rica received nearly 28,000 new applications from eighteen countries in 2018, nearly reaching Mexico's 29,544 new asylum applicants from twenty-six countries. Panama likewise encountered a spike in applications reaching 10,753 from twelve countries.[53]

Bowing to Trump's tariff threats, Mexico has become further implicated in the externalization of U.S. borders through the "Remain in Mexico" policy. Officially called the Migrant Protection Protocols, this U.S. policy requires individuals who seek asylum at a port of entry or who are apprehended near the U.S. border to remain in Mexico as they await a hearing with a U.S. immigration judge to adjudicate their asylum claim. In turn, Mexico agreed to provide a one-year humanitarian visa to U.S. asylum applicants and to deploy the Mexican National Guard to patrol Mexico's northern border. At the time of writing, legal challenges to these policies in Mexico and the U.S. are proceeding through the courts.

Under Programa Frontera Sur and these subsequent policies, the border has been *externalized* and delocalized physically due to increased enforcement of U.S. immigration policy through border arteries in Mexico. Just as the 1986 Immigration Reform and Control Act bolstered the militarization of the U.S.-Mexico border, the PFS seeks to securitize not only zones of transit but also the Mexican-Guatemalan border, which has become a site of enhanced enforcement and regulation of Central American migration, and more recently the Guatemala–El Salvador and the Honduras-Nicaragua borders. Under pressure from the United States, the Guatemalan government has taken to heightening enforcement and surveillance of non-Guatemalan nationals who might be migrating through the Guatemalan countryside en route to the United States. This includes citizens from the signatory countries of El Salvador, Guatemala, Honduras, and Nicaragua who—according to the Convenio Centroamericano de Libre Movilidad (Central America-4 Free Mobility Agreement) signed in 2006—are specifically permitted free circulation without checkpoints or restrictions of movement.

In 2019, the Trump administration began crafting a series of bilateral agreements seeking to further externalize U.S. borders. In Guatemala, in violation of a Constitutional Court injunction requiring prior congressional approval, the Morales Administration signed an agreement with the United States confirming that Guatemala would serve as a safe third country for asylum applicants from Honduras and El Salvador. Under pressure from the business elite, Morales claimed that he sought to evade Trump's threats of potential tariffs on Guatemalan goods, taxation of U.S. remittances, and a ban on Guatemalan nationals traveling to the United States. The Trump administration signed analogous agreements with El Salvador and Honduras, requiring asylum seekers traveling through that country to seek protection there. This means that if individuals first passed through a signatory country, they would be ineligible to seek asylum in the United States. The Honduran agreement uniquely stipulates that a failed asylum petition in Honduras renders individuals ineligible to apply for asylum in the United States.

Across each year of fieldwork, I encountered an increasing number of police checkpoints along roads in the department of San Marcos, which borders Mexico, stopping *camionetas* (public buses) in search of Salvadorans and Hondurans. On one occasion, five officers dressed in black uniforms and carrying shotguns boarded the bus, removing two young men. *"Buscan mojados del Salvador y Honduras; La Mesilla queda cerca"* (They're looking for wetbacks from El Salvador and Honduras; La Mesilla is nearby), a man sitting next to me explained. At the time, we were roughly one hundred kilometers south of La Mesilla, a border town well known for its thriving cross-border commerce. Nearly twenty years prior, Mexican authorities profiled Liseth for "looking Guatemalan" while she was legally exercising her right for refugee protection in Mexico. Now, profiling those who "look" Salvadoran or Honduran, police interrogate Central Americans despite their right to free movement in Guatemala. Legal rights were not respected in the era of Liseth's childhood, and they are not respected now. The men were loaded into the back of the police pickup truck. The *camioneta* rolled on.

THE ALLIANCE FOR PROSPERITY

Although Programa Frontera Sur and the CAM program were makeshift responses to child migration, they reflect larger trends in the U.S. securitized approach to migration management and the externalization of borders that have grown since the armed conflicts in Central America. The centerpiece of a more sustained regional response to child and family migration is the Alliance for Prosperity Plan in the Northern Triangle. Announced in late 2014, the Alliance for Prosperity is a five-year, joint regional plan between El Salvador, Guatemala, and Honduras that seeks to enhance public security in the region and to deincentivize migration through "development." With $495 million of funding in 2015, $750 million in 2016, $655 million in 2017, and $615 million in 2018, the APP aims to (1) develop human capital, (2) improve public safety and access to the justice system, (3) foster the productive sector, and (4) strengthen public institutions.[54] The Alliance for Prosperity purports to move away from earlier regional security efforts of the Mérida Initiative in Mexico and its rebranded successor, the Central American Regional Security Initiative (CARSI), to instead respond to a "citizen security crisis" through combatting corruption, enhancing "public safety," and "strengthening institutions."[55] The APP is reminiscent of John F. Kennedy's Alliance for Progress in the 1960s that paired enhanced economic cooperation between the United States and Latin America with propping up dictators who purported to curb the threat of communism.

"Citizen security" emerged as a concept when Latin American nations transitioned from authoritarian to democratic regimes. It seeks to distinguish historical violence under claims of "state security" or "national security" of authoritarian regimes from the security of individuals and social groups to live free from crime under new democracies, and to diminish the former and accentuate the latter. In postconflict Guatemala, state violence and crime are often difficult to parse apart. In recent years, murder rates have surpassed levels during the armed conflict, and in response, the state has resumed war-era *mano dura* (iron fist) approaches to public safety. The Guatemalan state has called upon the U.S. military to train the notoriously brutal special forces known as Kaibiles, which were responsible for the torture and killing of thousands of Indigenous peoples in Guatemalan during the armed conflict, now to confront drug cartels.[56] In practice, the APP fuses undocumented migration with transnational gangs and drug cartels, arguing that combatting migration is a first step in engaging foreign investment, a similar claim made under CAFTA-DR. In this way, we see the formalizing of the securitization of aid in the region. That is, foreign aid is contingent upon proscribed security initiates that Central American governments are obligated to implement in turn for needed development aid—the proverbial carrot and stick.

For example, 25 percent of APP funds are contingent upon Central American countries undertaking efforts specifically to deter migration, including informing citizens of the dangers of immigration to the United States, combatting human smuggling and trafficking, improving border security, and cooperating with the United States to facilitate the deportation of newly arrived migrants.[57] The remaining 75 percent of APP funds is contingent upon a series of neoliberal policies to combat corruption, enhance tax reform, train law enforcement, and pass specific fiscal, commercial, and investment legislation identified by the

United States as critical to support foreign investment. This aid conditionality provides the United States leverage to ensure that Central American governments are making progress on a series of sixteen issues. One of these issues was a series of antismuggler laws and penalties for parents whose children arrived unaccompanied, as discussed in chapter two. Another issue is the set of policy interventions directed at international call centers and *maquiladoras* (tariff-free factories). In 2017, the Guatemalan legislature passed a series of policies that sought to more tightly regulate taxable income from *maquiladoras* and workers, in an industry that has been declining in recent years. USAID officials shared with me that Guatemala's receipt of APP funding and foreign aid was contingent upon the Guatemalan government passing these probusiness and proinvestment policies.

A coalition of Central American NGOs, all of which were excluded from the formulation of the APP, explained in an open letter, "the Plan reinforces the same economic policies that have resulted in skyrocketing inequality, widespread abuse of workers' rights and increased violence against labor leaders, and forced displacement throughout Mesoamerica."[58] Here, coalition members reference the APP's push for the privatization of public services, the centerpiece of previous structural-adjustment programs that the International Monetary Fund and the World Bank historically have utilized to jumpstart stagnant economies and to orient national economies to the "free market." Scholars have demonstrated how these structural adjustment programs have disproportionately affected the poor, weakened the social sector, and intensified social inequality in Latin America, Africa, and Asia.[59] Immigration advocates argued that the APP is more of the same with the continued privileging of private interests of the elite over the needs of Indigenous communities.

With 60 percent of the APP budget allocated to further securitization of the region, including $222 million for international narcotics control in 2015 alone, the APP invests very little in social and economic programs that address the needs of communities from where people migrate.[60] Some modest efforts have been made to create alternatives to migration via USAID funding, largely centering on the ¡Quédate! (Stay!) initiative and apprenticeship programs for young people, to which I turn in the next chapter. However, when compared to the securitization investments allocated to the Alliance for Prosperity, these efforts are saturated with empty promises. Without considering the social dimensions of emigration from Central America, the APP fails to address the need for livable wages in dignified working conditions, social and health services, social protections, and inclusion of Indigenous communities in political life—the very exclusions young people in San Juan Ostuncalco denounced as they discussed the ideal social conditions embodied in *el buen vivir*. Now, several years since the immediate influx of development aid and humanitarian interventions of 2014 and 2018, few effective long-term alternatives to migration exist for young people and their families. What remains are policies and practices that reinforce militaristic approaches to human movement and relocate the spectacle of the border farther south. In spite of the APP's claims, Central Americans are no more secure than prior to the APP, nor are the thousands of other migrants now transiting through Central America and Mexico.

CHAPTER 4

¿QUÉDATE Y QUÉ?

IN GUATEMALA, securitized migration management under the Alliance for Prosperity Plan (APP) and its predecessor, Central American Regional Security Initiative (CARSI), have overshadowed more traditional development initiatives. But is this simply a question of misguided proportionality? When given the human and financial resources, can development actually curb migration? This chapter explores this question by tracing two development initiatives that explicitly claim to support unaccompanied children deported from the United States and Mexico, to reintegrate them into their communities, and to create alternatives to (re)migration. The first is a joint USAID and IOM effort to build the capacity of the Secretaría de Bienestar Social (SBS, Secretariat of Social Welfare), which receives unaccompanied children deported from the United States and Mexico and is charged with the "family reunification" of deported minors. To illustrate this family reunification initiative in action, I recount the experiences of sixteen-year-old Delia as she moves through multiple institutions across geopolitical space and how she experiences the program. While each experience of migration and return is unique, Delia's is representative of how many young people described to me their experiences of "reunification" within SBS facilities in Guatemala.

What follows is a synthesis of Delia's narrative as she is deported from an Office of Refugee Resettlement (ORR)–subcontracted facility for unaccompanied minors run by an NGO in Chicago and processed at the Guatemala City Air Force base where I first met her. While written chronologically for the reader's clarity, Delia's narrative did not unfold linearly or at once. The narrative was compiled over several conversations with Delia and her family within Guatemala's SBS facility and in subsequent visits in their hometown of Sibinal in the department of San Marcos over three years. Throughout, I seek to convey Delia's experiences with the unease, ambivalence, and agony she and her family shared with me. I supplement the narrative with ethnographic details from my prior research within the very Chicago facility where she was detained and from firsthand observations at Guatemala City's Air Force base and SBS facility where she was held until her parents arrived from Sibinal.

The second development initiative is called ¡Quédate! (Stay!), a program specifically designed for young people like Delia to "reintegrate" into their families and to create "alternatives to migration" for children. Although not the Guatemalan government's first foray into development initiatives targeting child migrants, ¡Quédate! garnered uncharacteristically high levels of public attention from Guatemalan officials and financial support from USAID and IOM. The discourses undergirding the ¡Quédate! program, like those of the well-funded Dangers Awareness and Know the Facts campaigns, however, fail to grasp why young people migrate. Moreover, they ignore the reverberating and enduring impacts of detention and deportation on young people and their families. Taken together, these development initiatives—from conceptualization to implementation—reinforce historical social hierarchies between the ladino elite and Indigenous peoples and reify their migranthood. Without addressing the social inequalities woven into state institutions, these development initiatives fail to effectively support young people's right to *not* migrate.

DELIA: "IT'S TIME."

The mattress creaked as Delia rolled over. For the last three months, she had not slept well—the uncomfortable mattress, the buzz of the neon lights from the hallway, and the snores of seven children sleeping on bunks in her room were unsettling, but the screams of kids waking from nightmares were worse. Their cries were filled with fear, panic, and pain. Sleep deprived, Delia was given a sleeping pill by a psychiatrist, which "made me feel like a zombie. I couldn't lift my head without it pounding. It's not for me," she described.

Delia lay awake as she often did, thinking about returning to her hometown outside of Sibinal on the Guatemala-Mexico border. "I really missed my parents and my little sister, and my mom's cooking. The tortillas in the shelter are like cardboard, and so much rice. I miss nighttime, bundling up in my sweater and sitting outside in the courtyard in darkness, looking up at the sky. There [in the detention facility], the light is always on. I am never alone."

At 2 a.m., a staff member shook Delia awake. "Get up. Get your things. It's time." Disoriented, Delia asked, "Time for what?"

"For your flight to Guatemala." Delia was being deported.

Her bunkmate Amelia stirred, waking to the sounds of Delia stumbling to get dressed. "She gave me a hug and we started to cry," Delia recalled. It had only been four months, but detention, or "shelter care" as the NGO staff euphemistically termed it, had made Delia and Amelia inseparable. They comforted each other when they were frustrated at the uncertainty of their futures, craving forbidden coffee, bored by the same action movies blaring on repeat, or homesick for their friends in their native Guatemala. "It's like they couldn't decide if we were babies needing to be burped or someone who couldn't be trusted."

Delia's unannounced, predawn departure prevented her from saying goodbye to her new friends and from mentally preparing for return. "It was a difficult time. I wanted to stay in America but not in *that* place. I made friends there and didn't want to say goodbye. I didn't know what would happen to them or if I'd ever see them again. They became my family there, only they know what it was really like, but I also missed by family and my country. It was confusing." She knew the day was coming, but the facility staff had not warned her of the date or time of her imminent departure.

"If kids knew they were leaving tomorrow, they would abscond today," a facility administrator justified. Relegated to knockoff Crocs to deter escape in Chicago's wintery mix, Delia put on jeans and a light-blue tee shirt. Finally, she cast off the primary-colored sweat suit with "48" written in black marker on each piece of clothing. "Number forty-eight? I have a name, you know," she later indignantly told me. She threw her few personal belongings in a black trash bag, and the facility's transportation coordinator, a former Army private, drove her to Chicago O'Hare airport.

Delia was detained in one of over one hundred ORR facilities run by NGOs across fourteen states. She had been apprehended by the Border Patrol near Nogales, Texas, after a month of traveling by bus and train through Mexico. She had hoped to reunite with her older sister living in Maryland, but when her sister did not complete the necessary paperwork to secure her release, Delia decided to request voluntary departure rather than remain in detention.

Delia describes her experience at the Chicago O'Hare airport, "It was quiet, eerie really. Stores were locked up. There weren't people at the counters. I'd never been on an airplane before, so I was nervous. We flew to Arizona and then waited awhile." Delia was accompanied by the transportation coordinator on a commercial airline from Chicago to Mesa, Arizona, one of ICE Air's five U.S. hubs, where she boarded a chartered flight to Guatemala.

In 2013, when I first observed deportation flights landing at Guatemala City's Air Force base, there were one or two flights per week. Two years later, when Delia returned, flights arrived almost daily. From 2010 to 2014, ICE Air deported 930,435 individuals to 185 countries, with Guatemala consistently being the most frequent destination for flights.[1] Since 2015, ICE Air has deported approximately 100,000 people annually. Individuals may be deported on commercial aircrafts, via ground transportation, or on foot at ports of entry along U.S. borders—but these ICE Air flights are big business. ICE pays an average of $8,419 per flight hour regardless of the number of people the planes carry.[2] A 2015 audit by the DHS Office of Inspector General cited a need to fill the vacant seats.[3]

Delia described her flight:

The [transportation coordinator] handed some papers to immigration. The officer put a bracelet on me. It had my name, picture, birthdate, A [Alien registration] number. We all got them. I felt like tagged cattle. They patted me down to make sure I didn't have anything in my pockets. They even looked in my mouth. No one had shoelaces or belts. I was one of the last to get on with the other kids. In the back of the plane, there were mostly men but also a few women. They all had handcuffs—the ones that connect their feet to their wrists. One man looked like he just walked out of the desert onto the plane; he really smelled. Everyone looked tired and nervous, like me.

It was a long flight. I kept looking out the window. I've never seen clouds so close. I wonder what they feel like. I wanted to wade through them. They gave us a bag with a sandwich, a granola bar, and a bottle of water. I didn't realize how hungry I was. I hadn't eaten all day. A little before we landed, the officers took the handcuffs off of the adults, so they could eat.

The landing was a little scary, but it was kind of a blur. I was nervous, worried, excited, sad. I couldn't wait to see my family. I missed them so much. I had so much to tell them. But I know that I failed them and that they would be disappointed in me. I was disappointed in myself. I didn't know what would happen once I got home . . . how would we manage?

From the tarmac, I observed Delia, along with 130 other deportees, deplane from the innocuous blue-and-white 737 onto Guatemala City's Air Force base. Officials wearing white polo shirts and navy blue vests from the Ministerio de Relaciones Exteriores (MINEX, Ministry of Foreign Relations) directed return-ees down a metal staircase and into a nondescript cement building. Returnees shuffled single file, heads down.

Marimba music blared as the adults lumbered into the building. To one side, a Banrural counter advertised financial services to returnees, offering to exchange U.S. dollars to quetzales. On the other side, employment signs for a multinational call center were displayed: *"Encuentra las mejores ofertas de empleo en Guatemala"* (Find the best job offers in Guatemala) and *"Comienza con un gran empleo el día de hoy! Salario mensual. Qs.500.00 incluyendo bonos"* (Begin a great job today! Monthly salary: 5,500 quetzales [723 USD] including bonuses), enticing English speakers to work in Guatemala's growing industry of multinational call centers. In my observations at the military base over multiple years, including the day Delia returned, I never saw a representative sitting at the counter.

As the returnees sat down and awaited processing, a woman with sparkled eyeshadow and rosy cheeks enthusiastically cheered in a mixture of Spanish and K'iche':

¡Bienvenidos compañeros! ¡Bienvenidos héroes! Ricos o pobres, grandes o pequeños, hombre o mujer, lo que seas, son compatriotas. It ko chupan ri a tinamit ki kin ri ka winiäq. Ya estás en tu país y con tu gente. Este es tu patria.

Welcome, friends! Welcome heroes! Rich or poor, big or small, man or woman, whatever you are, you are compatriots. You are now in your country and with your people. This is your homeland.

I wondered, what good comes of deportation when men, women, and children are taken from their families, jobs, and communities in the United States? Why rejoice in plans thwarted by a busted taillight, a workplace raid, or for Delia, the suffocating heat of the desert while the Border Patrol lay in wait? "There is nothing to celebrate here," a man wearing a University of Texas tee shirt jeered from his white plastic chair.

The MINEX representative countered, "Because there are people who leave and never return. If you're sitting here in one of these chairs, you are someone who has risked a lot, someone who has sacrificed for your families and your communities. There is no reason to be ashamed." Indeed, many deportees are ashamed at their failure to remain in the United States, to remit enough to their families, to fulfill aspirations that spurred migration—be it a month or a decade earlier. Authorities would process the adults over the next three hours, asking questions, taking note of their names, communities of origin, and arrival details in an oversized accountancy log.

In interviews with staff processing returnees, I was repeatedly told that returnees were offered a menu of services—medical exam, mental health evaluations, bus fare to return to home communities; however, across my multiple observations over three years, I never witnessed these resources. At best, some migrants used the often broken pay phone or were offered an occasional brown bag filled with a sandwich and juice. More often, returnees were processed and released to the entrance of the military base, left to borrow a cellular phone to call a family member or to beg for bus fare. Recognizing the growing demand for services, some bus routes relocated to the front of the military base, as did several smugglers offering deals to return to the United States. Some deportees remigrated immediately; others returned home for several weeks or months before trying again.

Deported unaccompanied minors are processed differently than adults. I climbed into the back corner of a dark-blue minivan, sitting alongside Delia and eight other unaccompanied minors who were shuttled across town to a SBS facility called Casa Nuestras Raíces (Home of Our Roots). At the time, it was one of two SBS facilities that processed returned unaccompanied children in Guatemala. The Guatemala City facility receives children returned on ICE Air chartered flights and the occasional youth deported from the United States and northern Mexico on commercial flights into the international airport. The other SBS facility, located in the department of Quetzaltenango, receives youth returned by bus from southern Mexico. At Casa Nuestras Raíces, youth undergo screenings with a case worker, social worker, and on occasion, a psychologist. Asked a litany of the same questions over and over again, fatigued and anxious young people wait up to forty-eight hours for the arrival of family members, who often receive little to no advance notice of their child's arrival.

Delia would wait two days until her parents Rigoberto and Maria Isabel arrived. They had not been notified of the timing of their daughter's return and had to borrow money for the fourteen-hour bus ride from Sibinal to Guatemala City. Rigoberto and Maria Isabel were frightened by the trip; they had never visited Guatemala City and knew only of the notorious gangs that gun down motorists and the corrupt police that shake down bus drivers and their passengers. Tucked away in Zona 1 of the city, Casa Nuestras Raíces is not easy to find. After wandering through the city for three hours, Rigoberto and Maria Isabel arrived at the yellow building and rang the bell.

They were not allowed to see Delia immediately. Passing their *cédulas* (identification documents) and Delia's birth certificate through the metal bars, they waited. Unlike many families who do not have these documents, Rigoberto and Maria Isabel were fortunate; they had secured copies for their children several years prior when their eldest daughter sought asylum in the United States. After over one hour, Rigoberto and Maria Isabel were directed to a waiting area where they were instructed to watch a video playing on a small television hung on the wall. The video recounted the violence migrants confront en route to the United States—the harsh elements, menacing gangs, thieves hopped up on cocaine, and rapists at every turn. The video warned: "It is your responsibility to be good parents and to provide for your children. Do not send them into harm's way." The video failed to mention the 5,924 homicides in Guatemala in 2014.[4] Ignored was the statistic that 59 percent of Indigenous people live in poverty or Guatemala's skyrocketing unemployment and underemployment rates.[5] The varied reasons why young people migrate were overlooked altogether. Rather, it was Rigoberto and Maria Isabel who were to blame for their "uneducated and selfish decision to send their child to the U.S.," as a case worker explained to me within earshot of the couple.

This explanation was nothing new to Rigoberto and Maria Isabel; they had endured insults of being stupid, backwards, or *brujos* (witches)—in health clinics, government offices, and schools—because they are Indigenous. Within the walls of the facility, these historically rooted racist discourses are both egregious and mundane in the ways that staff talk about and interact with Indigenous parents and youth. In these interactions, I observed a pattern of demeaning behavior by SBS employees in threatening to call police on parents, to remove children from their custody, and to bring charges for smuggling their children. In more mundane ways, staff treated children and their parents with a lack of respect— refusing them food, being inattentive to needs for hygiene products, not allowing children to socialize with each other, refusing parents access to the facility's restrooms, and repeatedly scolding them for speaking in their respective Indigenous languages. At the video's conclusion, I observed a case worker proceed to lecture Rigoberto and Maria Isabel. "If your daughter migrates again, she will likely end up dead and it will be on your heads. God will not forgive you. And, if she is returned again, she and your other children will be taken from your custody. You will be sent to jail. *You* must be responsible for your child; she is *not* responsible for you."

After several hours, Delia was finally released to her parents. They embraced in the waiting room. We all were in tears. Speaking in Mam, Rigoberto and Maria Isabel welcomed their daughter home, thankful that she was safe and assuring her not to worry. Maria Isabel handed Delia her *güipil* (blouse), *faja* (sash), and *corte* (skirt) to replace her jeans and sweatshirt, telling her, "You should be proud of who you are and where you come from," Delia later translated for me. Her *traje* (traditional dress) also served a practical purpose—to conceal her migration from inquisitive neighbors who may be prone to gossip, as girls were often assumed either to be raped en route to the United States or to prostitute themselves to pay for their passage.

Attempting to explain the interaction to an outsider anthropologist, the SBS director commented to me, "See, they are forcing her to be something she doesn't want to be. They don't want to be modern."

Delia emerged from the restroom, dressed in her multicolored *güipil* and dark *corte*. She hugged me, thanking me for the hot tea and cookies I shared with her parents during their prolonged wait and promised to remain in touch. Turning to her parents, Delia whispered, "It's time to go home. We are not welcome here."

RETURN, REUNIFICATION, REINTEGRATION

In the United States, "voluntary departure" is the most common form of removal for unaccompanied children. Described as a discretionary "benefit" to those who have crossed without permission into the United States, voluntary departure does not carry a mandatory ten-year bar from future admissibility to the United States, yet young people do not experience it as voluntary nor as a benefit. Young people held in ORR facilities for unaccompanied minors routinely request voluntary departure because, simply put, they are tired of detention. In the Chicago-based NGO facility where Delia was held, her freedom of movement was restricted through tactics such as surveilling her actions and reactions via video cameras and "line of sight" observance; recording her sleep patterns, conversations, and phone calls in institutional files; and restricting access to information about her case—be it reunification with her sister, upcoming court dates, or her impending deportation. ORR has long shared the files of its NGO subcontractors with ICE. As I document in my earlier work, *Migrant Youth, Transnational Families, and the State: Care and Contested Interests* (2014) these files can be and have been used against children in immigration proceedings. In May of 2018, ORR and ICE signed a memorandum of understanding universalizing this previously ad hoc practice by mandating continual information sharing, often with devastating consequences for children and their families. Like Delia, young people describe ORR facilities not as "shelter" or as "care" but as "lost time," "traumatic," and "a nightmare I can't escape" and as places where "I am treated like a criminal . . . a threat" and where "I have no rights." Young people's social and emotional lives are ignored, just as Delia's name is discounted. In its place, number forty-eight.

These inhospitable conditions and prolonged detention motivate many young people to secure the quickest route out—voluntary departure. Such "consent" is coercive at best.[6] Because the U.S. Supreme Court declared deportation as a civil rather than criminal process, the state operates on the premise that unauthorized migrants "are not being punished; they are simply being regulated."[7] In this way, the juridical term "voluntary departure" accordingly sanitizes the violence inflicted by the full force of the state against an individual body[8]; it is jarringly discordant with the ways that youth like Delia describe their experiences of forced return.

In discussions of child migration in the United States and Guatemala, policymakers often utilize another euphemistic term—"family reunification"—for child deportations. The underlying claim, as anthropologist Shahram Khosravi argues, is that deportation "restore[s] displaced, out-of-place people to their 'natural' place of life, their 'home-land.'"[9] This is particularly pronounced for young people whereby family reunification promises to return children to their "natural" place within the family. Thus, in the state's framing, repatriation is a form of "care." These claims, however, belie the fact that U.S. immigration authorities in virtually all other contexts pay little to no regard to immigrant families, many of which include U.S. citizen children, by routinely and aggressively separating parents from their children. In the United States and Guatemala, Delia encountered discourses that oscillated between infantilizing youth to treating her and her family as a threat—unable to "decide if we were babies needing to be burped or someone who couldn't be trusted." In Guatemala, SBS officials met Delia's parents with suspicion and disdain—"uneducated and selfish." Cast as neglectful and ill-informed, their reunification garnered shame and threats, not a rightful return to family and homeland.

Reunification in the aftermath of deportation is indeed challenging, as there are very few ways young people and their families escape the deleterious effects of deportation.[10] For Delia, deportation had stark material consequences for her and her family as they sank into financial ruin while navigating the shared burden of migratory debt. These pressures are felt intimately as families confront financial hardships, the loss of actual or potential remittances, limited employment opportunities, and for many Indigenous families, the loss of social standing for failing to repay debts. With no institutional services following deportation, the conditions that lead to migration are compounded by financial debt enlisted to migrate irregularly. For Delia, the anticipation of reunification—of staring at the stars, eating her favorite foods, visiting with friends and family—is tinged with hardship and uncertainty.

The international migration sector has long discussed return and reintegration of refugees. The development sector in the United States and Central America has embraced the phrase "reintegration" as a buzzword for child deportation. This is particularly problematic for Indigenous youth. Reintegration presumes prior membership and belonging. For youth who have resided in Mexico or the United States for the majority of their young lives, Guatemala is their country of

origin but is not necessarily their country of membership, memory, or belonging.[11] Absent social support or family in Guatemala, connection to language,
cultural knowledge, and the bureaucratic evidence of citizenship, young people
like Liseth (chapter three) feel like foreigners in their country of birth. Indigenous youth who have resided outside of Guatemala, even for more abbreviated
periods of time like Delia, articulate historical and contemporary exclusions of
Indigenous communities that thwart "reintegration." A perpetually unattended
employment desk, an unavailable medical exam, transportation assistance that
never materializes, a relic of a telephone hanging on the wall—all are emblematic of the social neglect that Indigenous youth encounter prior to migration
and following return. There is no support to attend to the conditions spurring
migration nor the realities that confront migrants in their communities of origin following return. Instead, young people, and by extension their parents, are
held accountable for those conditions as well as the risks encountered en route.
Such moralizing likewise suggests that young deportees have exclusive control
over their lives before, during, and following failed migratory projects.

Eliana, a K'iche' undergraduate student who coordinated some of my meetings following a community survey in Almolonga (chapter six), asked, "How are
we supposed to belong to a state that, during the armed conflict, tortured and
murdered my grandparents, that massacred my community, that disappeared my
aunts and uncles, that sought to exterminate us from the land of our ancestors?"
For Eliana, reintegration presumes integration in the first place. As illustrated by
the director's accusations that Delia's parents resist modernity, Indigenous migrants
are subjected to demeaning and racist treatment in government facilities. Scholars
have long documented how Indigenous communities in postconflict Guatemala
continue to be expelled systematically from all areas of social and political life,
including the labor market, public education, health care, development initiatives,
and political participation.[12] SBS's development interventions are dimensions of
broader discourses that individualize the reasons for migration and presume that
familial disintegration is the reason for child migration in the first place.

¿QUÉDATE Y QUÉ?

In 2014, I attended a conference in San Marcos on the influx of international aid
focused on "social reintegration" initiatives for returning youth. The centerpiece
of the conference was the launch of a USAID-funded initiative called ¡Quédate!

(Stay!) administered in collaboration with the IOM and SBS. Since 2012, prior to the media hubbub around child migration, then First Lady Rosa Leal de Pérez had become the face of the plight of unaccompanied children returning to Guatemala. As SBS Secretariat, a position traditionally held by the president's wife, she publicly prided herself in "saving" unaccompanied children from dangerous fates and "rehabilitating" them following deportation. Leal de Pérez declared, *"Me duele en el alma ver los problemas a los que se enfrentan nuestros niños, pero juntos saldremos adelante de esta crisis."* (It hurts my soul to see the problems our children face, but together we will get through this crisis.)

The ¡Quédate! initiative was consistent with Leal de Pérez's affectionate paternalism toward child migrants and consistent with discourses that infantilized and pathologized young migrants and their families. Through glossy posters, brochures, radio announcements, and occasional community fairs, the ¡Quédate! initiative implored—or as some felt, commanded—youth to "Stay!" The prevention program, as it was framed, sought to educate communities on the differences between regular and irregular migration, the risk during the journey, the rights of migrants, and should those rights be violated, government hotlines for the national police, the state attorney, and SBS.

Joanna, a researcher with the Archdiocese of Guatemala whom I met early on in my research and again at the conference, disclosed:

> I don't have much hope for these proposals because, after all, she is married to a *militar* [military person]. She has the mentality that migration is bad. She doesn't realize there are no alternatives. We [in civil society] want to promote people's rights, including the right to not migrate. We can't criminalize children and their families because they migrate; it is a right just like other rights. Her overarching approach is to repress migration; that simply is not nor has been a viable alternative historically or in the present in Guatemala.

Joanna's distrust was rooted in the fact that Leal Pérez's husband, the now-ousted president Otto Pérez Molina, served in a number of feared capacities during Guatemala's armed conflict, including in the Kaibiles (special forces), as Director of Military Intelligence, and infamously as the chief officer representing the military during the Peace Accords. During the trial of former dictator Efraín Ríos Montt, the Guatemalan press accused then President Pérez Molina of attempting to derail the trial by publicly denying that the genocide took place.[13]

Indeed, long before his impeachment in 2015, civil society widely questioned the motives and policies of the Pérez Molina administration to effectively and judiciously respond to the needs of the Indigenous communities, whose extermination Pérez Molina pursued throughout his military career. These critiques continue to press his successors, Presidents Jimmy Morales (2016–2020) and Alejandro Giammattei Falla (2020–present), regarding their incompetence, willful neglect of Indigenous communities, and alleged large-scale corruption.

"The Guatemalan government has no policy on migration," I was repeatedly told by researchers, attorneys, NGO personnel, community organizers, and government bureaucrats throughout my five years of fieldwork. In 2001, the Guatemalan legislation under the administration of President Alfonso Portillo approved the Social Development Act (Ley de Desarrollo Social, Decree 42-2001), which included provisions related to migration. Despite repeated advocacy by coalitions of NGOs and researchers, there had been only sporadic provisions specifically related to trafficking until 2016, when a more comprehensive revision to the migratory laws was undertaken.[14] Its implementation, however, remains pending. In the absence of enacted policy on migration, the state implicitly encourages migration outflows as a means of generating economic support for the nation and tacitly accepts current regional and transnational migration practices. With an economic disincentive to deter transnational migration and corresponding remittances, the Guatemalan state, in effect, abdicates its responsibility to provide alternatives to would-be migrants and support for deportees. For unaccompanied children returned to Guatemala, migration policies face the added challenge of meaningfully integrating national child welfare policies, which in most instances also lack the necessary political will, institutional resources, and public attention.

In addition to the joint USAID-IOM workshops where I first met Liseth (chapter three), the ¡Quédate! program garnered considerable political attention in Guatemala City. The Ministry of Education offered advertising support in schools; the Ministry of the Interior provided radio frequencies to disseminate additional PSAs; and politicians jockeyed for financial resources. Even in some of the most geographically remote villages I visited, the purple and gold ¡Quédate! posters hung on walls of schools, churches, and municipal offices. The ¡Quédate! initiative included funding for a Centro Quédate, a training center located in Nahualá, that according to its director was intended to provide a "comprehensive education from high school through a Bachelor of Science and Letters in Productivity and Entrepreneurship to adolescents from fourteen to eighteen years of age."

Nahualá, in the department of Sololá, was a dubious choice for the placement of Centro Quédate given that Sololá experiences considerably less out-migration of children compared to communities bordering Mexico—with official counts estimating just twenty-nine unaccompanied children from Nahualá apprehended in the United States from 2007 to 2017. The center initially aimed to serve returned youth in the surrounding municipalities in the department of Sololá, which ranks ninth of twenty-two departments in out-migration of children, but staff were unable to locate enough deported youths to attend workshops. The program eventually expanded to young people without migration experiences in order to reach funding-mandated targets. The center provided workshops in computing, costume jewelry, piñata making, English, and hairdressing as well as training for small-scale electricians, all billed as "alternatives to migration." These alternatives, however, framed family-based agriculture as neither a viable nor valued option for young people. Among Indigenous communities in Guatemala, these messages over time seeped into the ways young people learned to (de)value the ancestral knowledge and labor of their elders.

Meanwhile, SBS received considerable financial support to renovate its two reception facilities in Guatemala City and Quetzaltenango in anticipation of receiving more deported children from the United States and Mexico. Notably, however, SBS did not receive funding to hire additional personnel or to instate much-needed follow-up services for youth returning to their communities. A long-standing director of an SBS facility confided, "We've seen children come through our doors two, three, even five times. Whatever is happening in their home and in their communities is not changing. We try to intervene, but there are so many kids, with so few resources to address their needs. My team does its utmost, but we simply don't have the support we need."

As a symbolic role, the first lady's position as SBS Secretariat lacks the institutional and financial power and support from key government departments— such as the Department of Defense, the Ministry of Foreign Affairs, the Office of the Attorney General, and the Executive office—to institute sustainable changes to the reception of and opportunities available to youth and their families. Instead, there are occasional spurts of short-term scholarships for children to attend school and monthly *bolsas seguras* (bundles of food) primarily in communities with elevated numbers of returned youth, but in my years of research, I observed little continuous or meaningful investment. The few social service organizations that at the time worked directly with returned young people did not receive any government support to continue or enhance their community-based efforts. An advocate in Xela explained, "The funds disappear into politicians' pockets in Guatemala City. They never reach the provinces."

At its core, the ¡Quédate! initiative implores children and adolescents to consider the risks and dangers of undertaking irregular migration and, simply, to stay put. Vanessa, a youth activist in Sololá, described, "It's like plowing the sea—a waste of limited resources and a total disregard for why we migrate in the first place." Vanessa remarked that in surrounding communities the launch of ¡Quédate! did not usher in any new school scholarships, programs to generate youth employment with livable wages, or funding for high-skilled training programs that might substantially alter the economic conditions that instigate migration. Rather, a limited number of youth (approximately one hundred in 2015, for example) were offered trainings in low-wage labor.

"Learning to make costume jewelry will not pay the 40,000 quetzales [5,260 USD] in migratory debt, and it will not offer economic stability for a family. It will replicate the same economic marginalization that their parents and grandparents confront," Vanessa critiqued. The ¡Quédate! initiative, she contended, ignores wholesale the security concerns of those youth who are forced to flee Guatemala without providing avenues for addressing the structural violence that undergirds the reasons for migration. *"¿Quédate y qué?"* (Stay and what?), Vanessa asked.

¡Quédate! was particularly fraught with misinformation, corruption, and inefficacy, and after two years of minimal activity, the initiative largely transitioned to a mechanism for distributing educational scholarships from foreign governments and for trainings of older teenagers through the Instituto Técnico de Capacitación y Productividad (Institute of Technical Training and Productivity). As with the Dangers Awareness and Know the Facts campaigns, that ¡Quédate! failed not only is emblematic of how the government and international development agencies ignore young people's experiences and perspectives, but also is revealing of how they divorce migration from structural factors that provoke it. Under the symbolic as opposed to legislative leadership of the first lady, SBS lacks the institutional power and financial resources to remedy structural inequalities that impact the lives of Indigenous youth and their families. Veronica, another youth activist and colleague of Vanessa's, contended:

> There is a need for a fundamental shift in governance. The current regime must move beyond telling young people and Indigenous communities what to do. It must stop protecting private and foreign interests. It must start supporting a school system that works, a health system that respects us, and jobs that are dignified. It must, and we must, start creating the conditions to achieve these goals. Without them, children and adults will continue to migrate.

The discursive and policy responses of the ¡Quédate! Initiative, as with the Dangers Awareness and Know the Facts campaigns, presume that misinformation or a lack of education are to blame for child migration, rather than, as young people attest, structural violence and social inequality.

CHAPTER 5

NEGOTIATING RETURNS

DEPARTURE, RETURN, expulsion, removal, repatriation, refoulement, reunification, reintegration. Just as migration has multiple meanings for Indigenous youth and their families, there is no single word that encapsulates diverse trajectories of removal nor of postdeportation life. This chapter traces how young people variously experience removal in their communities in the months and years following return—as children of *madres y padres deportadxs* (deported parents); as *llegadxs* (arrivals), or U.S. citizen children who accompany their parents to Guatemala following removal; and as *retornadxs* (returnees), or unaccompanied children who are deported. Conceptually, these multiple experiences of removal, either their own or of a family member, allow us to recognize deportation not as a singular event impacting an individual deportee but as a process with reverberating and long-lasting impacts on young people, families, and communities.

Methodologically, a longitudinal approach to the study of deportation across legal statuses is critical as the impacts of forced return, as well as the meanings of migranthood, shift over time and across citizenship status and geography. The immediate material deprivation and psychological trauma resulting from forced removal—one's own or a parent's—seep into relationships and influence one's sense of self and belonging. The conditions of removal and the availability of social and financial capital shape how young people are able or unable to pursue education or employment in Guatemala and how they cultivate or are isolated from peer groups. These outcomes are enduring on not just individual youths but also their families, and as we will see in chapter six, on communities. Youth, however, are not passive victims. As social actors, they negotiate legal processes, institutional actors, social and familial dynamics, cultural transitions, citizenship laws, gendered norms, and identity politics bound up in their experiences following deportation. They enlist a wide range of tactics and techniques to facilitate integration of their parents, siblings, and themselves in an effort to mitigate the profound material and psychological impacts resulting from removal. As criminologist Sarah Turnbull writes, young people "survive, adapt, (re)build their lives, (re)integrate, and carry on, even in difficult circumstances not of their choosing."[1]

Focusing on young people's experiences of removal across legal categories frees us from reifying their experiences into narrow juridical categories, which often perpetuate discourses of "deserving" or "undeserving" migrants in public policy. By holding unaccompanied children as uniquely deserving of specialized services and protections, in countries of either destination or return, public policy negates the need for protections and services for families or adults who find themselves in similarly perilous migratory circumstances or who likewise may confront violence and precarity following forced return. These artificial legal distinctions, often reified in migration scholarship and popular conceptions of migranthood, not only contribute to a hierarchy of vulnerability but likewise distract from the development and securitization policies that engender structural violence, violence that leads to (re)migration and is compounded following return.

MADRES Y PADRES DEPORTADXS

Migration research consistently frames children as dependents of parental decision-making, particularly studies of youth "left behind" by parents who migrate.[2] This research commonly details the adverse consequences of parental absence on children, including inflicting psychological trauma,[3] disrupting positive familial relationships necessary for healthy development,[4] creating tension on relationships with caregivers,[5] and impeding children's educational attainment.[6] Some studies, however, consider the effects differently, focusing on how parental migration actually enhances a child's social status and access to resources, often through remittances.[7] In spite of the profound social, legal, and emotional costs or benefits of parental migration, the experiences of children remain largely framed as the consequence of a parent's fate. Rather than being valued for their unique insights, perceptions, and experiences of removal, either a parent's or their own, youth are often thought of as merely representative of the impacts of parental removal. This overlooks that children are "pivotal points" shaping migratory decisions, household bonds amid parental absence, and integration following parental return.[8]

Fraught with anticipation and excitement for many youths, the return of *madres y padres deportadxs* (deported parents) also can bring anxiety and disruption to household relationships. Here, Diego, Ana, Clara, Magdalena, and Lorenzo share how they navigate the social, emotional, and material impacts of their parents' sudden return to Guatemala, often after prolonged absences, and how the meanings they ascribe to their parents' migration changed following deportation.

Diego

Diego, a sixteen-year-old, recounted his father Carlos's unanticipated deportation to Nuevo Progreso in the department of San Marcos in 2014. "Overnight, we couldn't pay our tuition, so I decided to leave school. I figured, better to spend the limited resources on my sister's education. She's always been better at school anyway. I figured I can work and help out and go back to school later if we find the resources." Upon apprehension and deportation, Diego's father was unable to access his meager savings tucked in a drawer in his Atlanta apartment; he did not have the requisite documents to open a bank account in the United States. A year later, with a modest monthly household income equivalent to $300, basic needs for food and transportation could not be met. As we walked around town with my children racing ahead, Diego pointed to a small storefront, describing, "I work [there] as a tailor's assistant. My mother wakes up at 2 a.m. to sell cilantro and potatoes at the market. My dad works as a *mojado* [derogatory term for day laborer]. It's just not enough." For Diego, his father's return was highly anticipated and welcomed after their eight-year separation. Diego described receiving his father with a confluence of emotions—anticipation, excitement, apprehension, and anxiety. Parental return brought noteworthy shifts in the family's everyday lives, especially the economic implications of his father's lost wages.

I first met Diego's father, Carlos, a year following his deportation in San Marcos's main plaza as my children protractedly deliberated, as they often do, the various flavors of *paletas* (popsicles) for sale. Standing next to us, patiently waiting for them to decide, Carlos introduced himself to me in fluent English. He was in San Marcos to pursue a business opportunity as a driver of school buses imported to Guatemala from the United States, he explained. A week later, I met with Diego and Carlos at their family home in Nuevo Progreso and would continue to meet with them yearly on subsequent research trips in the area. Carlos rifled through a tattered shoebox filled with important documents and *recuerdos* (mementos)—his *cédula*, a photo from his wedding, a letter from his pastor in Georgia, a Gallo beer sticker, and a series of carefully perforated white envelopes with documents from U.S. immigration authorities: a notice to appear, a change of address form, an order of removal. "Here it is," he beamed. "They may have taken the card from me, but I memorized it. This is my social security number." He ran his thumb over the prized nine numbers neatly written on a scrap of paper. Proud at his subversion, Carlos explained that he received a temporary work authorization and social security card after applying for political asylum. After losing his final appeal for asylum, he was deported.

When Carlos left Guatemala, Diego was eight years old. "At first it was hard," Diego reflected in 2016, now two years following his dad's return. "I remember being angry all the time. I was angry he never said goodbye. I wouldn't talk to him on the phone for months. I know now it was difficult for him too. . . . He's back but I don't really know who he is. It's like having a stranger waking up in your house. I don't know things I should know—like what he likes to eat or his favorite soccer team. He doesn't know me or my friends. We live in the same place but don't really talk."

Six months following this conversation, the family had to sell their van to pay for their grandmother's funeral. The sale had practical and symbolic significance. Now, Diego lamented, "Only an American flag and a box full of immigration papers are proof of his eight years in the U.S." Sinking deeper into poverty with each passing month, Diego and Carlos worried about their survival. While Carlos, who faced a ten-year bar from returning to the United States, was reluctant to remigrate, Diego was considering his first journey. "I just don't see another way."

Ana

In a workshop organized by a youth organization in Almolonga where I conducted a community survey (chapter six), seventeen-year-old Ana reflected on how her mother's migration to Louisiana shaped her childhood. "It's not easy growing up without parents around. No matter if they call each week or send money or clothes at the holidays, you always feel this hole in your life. I understand though, why she left. She did it to support us."

Ana later would describe to me how she negotiated her mother's physical absence, at times providing meaningful connections to her mother. "We used to talk over WhatsApp. I would tell her everything that was going on in [the community], all of the news, gossip, drama, you know. We'd talk about the latest scandals in *La Sombra del Pasado* [The Shadow of the Past, a soap opera] and what we thought would happen between [main characters] Cristóbal and Aldonza." In spite of her mother's physical absence, Ana maintained a virtual and emotional relationship with her via social media and instant messaging. Living with a maternal aunt and her three children, Ana found meaning in her mother's absence "to support us" when the family confronted the harsh realities of structural violence, which, for Ana's family, manifested as limited protections when Ana's father began to batter her mother. Ana's mother and grandmother tried to denounce the abuse to the police; instead, the police arrested them for making false accusations against her father and beat and detained them over three days. Out of fear of ongoing police harassment, and without sufficient income to support her children after Ana's father moved in with another woman in neighboring Zunil, Ana's mother migrated, leaving eleven-year-old Ana and her four-year-old sister in the care of their aunt and maternal grandmother.

In her mother's physical absence from Almolonga, Ana attempted to maintain her mother's connection to their family and community by sharing mundane happenings around town or plot lines of the nightly *telenovela*. This connection, Ana surmised, helped to ease her mother's reintegration into social and familial life following deportation. "It's not like she is a stranger to me. I may not know what she smells or feels like, but I know how she sounds and that she cares."

However, Ana acknowledged that her mother had changed in El Norte (the United States). "My mother dresses differently. She rarely wears *traje*. She told me that she couldn't wear *traje* in the United States because she would get harassed . . . Now that she is here, it's like she's still afraid to show who she is, who we are."

Other youths I encountered shared how their parents changed in the United States—how they forgot K'iche' or Mam or how they would rather speak English; how they no longer drank *atol* or ate tamales, and relied on Pepto Bismol to settle their stomachs that had grown unaccustomed to Guatemalan food; and even how life in the United States changed their race—becoming either "whiter" from endless hours working inside factories or darker from working under the blazing sun as agricultural laborers. From penchants for food, music, and dress to noteworthy modifications in language, race, and cultural identity, many youths noted significant differences in their parents following their return. These changes redefined young people's relationships to their parents, at times creating social and emotional distances and eroding trust as they adjusted to life together.

Despite their close relationship and regular communication during her mother's absence, deportation devastated Ana's mother and, in turn, Ana. Describing the immediate impact of her mother's deportation six months prior, Ana explained:

> When my mom was returned, I smiled every day. I was so happy to see her, to hug her. But it isn't easy. I know she had a life there and she misses it. She loves us and wants to be with us but just yesterday I saw her with this look, thinking of somewhere else. She's not here. It's her turn to feel that hole. I try not to take it personally, but it is hard not to.

Just as Ana created opportunities for belonging during her mother's physical absence, she likewise brokered her mother's reintegration following return. Ana encouraged her mother to play with her children, join in community meetings, attend church, or go for a walk. "She can't stay inside all day. She needs to get out," Ana diagnosed. Ana tried to empathize with her mother, insightfully noting the challenges her mother faces in being separated from her partner and another child, a U.S. citizen, who remain in Louisiana.

Clara

Nineteen-year-old Clara and I chatted as she tended her family's corner store in San Juan Ostuncalco. Her aunt Estela, an area schoolteacher who collaborated on a multimedia elicitations workshop (chapter two), introduced me to Clara during one of our planning sessions at the family's store. I marveled at Clara's capacity to multitask—always moving at a frenetic pace, arranging products on a shelf, cleaning the counter, sweeping the floor, caring for her toddler brother—yet never once interrupting our conversation. Clara would later describe how her life changed since her father (Estela's brother-in-law) was deported after eleven years in Georgia. Now, two years later, Clara laughed:

> Growing up, I've been able to do what I want. My mom was never strict, so we could go out with our friends and have fun. Nothing crazy; I'm a good girl, I swear! Now that he's back, he has all of these rules . . . a curfew, how to dress, how to talk, what to do around the house. Now I have to sneak out when he's sleeping, tell him I'm with my cousins when I'm with my friends, invent errands just so I can be free.

Clara animatedly described strategies she and her sister devised to outsmart their father—the opportunities they created to go into town or to steal away with a boyfriend for an afternoon, the text messages they deleted, how they concealed the latest fashion trend underneath their *traje*. As her father sought to reassert control over the household, Clara relied on her expansive social network of friends and extended family to adjust to a new life with him. Estela attempted to intervene on her behalf with Clara's father, explaining new clothing styles and encouraging him to trust Clara, who was a dutiful and smart daughter. Clara's friends helped her to conceal activities that her father might disapprove of. Her young cousin even volunteered to take her shift at the store so that Clara might attend a dance at the local community center, an activity her father forbade.

Clara paused, hands in midmovement as she arranged packages of instant soup on the shelves: "I respect him and defer to him because he is my father, but I don't talk to him about my problems or what I need. I'm not sure if I can trust him. Honestly, I'm not sure if it is better now that he is here." Her father's return marked a shift in her dress, movements around town, and peer socialization. Her everyday life now involved new strategies to maintain former freedoms that her father sought to curtail. Notably, his return also brought into focus her struggle to rebuild a trusting relationship with her father, starkly questioning if her life was improved by his presence.

Clara is not alone in recounting the tensions that migration brings to family unity. She and others describe an emotional wedge between children and their parents and the resentments that absence and return incite. However, Clara also acknowledged how she and her sibling benefited from her father's migration, including the ability to attend a local private school and opening and maintaining the family store, made possible through remittances and ongoing family conversations about the importance of education. These "benefits" do not negate the emotional toll that migration took on Clara and her family; however, the impacts are situated in a context of limited financial and educational resources available to young people in San Juan Ostuncalco, a context that sparked her father's migration over a decade prior.

Magdalena and Lorenzo

Magdalena took a manila envelope out of her oversized gray purse and handed it across the table of a corner diner in Chicago where we met for coffee. She asked if I could deliver it to her family in San Marcos when I traveled to Guatemala the following week. The envelope contained photographs of her in front of Chicago's infamous "bean" sculpture and another of her sitting on a red Mustang with Montrose Beach in the background. It also contained $350 in remittance—money she earned from caring for an elderly man on the city's affluent North Shore. The remittances, she said, were to help her family rebuild after the 7.4 magnitude earthquake in San Marcos in 2012 that left devastation and thirty-nine dead in its wake. When Guatemalan authorities designated their home for demolition, Magdalena decided to migrate to the United States. "The government said they would tear down our home because it was a danger to us. How is being thrown out on the street any better?" she blasted. Without a legally required *consulta comunitaria* (community consultation), the department of San Marcos government decided to condemn homes impacted by the earthquake but failed to provide temporary housing or support for reconstruction. *"Así es en Guatemala"* (That's how it is in Guatemala), Magdalena explained, resigned not just to an absence of state support but likewise to the government's policies adversely impacting Indigenous communities. "The government said they didn't have the resources to help us, but [President] Molina still managed luxury vacations while we suffered," she sighed.

Over the next three years, I would come to know Magdalena's family in San Marcos, including her younger brother Lorenzo. Lorenzo is a jubilant, quick-witted boy who incessantly asked questions about me, my children, and life in America. "Does everyone in the United States have their own car? Have you ever met Angelina Jolie? I'd like to meet her . . . maybe she'd adopt me. Do Americans really hate Latinos? Are you a socialist? Why are your kids brown?" On Lorenzo's fifteenth birthday, their father was deported after ten years in the United States, leaving Magdalena with the responsibility of supporting the family. Their father had worked at Case Farms in Ohio, a chicken-processing plant notorious for its egregious and repeated Occupational Safety and Health Administration (OSHA) violations, including more than 750 workers suffering amputations from 2010 to 2017.[9] Their father was one of dozens of Guatemalan immigrants who had relocated to Ohio in response to the company's recruitment of undocumented workers, Lorenzo explained. He spent his days in the evisceration department, transforming defeathered chickens into the neatly butchered meat sitting on grocery store shelves. "To this day, he won't eat chicken. He says it was backbreaking and vile work."

Sitting in his family's courtyard, Lorenzo recounted how his relationship with his father had grown tense since his father's return:

> When my dad was gone, it was hard but now that he is back, we are all nervous. When he drinks, he is violent. He yells at us, hits my mother. When he was in Ohio, we had food to eat, even meat every so often. We went to [private] school; we even went out to eat on occasion but now we don't. We are afraid if we do anything wrong, he'll get mad. I wish he would leave again.

For Lorenzo, his father's return was plagued by previously absent, intrafamilial violence. Lorenzo is not alone in his account of parents returning with addictions they acquire in the United Sates. In fact, many in highland communities associate alcoholism, drug addiction, and sexually transmitted infections with the risks of migration to the United States. Following deportation, Lorenzo described how their father entered into a deep depression and turned to alcohol to cope with the loss of income and his life in the United States.

For some young people, parental migration is a welcome reprieve from household violence. No longer able to assert direct control, the migration of an abusive family member may provide safety or independence that might not have previously existed. Some women recount having more autonomy, greater discretion in running the household, and freedom from the immediacy of physical and psychological violence of their spouses. Others describe how, in the physical absence of a spouse, neighbors may police their behavior or in-laws may control remittances. In Guatemala, women and girls are subjected to various forms of gendered, structural violence, including sexism, domestic violence, psychological abuse, sexual harassment, and rape. With authorities failing to protect women and children from abusers, and in the absence of an effective judicial system to hold perpetrators accountable, the very social institutions intended to protect women and children instead inflict violence on them. As scholars detail, this gendered violence extends beyond the acts of abuse and the impunity of abusers, manifesting as enduring health impacts such as injury, chronic pain, sexually transmitted infections, depression, and posttraumatic stress disorder.[10]

Lorenzo's father had not been abusive prior to his migration. Rather, as Lorenzo assessed, the effects of deportation created a pressure cooker in which stress, debt, and depression spawned his father's substance abuse and violence. His father's deportation threw into stark relief the family's precarious economic situation, with direct consequences on Lorenzo's schooling. No longer able to afford school fees, he dropped out. Now, Lorenzo sought work as a day laborer but with limited success due to his scrawny stature and lack of agricultural experience. His education, a luxury for many, had impeded his agricultural knowledge and, in turn, limited his opportunities for work now that school was no longer a possibility.

Across the experiences of Diego, Ana, Clara, Magdalena, and Lorenzo, we see how deportation intimately impacts young people even if they do not migrate themselves and how the conditions of structural violence that led to parental migration are compounded by deportation. While young people initially may be eager to reconnect and to share physical expressions of love and affection with *madres y padres deportadxs*, they simultaneously confront the impacts of extended separations, weakened attachments, and at times, resentment for not fulfilling highly anticipated expectations of reunification. Young people are forced to adjust to life with a new household member whose absence or virtual presence they had grown accustomed to. Across these varied experiences of parental return, young people absorb the stress, depression, and anxiety of a parent who is deported. Like Ana, young people likewise may provide essential emotional support to parents who struggle with the stark realities that accompany forced return. Young people rely on their broad social and kinship networks of grandparents, aunts, uncles, cousins, siblings, and peers as they navigate new household dynamics. Ultimately, young people come to understand parental migration—its causes and consequences—in new ways.

LLEGADXS (ARRIVALS)

Many U.S. citizen children remain in the United States following parental deportation, at times living with a single parent, a relative, an older sibling, or family friends. Others may enter into state foster care. All too common are the experiences of parents like Encarnación Bail Romero, a Guatemalan mother who was detained following a workplace raid in Missouri in 2007. Her son, eleven months old at the time, was entrusted to the care of family and friends until a judge decided to place him in foster care. From immigration detention and following deportation, Bail Romero attempted meaningfully to participate in legal proceedings regarding the care and custody of her son; however, a judge ultimately terminated her parental rights, framing her detention as constructive abandonment.[11] A white family in rural Missouri adopted her son, and Bail Romero's appeals to regain custody have since been exhausted. In the legal realm, the detention and deportation of parents routinely are framed as forms of abandonment, framings that resulted in an alarming 5,100 children entering state child welfare systems in 2011.[12] While there are no current U.S. data on the numbers of children entering the state child welfare system following parental deportation, the Trump administration's "zero tolerance" policy has resulted in dozens of children remaining "ineligible for reunification" almost a year later and in defiance of a federal court order.[13]

The estimates of U.S. citizen children who accompany their parents following deportation from the United States are staggering—over six hundred thousand children just to Mexico in the last decade.[14] While the research and available data predominantly center on the experiences of children in Mexico, many analogous obstacles confront U.S. citizen children in Central America.[15] U.S. citizen children who are de facto deported,[16] that is, those who follow their deported parents to the parents' country of origin, must navigate institutions in a new country in securing identity documents, establishing citizenship, enrolling in school, and even learning a new language. Young people simultaneously confront the often turbulent emotional terrain of arriving in a foreign country amid feelings of isolation from peers, family, and culture along with the everyday realities of structural violence in Guatemala—despite claims that they are returning "home." Carla, Sonia, Antonio, and Julian, young U.S. citizens who were de facto deported to Guatemala following their parent(s)' removal from the United States, share how they negotiate new institutions, family formations, and peer groups and how these realities influence their identities, relationships, and sense of belonging in their adopted country.

Carla and Sonia

Carla and her younger sister Sonia were eager to speak of their lives in Nebraska as we sat in a community library in Zunil in 2017. Their uncle, a friend of mine who worked at an agricultural cooperative I frequented in Xela, introduced me to his two nieces who had arrived from the United States. Following their father's deportation to Guatemala in 2013, their mother struggled to support Carla and Sonia in Nebraska for two years. Unable to pay rent, a financial challenge compounded by the expense of their father's third failed attempt to return to the United States, the girls and their Mexican mother decided to join their father in Zunil. Upon arrival in Guatemala in 2015, Sonia recounted crying often, initially afraid to leave the house and fighting often with her parents. Carla described in English their first months in Guatemala:

> It was really tough. My parents fought all the time. My mom didn't like it. It is so different. People treated her poorly because she's Mexican, and we're not from here. For me, it's been an adjustment . . . even little things like not having a refrigerator for our food or to kiss adults' hands after I finish a meal . . .

or going to the store. When there isn't enough money to buy something for everyone, we can't go.

In addition to differing economic realities and social practices, Carla and Sonia also confronted interrelated institutional obstacles, including securing identification documents, health care, and school enrollment. "The school said we need a *cédula* [identification card], and RENAP [national registry] kept saying we don't have the right documents to get a *cédula*. We spent so long trying to get my dad the right documents [in the United States], and now we're the ones without papers [in Guatemala]."[17] Schools are sites of pronounced tension as foreign citizens must present a series of legal and institutional documents to school administrations that are ill-equipped to verify documents or to ascertain equivalencies. Without copies of their U.S. birth certificates or the requisite consular documents, Carla and Sonia were unable to secure the Guatemalan national identification document necessary to enroll in public school. Only after their father bribed a RENAP official six months later were they able to obtain the requisite documents to begin school in Guatemala.

When asked to share their impressions of school, Sonia chimed in: "The other kids would make fun of us when we'd speak English. But some kids were curious about us and asked us lots of questions. For me, the biggest shock was that there is no water in the school, no library . . . even the English teacher couldn't speak English."

Statistics from the Guatemalan Ministry of Education indicate that in 2010, by the sixth grade, only 45 percent of students reached national mathematics standards and only 30 percent reached national reading standards.[18] Middling performance by the schools notwithstanding, families are asked to purchase desks, writing materials, and uniforms for their children, making the nation's "free and compulsory" school attendance a financial impossibility for many. Guatemala's 1996 Peace Accords called for the incorporation of a multilingual educational model, but public schools remain ill-equipped to support Spanish-language learners and English speakers such as Carla and Sonia. While the rates of primary school attendance have risen in recent years, the poor quality of education—particularly in rural, Indigenous communities—persists, leading to a growing privatization of education across the country.

Despite the school's stark conditions, so different from those they had encountered in Nebraska, Carla and Sonia's parents encouraged them to focus on their studies. Carla explained, "I want to continue studying so that I can teach, I can travel, go new places but I'll always have a job." She described how her father pressured her to pursue a career as an educator rather than a musician, as she had dreamed. Albeit reluctantly, she grew to appreciate the career choice and the opportunities and security it might bring. Carla's desire for a consistent income contrasts the employment realities of her parents. Her mother's income from the produce she sold at the local market fluctuated. Her father worked collecting iron to recycle.

As a result of their unstable economic situation and struggles to adapt to a new home, Carla and Sonia shared how they have grown closer. Sonia explained:

> My sister really helped me. Everything was new, but Carla was always supporting me and encouraging me. She understands best how I'm feeling when no one else does. I couldn't survive without her. Our parents have their worries—they are working hard to support us and to make this work—but they don't always get ours. How could they?

With her sister's support, Sonia described gaining more confidence, emerging from their home, attending classes, and eventually befriending her English teacher. Recognizing their precarious living conditions and their parents' ongoing efforts to eke out a living, Carla and Sonia adjusted their expectations of their parents and instead relied primarily on each other for emotional support. Together, they negotiated school and peer relationships in a new country with different languages, customs, and economic realities.

Antonio

I met seventeen-year-old Antonio at an internet café in Xela in the department of Quetzaltenango. Overhearing me assuring my eldest daughter again, this time in English, that I was *almost* done with work emails, he asked in English: "I'm from New York, you?" Antonio traveled to Guatemala to reunify with his mother, who had been deported following a workplace raid three years prior. Initially, Antonio remained in the United States with his father, but his relationship with his father grew tense. "My mom is the glue. My dad and I, we never really got along. He doesn't like how I dress, what music I listen to, who I hang out with. I can never do anything right by him. He just doesn't get me, and truthfully, I don't get him." Recalling when his father began dating another woman, Antonio chuckled. "I didn't want to deal with his shit, and he didn't want to deal with mine."

For Antonio, the decision to move to Guatemala was an impulsive one. He and his father got into an especially toxic fight one night when Antonio blew through his curfew. "I laid it all out and he didn't like what I had to say," Antonio explained as he fidgeted with a loose button on his rain jacket. Antonio stormed out, only returning a few days later to collect his belongings. He couch surfed until his parents agreed to buy him a one-way ticket to Guatemala. Antonio would later explain, "My mom always told me about Guatemala—the land of eternal spring—and how beautiful it is. I always had the illusion that I'd come here to visit. But only to visit."

When I saw Antonio a year later, he had found a job at a local call center, a coveted position among English speakers, where he earned the equivalent of $500 per month, well above the national monthly minimum wage of approximately $360. Praised by his mother for being "a good son who avoids trouble and works hard," Antonio's new income allowed him to buy a used motorcycle and to support his mother with monthly rent. Feeling most comfortable with the English-speaking tourists who frequent the highland city, he began dating a white woman from Wisconsin, much to his mother's delight. Despite appearances of being well adapted, Antonio wondered aloud: "What the hell am I supposed to do *here?*"

Although he was able to avoid many of the institutional challenges that confronted Carla and Sonia, Antonio struggled to belong in his adopted country. Even with his relative material success and a growing peer group, Antonio felt out of place and without purpose. While having escaped the pressures of gangs in New York, he now faced increased pressure from his supervisor at the call center, a gang leader, to join the MS-13. Struggling with social isolation in his personal life and fear in his workplace, Antonio planned to return to the United States but could not bring himself to tell his mother.

Julian

Born in Colorado, eighteen-year-old Julian described his experience living in a small border community near Tacaná in the department of San Marcos following his father's deportation the previous year. I met Julian during a meeting of deportees with a Canadian filmmaker who hoped to make a documentary film on deportation to the region. Julian and I served as impromptu English interpreters. During the meeting, Julian explained how before joining his father, he spent several weeks reading about Guatemala's history of colonialism, genocide, and violence, conditions that incited his father's migration in the 1990s. Following his father's arrival in Guatemala, Julian desired to (re)discover his Indigenous heritage. "I didn't work in the United States but here I am learning how to work the fields. It hasn't been easy but I'm learning about the land, my culture, and what it means to be Indigenous. I even speak a few words of Mam . . . I'm learning that although we have little, we have something."

During a break from the meeting, he described to me how two fading family photographs had sat on the mantel in the Denver apartment where he grew up, but his parents did not talk about their lives in Guatemala. On the rare occasion when Julian would ask, his father's responses were monosyllabic. His mother would say, "It was another life" or "It doesn't matter now," Julian recalled. His parents encouraged him to go to school and to make American friends. They sat him in front of the television so that he would "speak English like a native," Julian recounted. "I was their American kid. I got America in ways that they never would, and they probably felt the same way about Guatemala . . . that I'd never really understand if I didn't live it. But, here I am. I'm livin' it!"

In subsequent conversations over the years, I would come to learn that in the absence of friends and the attractions of urban life, Julian focused his attention on "discovering my identity." He joined a small group of young people who sought value in their histories and Maya identities. For Julian, this meant learning how to cultivate corn, talking to elders about the meanings of colors and images depicted in weavings, participating in ceremonies, attending community events, and meeting regularly with a local spiritual guide to learn the Mayan calendar and to practice cosmovision. "To me, this means that I see and feel the world in connection to my ancestors and to the universe . . . to channel the energies and the spirit where everything is connected and nothing is left out," he explained. Julian drew strength from his *nahual* (energy or spirit) of *Iq*, which "like the wind, is known for its energy to adapt to new situations and its sacred and purifying breath," he explained. Julian began to resignify his experience of de facto removal as a return to his ancestry and his Indigenous identity—an awakening as he came of age in a new country.

When I marveled at his ability to find solace in such challenging circumstances, Julian was quick to footnote: "But it isn't always pretty." Battling with both the tedium of small-town life and the discrimination he encountered as simultaneously *Indigenous* and *foreign*, he shared, "I don't feel like I really belong anywhere."

Young people who are de facto deported share in the challenges of adapting to a new life following parental deportation. Carla, Sonia, Antonio, and Julian describe learning to navigate new material realities and at times tumultuous social contexts, peer groups, and family dynamics. They also confront institutions that may impede their access to public goods such as education and health care and their ability to secure citizenship documents in their parents' home countries. In the process, young people recount the vital support provided by siblings, parents, extended family, teachers, and mentors as well as by learning about their histories and cultural identity—all critical to forging a sense of purpose and belonging over time. As Julian reminds us, experiences of vulnerability and exclusion are intertwined with experiences of inclusion and strength because "everything is connected, and nothing is left out."

RETORNADXS (RETURNEES)

Just as there is a dearth of statistics on the number of children impacted by parental deportation and children de facto deported from the United States to Guatemala, there are also few available data on the number of children who are themselves officially deported from the United States or Mexico. Statistics of unaccompanied children removed from the United States are difficult to determine, as they are disaggregated between voluntary departure as opposed to deportation. Children's legal cases may drag on for years, leaving these data difficult to trace reliably over time. Statistics from Guatemala's Dirección General de Migración (General Directorate of Migration) indicate that the United States deported 2,715 unaccompanied children to Guatemala from 2012 to 2018, yet these data do not include children deported within families nor those who are deported upon turning eighteen years old. Data from Mexico additionally reveal that from 2014 to 2018, 145,755 children (accompanied and unaccompanied) were deported from Mexico to countries of origin, with 45 percent being from Guatemala. Twenty-three percent of all children deported from Mexico were unaccompanied minors from Guatemala.[19]

Deportation inflicts violence on the bodies of migrants and reverberates in families and communities of return. For youth, apprehension and removal may thwart efforts to seek and maintain family reunification, disrupt future employment or educational plans, and limit the ability to support family, escape poverty, and ensure safety. Removal may be accompanied by feelings of guilt or shame at failing to arrive—and remain—in the United States. Like Delia's experience discussed in chapter four, there are also salient racialized discourses that shape young people's experiences of return in government-run reception centers in Guatemala. As we see in the narratives that follow of Camila, Rodrigo, and Elder, these discourses powerfully influence young people's experiences of return over time.

Camila

Criminalized by government bureaucrats and often ostracized by their communities or even families, unaccompanied youth return to a complex landscape of government surveillance, limited support services, and considerable stigma associated with deportation. Camila, a fourteen-year-old who was deported from Houston, described her deportation flight to the Guatemala City Air Force base, "I was scared. I've never been on a plane and behind me were these men [adult deportees] with handcuffs. We arrived, and the guards signed some papers, pushed us off the plane, and then slammed the door. They didn't even get off the plane, like they'd get sick if they stepped foot in Guatemala." Quickly shuttled to SBS's facility where I met her in 2015, and analogous to Delia's experiences (chapter four), Camila described undergoing a series of humiliating experiences—from the absence of food to the way professionals ridiculed her and the criminalization of her Indigenous parents—while waiting for them to arrive at the facility.

Many young people describe the return to their home communities in Guatemala following deportation as distressing. Surrounded by rumors of delinquency, failure, and for girls, allegations of prostitution and promiscuity, deported youth may be assumed by their community to have committed a transgression of the law or to have succumbed to a moral weakness such as drinking or taking drugs, thereby warranting their detention. In spite of rising numbers of deportees to Central America, there is little distinction between youth who enter immigration detention due to unlawful presence and those who are charged with committing a delinquent or criminal act in the United States. In many ways, this reflects U.S. social and legal discourses that also conflate illegality with criminality.

In Guatemala, migrant youth and their families recognize that migration is costly and risky. In my interviews with young migrants, many youths and their families collectively discuss the decision to migrate, weighing, for example, a child's age and earning potential over that of older family members; Spanish-language ability—a skill necessary to negotiate migration through Mexico and to navigate everyday life upon arrival; character amid the temptations of alcohol, drugs, sex, and consumerism associated with the United States; and gender, given the stark realities of sexual abuse and rape that place female migrants at increased risk. Camila is not an exception. "My family picked me because they know they could trust me. They knew I wouldn't forget them. I remember my mom asking me if I really want to go and I told her, 'No, but I will go anyway, for my family.'"

As discussed in chapter one, most often, though certainly not always, youth ultimately identify the decision to migrate as a collective investment in the family's future, a gesture of their parents' trust in them to provide for their families, or a long-held promise to reunite *allá* (over there). For many young people, deportation generates feelings of failure, shame, and guilt for not reaching the United States. Camila hid in her home in Pajapita for four weeks upon her return, embarrassed and ashamed by what she viewed as a personal and spiritual failure. "Maybe I didn't have enough faith or didn't believe enough that God would watch over me." Indeed, this is a message I have witnessed conveyed from the pulpit of her evangelical church in San Marcos—that a migrant's failure to arrive safely is emblematic of a lack of faith in God. It was a variation of a sermon I would hear throughout the region.

Camila did not realize, and her pastor failed to admit, that she had very little chance of arriving in the United States. Neither she nor her pastor recognized the militarization of borders and transit arteries through Mexico, leading Camila to internalize her deportation as if it were a personal failing. Nor did they identify the structural violence that compelled her migration or the policies that made her arrival highly improbable. Instead, Camila vowed, "Next time, I will pray harder."

Rodrigo

Deported from Mexico to Guatemala after two failed attempts to migrate to the United States, fifteen-year-old Rodrigo spoke from the SBS facility in Xela where I first met him. "I am ashamed they caught me. We mortgaged our land.

My family depended on me to work hard and to support our family, but now this. *Soy un fracaso* [I'm a failure]. I don't know what to do." Because of the unlikelihood of arriving in the United States, coyotes offer prospective migrants three attempts to reach the United States from Guatemala. After his third and final attempt, Rodrigo grappled with the decision to try again. The family's mortgaged land had been his inheritance—it was the land where he might build his home and start a family. Now, with the land in peril, he weighed the risks. It is important to note that Rodrigo never envisioned his migration as a rejection of "home"; instead, it signified an investment in his family's well-being and his own future. His forced returns powerfully complicate his sense of place and future.

In some instances, home communities associate youths' experiences in the United States as a sort of contamination, one that results in a suspicious "loss of culture" upon returning home. Such was the case with Rodrigo, who returned to Guatemala with an iPod shuffle and camera and who grew resentful of his parents' inability to provide even for his basic nutritional needs. His mother explained to me, "He is not the same as before. He looks different. He speaks different. I see him, but he is not here." To his mother and others, that Rodrigo wore his pants slightly lower, purchased hair gel from the town store, and offered little enthusiasm for subsistence farming marked the corruption of his identity.

What is perceived as a "loss" by home communities is, however, a set of behaviors and social values reinforced in the United States. In detention facilities for unaccompanied minors, for example, behavioral modification programs incentivize "good" behaviors, such as obedience to daily hygiene regimens, cleaning one's room thoroughly, learning English, eating a full plate of food, drinking milk, making eye contact, and shaking employees' hands firmly. A three-page list of rules in English and Spanish posted on bulletin boards throughout an Illinois facility for unaccompanied minors where I previously conducted research delineates acceptable versus unacceptable behaviors.[20] Incentivized by daily earnings of two dollars and regular shopping trips that allow the purchase of iPods, MP3 players, watches, jewelry, and hair products, detained youth are socialized as would-be consumers. The impact that such behavioral modification programs, institutional values, and consumption practices have on children after they rejoin their families following deportation is never considered.

When I saw Rodrigo a year later, he mumbled, "I am worse now. I can't make enough here to survive. I mean, I want to help my family and to work but earning 50 quetzales [6.50 USD] a day selling empanadas or growing *milpa* [maize] or even selling in the market. . . . it doesn't make a difference. I failed. I know I failed. I will make it right again. I will."

Elder

"It was really difficult at first. Still is, honestly," Elder confided. It had been two years since his deportation from the United States to San Pablo in the department of San Marcos. He had been living in Utah with a maternal uncle for two years, working on a cherry farm. "My shoulders still hurt. I'm used to cities, so it was all new to me, but I got used to it. It was better than working with smelly cattle; I did that for a week and couldn't stand it. With the farm work, at least I was able to attend English classes on the weekends and occasionally go out."

Apprehended in a workplace raid, at fifteen years old, Elder was placed in a federal facility for unaccompanied minors in Los Fresnos, Texas. He was held there for five months until deported to Guatemala City in 2014, where I met him in the SBS facility. "Detention was cruel. I knew Americans hated us, but I didn't get how much until that place . . . We were treated poorly. Kids teased me for everything—my height, my nose, how I speak Spanish, and the staff didn't do anything to stop it. There was one staff member who was nasty; he called me a *maricón* [faggot] and teased me about whatever, anything really. I couldn't wait to get out."

Elder did not remember his father, who separated from his mother when he was one year old. At sixteen years old, Elder lived with his mother, new stepfather and newborn stepsister. Elder had a tense relationship with his stepfather; their fights were frequent and at times violent.

> I went back to school, but I just didn't see the point. If I'm honest with my-self, I was angry and depressed. One day I got in a fight with [my stepfather], so he refused to pay the school fees. I left school three months before finishing *secundaria* [high school]. He doesn't want me. He's got my mom and his kid; I'm just a nuisance to him. I'm an expense he doesn't want. My mom tries to smooth things over, but it's easier if I work here and sleep in the back [point-ing to a cot just behind the curtain divide in the store].

His mother had run a store for nearly a decade, but with a new and much younger husband and a newborn, she turned its day-to-day management over to Elder. Standing behind the store counter dressed in black jeans and a black tee-shirt, Elder contrasted the brilliantly colored store. While he attended a customer, I gazed at the thirteen varieties of chips hung in orderly rows, the dried foodstuff stacked neatly on the shelves, and the line of florescent-colored cleaning supplies arranged in rainbow order. Elder took pride in his attention to detail.

Returning to school had been difficult. He was ridiculed for acting effeminate and ruthlessly teased for his thirty-nine-year-old mother marrying a man twelve years younger. It took a substantial toll. "Sometimes, I'm just tired of it all—the jokes, the bullies, my stepfather. I don't want to be here. I am physically living here but I'm not really *here*, understand? My mind is somewhere else. I want to make something of myself, to be someone, and I don't think I can do that in San Pablo." He was on his fourth cellular phone—each previous one having been taken by bullies or local gang members, a sometimes difficult distinction to make. The extortion of the family business was especially troubling to Elder and his mother. Initially they paid 20 quetzales (2.60 USD) each week to ensure his safety and the safety of their merchandise. As the store became more profitable, the *multas* (fees) rose. "What can you do? It's the cost of business here," his mother explained to me.

When I last visited Elder in 2016, he had just started a new private school. Upon hearing of the insecurity at the public school, his uncle in Utah remitted money so that Elder could attend classes in the afternoons. His mother covered his afternoon shifts at the store. Otherwise, from 7 a.m. until 11 p.m., Elder tended the store. The money he earned went directly to paying down his migration debt although his grandmother slipped him a few quetzales when she received remittances from Elder's aunts and uncles. With the help of his uncle, Elder hoped to pay off the debt in four years' time. "School is fine now. I am learning industrial arts which is pretty interesting and making a few new friends. It's still pretty lonely. I don't know if I'll go back to the United States. For now, I'm just here."

Within six months of our visit, Elder was killed in an attempted robbery at the store. His mother said three young men hopped up on drugs entered the store waving a gun. The police never found the assailants. "I doubt they even tried," she wept. Using the common refrain, she lamented, *"Así es por aquí."* (That's how it is around here.)

During his short life, Elder contended with various forms of violence—routinized and spectacular, physical and psychological, interpersonal and structural—across Guatemala, Mexico, and the United States. He contended with poverty, homophobia, racism, bullying, gang violence, domestic violence, and institutional violence, yet his death was dismissed by both his mother and the state as attributable to a few youths with ready access to drugs and guns. Elder's life and death is a testament to the depoliticization of crime in the neoliberal era in which acts of violence are perceived as random and accordingly dismissed, rather than attributed to the state's systematic failure to ensure Elder the right to not migrate or, in the least, to hold his assailants accountable for his murder.

EN LA LUCHA VIVIMOS

Young people experience removal in Guatemala in various ways, whether as children of deported parents, as U.S. citizen children who are de facto deported, or as unaccompanied minors who are themselves deported from the United States or Mexico. Yet across these experiences are critical commonalities. For one, the material changes wrought by deportation profoundly impact young people's everyday lives, including their access to food, shelter, and health care; pursuit of education or employment; and migration decisions, either their own or a family member's. Through deportation youth also experience consequential realities of structural violence. By examining in particular youths' negotiations of legal processes and institutional actors, we see how regulatory bodies, citizenship laws, schools, employers, and police often enact and compound violence that limit youths' rights across multiple nations. As Diego, Ana, Clara, and Lorenzo pointedly attest, there are also sustained social and emotional consequences of deportation—nuanced and intimate consequences that alter youths' personal relationships as well as their own sentiments of self-worth and belonging.

While the enormity of the structural violence confronting youth easily subsumes hope and the right to not migrate, and although alternatives to migration are few, scholar Lisa Marie Cacho reminds us that "empowerment is not contingent on taking power or securing small victories. Empowerment comes from deciding that the outcome of struggle doesn't matter as much as the decision to struggle."[21] In spite of the emotional ramifications of deportation on the lives of young migrants and their families, many youths like Antonio, Elder, and Camila continue the struggle—for survival, to support or start families, or to better their lives through education, labor, and self-sacrifice. They find strength and resilience in their social obligations to family, their own young children, their faith, their indigeneity, and the re-signification of their or their parents' migranthood.

Consider how youth like Carla, Sonia, and Rodrigo learned to navigate new and complex institutional, economic, and emotional terrains. They nurtured relationships with parents, deepened bonds with siblings, met extended family, and built rapport with new peer groups and mentors. Some (re)discovered Indigenous identities, learned ancestral cultural practices, and developed linguistic knowledge. Julian reflected as we walked through a cornfield he helped to cultivate, *"En la lucha vivimos."* (We live in the struggle.) That these creative and even resilient experiences exist alongside, and often in spite of, the constraints imposed by deportation deserves more scholarly and political attention. Only by sustaining our attention to the everyday struggles and triumphs of young people over the different courses of deportation over time, might we begin to recognize youths' lives and contributions on a global scale.

CHAPTER 6

DEBT AND
INDEBTEDNESS

"WE DON'T OFTEN GET anthropologists here and this is fascinating, thorough research. But what about the quantitative data?" a State Department officer inquired. It was 2014 at the height of the influx of child migrants from Central America, and I had just briefed the U.S. Department of State and USAID on my first two years (2013–2014) of research on child migration and deportation in Guatemala. I was grateful for, and quite nervous at, the unique opportunity to reach policymakers with this research. Interweaving narratives from young migrants and deported youths with interviews with stakeholders, I shared findings that development initiatives designed to create alternatives to migration—alternatives ranging from extractive industries, free trade zones, the ¡Quédate! initiative, and nonagricultural programs in communities where I researched—stimulated rather than deterred the migration of Indigenous youth. I detailed how nearly 60 percent of the Indigenous youths participating in my study enlisted debt to manage everyday precarity and, absent a social safety net, how this debt led to transnational migration. With the increasing use of deportation, I explained, upon return they became ensnared in an ever-deteriorating cycle of deportation and remigration, of either themselves or their siblings.

As an ethnographer who engages in critical policy analysis, I am accustomed to such requests for quantitative data. Indeed, the scarcity of publicly available data on child migration is a perpetual frustration of mine. Ethnography offers depth and breadth of context often missed by quantitative data, but ethnography is not generalizable, as the State Department officer desired. My localized findings could not be applied to the entirety of the country, nor as so often is problematically done, to the greater region. The question, however, did spur me to reconsider questions of scale—how does child migration and deportation impact Indigenous communities? I had spent considerable time focusing on the intimate and interpersonal impacts of migration and deportation on individual youths and their families and analyzing the structural forces that result in child migration, but how did these impacts and forces shape community dynamics, social values, and cultural practices over time? This chapter endeavors to explore these questions by sharing findings from a household survey I conducted in 2016 in the community of Almolonga, a peri-urban, K'iche' community in the department of Quetzaltenango. It likewise grapples with how anthropology as a discipline might at once be rigorous, applied, and responsive to public policy's need for contextualized data. The survey provides insight on the community-level impacts of migration and deportation and explores local critiques of migranthood and development in the highland town of Almolonga.

Authorities and development experts in Guatemala hold Almolonga as an alternative to migration, as it offers a prosperous example of a globalized, agrarian-based economy. Known as the "Hortaliza de América" (Breadbasket of America), Almolonga maintains a thriving agricultural economy. Employment opportunities are abundant and include harvesting multiple seasons of crops, selling in local markets, and two-way commerce with Mexico and El Salvador. In the past fifteen years, Almolonga has experienced a population surge, largely due to internal migration by Guatemalans seeking employment. The town is well known for the size of its produce, which people largely attribute to God's material reward for the town's "transformation from a community plagued by alcoholism, adultery, witchcraft, and sorcery to a community of devout evangelical disciples," as a community elder and locally ascribed town historian explained. With 90 percent of Almolonga's residents self-identifying as evangelical Christians and over fifty officially recognized evangelical churches and one Catholic church, there is also notable institutional leadership in the community. Yet, in spite of these promising aspects, Almolonga continues to experience significant out-migration of young people. As our survey found, roughly 19 percent of transnational migrants and 18 percent of seasonal or regional migrants from Almolonga are younger than eighteen years old at the time of migration.

Pairing quantitative findings with ethnography and interviews, this chapter examines how Indigenous households manage precarity in everyday life and the tactics they enlist to mitigate the impacts of structural violence. In particular, I trace the ways K'iche' families enlist borrowing to navigate precarity and how the growing prevalence of financial institutions and organizations engaged in the issuing of credit are eroding long-standing norms of interdependency and collectivity. Even in communities like Almolonga, seemingly successful and thriving, the absence of social welfare services and government investment leaves families to construct some semblance of home and community amid what, as anthropologist Anna Tsing writes, is "life without the promise of stability."[1]

The precarity of everyday life demands imagination and resourcefulness. In Almolonga, and consistent with the experiences of many highland communities where I work, assuming debt is a strategy for collective survival. Among wealth-constrained families in Guatemala, debt-financed migration entails the assumption of monetary debt to finance irregular movement across international borders. While, historically, individuals or families have secured loans from family and friends, increasingly they turn to high-interest loans from unregulated or loosely regulated institutional actors—such as *prestamistas* (moneylenders), notaries, cooperatives, and banks—using land, homes, vehicles, or goods as collateral. If a migrant is deported, usurious monthly interest rates that families face often make remigration the only viable means for debt repayment. What results is a cycle of migration and deportation, each attempt compounding the conditions that instigate migration, while at the same time enhancing the vulnerability of migrants by compelling them along less secure migratory routes with more predatory smuggling networks. Since migration-related debt in Almolonga is typically assumed collectively by Indigenous families rather than by individuals, the effects of this debt seep into intimate familial relationships with lasting impacts on their well-being and sense of belonging within the community. In turn, this phenomenon impacts the community, resulting in inflated land prices, intensified social inequality, an erosion of social networks, and a growing exodus of youth. What emerged from the survey were fundamental challenges to popular perceptions of migranthood that correlate transnational mobility with material success. In addition, community members offered substantive local critiques of how development fails to connect to the everyday realities of Almolonga, and how securitized responses to migration and deportation beget everyday precarity in Guatemala across generations.

COMMUNITY SURVEY

In the summer of 2016, I led a team of eight interdisciplinary research assistants (six Guatemalan researchers and two U.S. graduate students) in conducting a household survey in Almolonga. The survey design was based on two years of prior research that included interviews with several youths who were deported to Almolonga, ongoing conversations with community members and local leadership, three small-group meetings with community members, and consultation with an Indigenous organization serving deported youth in neighboring Xela. The survey covered a wide range of themes, including basic household demographics, education, health, food security, land ownership, public service, crime, migration and deportation, remittances, and civic participation. The survey instrument was later refined with support of members of our largely Indigenous, multilingual research team, who generously shared their personal, professional, and linguistic expertise in community-based initiatives.

With the approval of Almolonga's mayor and his municipal council, the Community Council on Urban and Rural Development (Consejos Comunitarios de Desarrollo Urbano y Rural, COCODE), and key religious leaders, our team conducted 148 household surveys. We enlisted a randomized sampling design to select households geographically distributed throughout the boundaries of the municipality of Almolonga, including its two villages of Las Delicias and Los Baños, as indicated in Guatemala's most recent census of 2002. Surveys were conducted during weekday hours (8 a.m. to 5 p.m.) in respondents' homes, with occasional evening or weekend interviews upon a household's request. Some sectors of Almolonga likely are underrepresented in survey findings, namely those who seasonally migrated during the period of the survey and, given the weekday hours of the survey, laborers (predominantly men) who tended to work in the fields in the morning. Participation was voluntary, and respondents could refrain from answering any question(s) or stop the survey at any time. The duration of the in-person survey ranged from one to four hours depending on the detail of responses to open-ended questions. At times, multiple family members participated collectively and individually in answering survey questions. Notably, several young people (ages thirteen to eighteen) provided information with the consent of their elders. As a household rather than a family survey, we included information regarding all persons who physically resided in the household for at least three of the previous twelve months. In teams of two, we verbally administered surveys in Spanish (82 percent), K'iche' (11 percent), or a combination of languages, namely K'iche', Spanish, Mam, and English (7 percent), depending on the respondent's preference. We compensated participating families with 60 quetzales (7.90 USD) for their time (whether they completed the survey or not) and contributed an additional 140 quetzales (18 USD) in materials, workshops, and equipment according to the community needs identified by respondents in the survey.

In addition to the survey, the research team conducted semistructured interviews with twenty-six key community stakeholders, including municipal officials, COCODE members, church leaders, local historians, teachers, business owners, bankers, attorneys, a judge, health-care providers, midwives, and traditional healers. We also conducted several in-depth follow-up interviews with survey respondents who had experienced migration and/or deportation. In 2017, I conducted two focus groups and, with the support of an Indigenous organization from neighboring Xela, we held five workshops with youth (aged thirteen to seventeen) to explore themes of child migration, identity and belonging, and the K'iche' language. In 2017, I also conducted interviews of twelve Almolonguenses living in and around Portland, Oregon. Six months following the survey, three members of our research team reassembled in Almolonga to share preliminary findings and to seek community input through a series of public presentations and community meetings. We incorporated this analysis into our final bilingual report, which was shared with the community, municipal leaders, departmental policymakers, and in 2018, in a subsequent briefing of USAID and the U.S. Department of State. In the summer of 2019, I returned to Almolonga with an interactive art installation that emerged from the survey and subsequent collaborations and which, with the community's approval, had been circulating in various universities, libraries, and community centers in the United States. Through these varied efforts, I sought to collaboratively analyze the data, to reach a broad and more diverse public, and ultimately to return the research to the community to which it belonged.

A CAUTIONARY TALE

Within the first week of the community survey, each member of our research team returned to our offices with fragments of a story about Ana Petronila Xiap Machic, a thirty-seven-year-old Almolonguense who died while crossing the Río Bravo along the U.S.-Mexico border in 2015. Ana's neighbor, Silvia, whom I would meet in a community gathering the following year, shared the fullest, single account of Ana's deadly journey and its aftermath. Silvia described:

> She was trying to meet her husband over there. Rumor was that he had already found a new wife and had forgotten them, but Ana did not think so. Besides, her family was in debt and they could not pay. The remittances had dried up, so she had to do something about it . . . to make it right. She hired a local smuggler to transport her and her son Pedro. They traveled for thirty days with a group of migrants before reaching the Río Bravo. Pedro crossed first and waited on the other side; he had made it to the U.S., you see. I'm sure he was relieved to finally be in El Norte [the United States] and to know he would see his father soon. He had not seen him in years. But there was a strong current. Almolonga is the place where water flows,[2] but we do not swim. Pedro watched his mom drown; her body carried away before his eyes. He was twelve. I can only imagine his suffering—to lose a father to migration and now to witness his mother disappear. If you are lucky, migration brings remittances, but over the long run, nothing positive comes of migration.
>
> Pedro walked all night; he had to, but la Migra [immigration] would soon arrest him and return him. A fisherman found her body the next day. The consulate was supposed to send her body, but it takes some time to get the proper papers. Papers . . . alive or dead . . . it's all about the papers. And, look, it's expensive to return a corpse but cheaper than a live body. ¡Púchica! [Oh my gosh!] Here in the community, we pressured the pollero [smuggler]. He didn't want to return the money to the family. He said it was not his fault . . . that he got her to the border and the boy to the other side . . . that there are

risks . . . that the family still owed him the money. Disgraceful, really. We told him we would ruin his name and his business . . . we'd make an example of him. Without the money, the family would never have been able to bury her; the debt would have sunk them, too. But he was convinced to return some of the money, so they could care for their orphan grandson. The family does not like to talk about it now. Who would? *Es pesado* [It's heavy]. It's just too much.

In Almolonga, Ana's life and death are a cautionary tale of the dangers of migration. For many, her life was emblematic of the risks of migration—of migrants who forget their families and start new ones, of children who forget their parents after prolonged absences, and of families that disintegrate under the strain of distance and time. "Ana was foolish," another community member told us, "to take such an unsafe journey, as a woman and with her son, no less, in search of a man who has long forgotten her." Others empathized with Ana and her family's complicated predicament—longing to reunite with her husband after nearly a decade apart, the necessity of providing for her son amid few viable economic opportunities, and the crushing weight of financial debt. "It just isn't worth it," another neighbor tsked. Ana is one of the 15 percent of migrants from Almolonga who are women, nearly half of whom identified a desire to support their children following marital separation or single parenthood.

So, too, Ana's death was representative of the risks of migration, the exorbitant financial costs of the illusive American dream, and the unscrupulous dealings of smugglers, even trusted ones. Only under the community's threats of punishment—in this case, the threat of necklacing the smuggler with a gas-filled tire and setting it aflame—did the smuggler relent and return some of the family's money. As Silvia inferred, the stark irony remains that in death Ana travels more easily and garners more documentation as a corpse than as a migrant. Indeed, the costs of repatriating a body from the United States to Guatemala at the time was roughly $5,000, under half of her smuggling fee.

Ana's death is also illustrative of the unanticipated and rippling effects of debt on households. Three years prior, her family had secured a loan from a local cooperative to purchase agricultural supplies for an upcoming harvest of cabbage and carrots. When the harvest failed due to a drought, her family was unable to keep pace with the 10 percent monthly interest. With a quickly ballooning debt and only a trickling of remittances from her husband in the

United States, Ana and her family decided that she and her son should migrate. Her parents mortgaged their family home to pay for their journeys.
Following Ana's death, Pedro was detained as an unaccompanied minor in
an ORR facility in Texas and was later deported to Guatemala. Ana's tragic
drowning compounded by their ongoing financial debt continued to weigh
on their family.

In response to Ana's very public death, a legislator from the department of
Quetzaltenango whom I interviewed questioned, "Why would anyone leave
Almolonga? *Hay condiciones para vivir. Hay desarrollo.*" (There are means of
survival. There is development.) He attributed these conditions to Almolonga's booming agricultural production, industrious Almolonguenses who rise
at predawn to begin work, and the inflow of remittances from Portland,
Oregon, where there has been a relatively well-established Almolonguense
community since the 1990s. In Guatemala, financial remittances resulting
from migration are often extolled as primary drivers of development and
tangible benefits of migration. Many actors have a stake in the growing flow
of remittances—and the issuing of credit to facilitate (irregular and state-
sanctioned) movement of people across borders—including banks, money
transfer companies, moneylenders, multinational corporations, cooperatives,
churches, communities, and beneficiaries themselves. At the household level,
Almolonguenses who were surveyed identified the benefits of migration as
modest improvements in living conditions (23 percent), including the purchase of land and vehicles and the construction of homes; repayment of debts
(21 percent), including debts incurred for a wide range of reasons, such as
health care, death, failed crops, and debt-funded migration; improved education (6 percent); and providing for family (8 percent). Some households
(2 percent) indicated that there is little to no positive effect of transnational
migration, citing the adverse consequences of addiction, depression, family
disintegration, and financial debt.

While development discourse lauds financial remittances from migrants as
having a significant benefit to the community and to the nation, Almolonguenses were hard-pressed to identify community-level benefits to migration. "Only
families benefit, not communities," we were told repeatedly. The majority of
surveyed households view migration to the United States with resoundingly
negative effects on the community. Only 3 percent indicated that remittances

assist in development of Almolonga, namely roads and water projects. In contrast, when asked to identify the negative impacts of migration on the community of Almolonga, respondents were quick to identify that remittances inflate land prices (13 percent) and that deportees and their families may lose their land when unable to repay loans. Respondents also recognized how family disintegration (29 percent) impacts the health and well-being of the community, as family breakdown shapes young people's education, health, and life prospects. Over the long term, they attested, there are adverse intergenerational consequences of migration in Almolonga.

Local and national bureaucrats claim that, as the breadbasket of Central America, Almolonga enjoys an abundance of jobs, *condiciones* (favorable conditions), and *desarrollo* (development). However, as a resident explained: *"Sí, hay trabajo pero no hay empleo con condiciones dignas."* (Yes, there is work but there isn't employment with dignified conditions.) In Almolonga, poverty remains significant and livable wages are scarce. The average monthly household income is 800 quetzales (105 USD) per month for an average of 6.3 individuals per household, with 79 percent of participating households earning under 1,000 quetzales (131 USD) per month. Only 5 percent of the surveyed households cumulatively earned the national monthly minimum wage of 2,742 quetzales (360 USD). For young people in particular, they are caught in positions of precarious and at times hazardous employment. As youth in Almolonga recounted, working conditions are often dangerous, workplace abuses are common, and withheld or garnered wages occur frequently. With few opportunities to denounce workplace abuses, people make a consequential distinction between "work" and "employment" rooted in an awareness of a desire for dignified conditions—that is, a safe workplace free of harassment and discrimination and in which they are consistently paid a fair wage.

That several community members lamented the dearth of government initiatives to generate dignified employment is indicative of the state's apathy toward the needs of Indigenous peoples. The state, they highlighted, at once celebrates migrants' financial remittances while discounting its own responsibilities to provide for its citizenry. Several residents cited President Jimmy Morales's 2016 offer of cheap (read: Indigenous) labor to the Trump administration: "To the gentleman who wants to build a wall, I offer cheap labor. We have high-quality labor, and we'll gladly build. Tell us the dimensions, and we know how to do it."

With an economic disincentive to deter transnational migration and correspond-ing remittances, combined with a disparaging view of Indigenous people's labor, respondents described how the Guatemalan state has abdicated its responsibility "to provide alternatives" to would-be migrants, "to monitor the banks and the cooperatives," "to hold accountable lenders who take advantage of Indigenous communities," and "to provide real support to deportees."

DEBT-DRIVEN MIGRATION

In Almolonga, debt-driven migration involves a diverse cross-section of actors and institutions. For youth and their families, transnational migration is un-derstood as a risky endeavor requiring the acquisition of sufficient resources and, increasingly, the incursion of considerable financial debt and social in-debtedness. In migrating to the United States, for example, Almolonguense youth and their families described the necessity of securing the financial capi-tal to contract one of the three well-known and respected *polleros de confianza* (honest or trusted smugglers) and of having the social capital to secure hous-ing and employment immediately upon arrival. While coyotes have a vested financial interest in ensuring arrival on the first attempt, this does not deter attacks, injuries, kidnappings, rape, and theft by the cartels, police, smugglers, or other migrants.

Irregular migration from Guatemala with any measure of certainty or safety, even if aspirational, necessitates access to substantial social and financial capital. Families in Almolonga report mortgaging their land, pooling funds from friends and family, and borrowing heavily from local moneylenders, no-taries, attorneys, or increasingly, banks, cooperatives, or evangelical churches. In the past, families recounted borrowing funds primarily from family and friends or via remittances to pay for smuggling costs; now they frequently turn to institutions and other community actors. As discussed in chapter one, legacies of discriminatory land reform among Indigenous communities across the highlands of Guatemala shape the capital resources available to families for daily survival.[3] As a result, families like Ana's commonly utilize land as collateral to fund undocumented migration. For those who do not own land, unauthorized migration is often an impossibility outside of the occasional caravans, which help to bypass most smuggling fees and provide a modicum of safety.

Some community leaders in Almolonga noted that lending practices related to debt-driven migration have led to shifts in, and at times a consolidation of, land ownership. The prevalence and scale of these shifts, however, remain difficult to trace due to opaque processing of land titles, restricted access to department-level data, and limited monitoring of predatory mortgage practices. Although the Registro General de la Propriedad, a national land registry, seeks to track property titles (known as *certificaciónes del historial de la finca*) and to regulate the once frequent practice of mortgaging one's land multiple times, the practice continues.

NGOs and cooperatives are also involved in the financing of irregular migration from Guatemala. Anthropologist David Stoll argues that following the armed conflict, an enthusiastic influx to Nebaj of microcredit projects aimed specifically at Indigenous women resulted in their greater access to capital. According to Stoll, some entrepreneurial Indigenous women converted these funds into a series of loans akin to a pyramid scheme, with incrementally increasing interest rates to fund transnational migration. This led to the considerable outmigration of primarily Ixil men aged fifteen to thirty. Stoll argues that increased access to credit in Nebaj, alongside fewer opportunities for low-waged labor in the United States, has led migrants to default on loans, which has created rippling economic impacts.[4] In contrast to Nebaj, Mam and K'iche' communities in the departments of San Marcos, Totonicapán, and Quetzaltenango, which includes Almolonga, have not been flooded with equivalent development aid. While microfinance indeed is in vogue, microcredit loans from NGOs across these departments rarely exceed 600 quetzales (79 USD).

That said, directors of three cooperatives functioning in Almolonga whom I interviewed describe awarding loans for infusion into local businesses or agricultural production while candidly admitting their implicit knowledge that these loans fund migration. As one local cooperative director described, "Nobody comes to say, 'I need to send my son to the United States, and I need money quickly.' But we know the realities of our community and we know that people need access to money to migrate. We don't ask, and nobody asks us." Only recently has the Coordinación de Organizaciones No Gubernamentales y Cooperativas (Coordination of NGOs and Cooperatives) begun to clamp down on these transactions through audits, site visits, and repealing the business licenses of cooperatives that knowingly engage in funding migration.

The regional director of a national cooperative that recently had opened a branch in Almolonga described:

> Almolonga is a booming market for us, as people need capital to cultivate crops, transport goods, and export products. We also see a growth in small businesses that would benefit from ready access to capital. Almolonguenses are industrious people. They work hard and are God-fearing, but historically Almolonguenses do not have a repayment culture, which is one of the reasons why it took us some time to open up an office there. It is definitely a consideration when we evaluate potential clients.

The director's reference to a "repayment culture" is rooted in a prominent idea within the microfinance sector that lenders must break borrowers' ambivalence toward repayment, an ambivalence characterized by viewing loans as handouts not necessitating reimbursement.[5] The development logic argues that institutions must cultivate "credit discipline" among its borrowers.[6] Notably, the absence of a "repayment culture" implicates the individual borrower rather than the conditions that lead one to borrow or the feasibility of earning the level of wages needed to repay it. Moreover, pejorative assertions that Indigenous people are "lazy" or "helpless" and whose cultures are "full of vice," as I heard throughout my research, problematically underpin these disparaging development logics in Guatemala.

Financial institutions are not to be outdone. Banks market insurance packages to would-be migrants and their families, undertaking to repatriate the bodies of migrants if they should die en route to—or in—the United States, covering costs that now reach $12,500. To rival the profits from the wire transfer services of MoneyGram and Western Union, banks have created "migrant accounts" that allow U.S.-based migrants to deposit funds for immediate access by family members residing in Guatemala, all for a sizable monthly fee. Bank loans previously taken out to fund irregular migration are now expressly prohibited by Banco Industrial, Banco G&T Continental, and Banrural, Guatemala's largest banks. A Banrural executive explained the policy change in lending: "With increased enforcement of the border compounded by the decreasing demand for low-wage labor in the United States, migrants defaulting on their debts grew commonplace. This led banks to further restrict our lending and enhance our requirements for lenders." However, interviews with local bank managers and deported migrants within and beyond Almolonga reveal that the practice continues. In fact, 31 percent of surveyed households that had enlisted loans utilized bank loans from Banrural to fund irregular migration.

In Almolonga, some evangelical churches also manage migration with increasing frequency and intensity. A pastor at one the largest churches shared:

> We guide families on who to trust and how much to send and when. Unknown smugglers can deceive families into sending all of the money up front, so we try to help guide their decisions that you only send a little bit first, more when they get to the border, and more once they actually arrive in the United States. Some smugglers will want to take them on routes through Salamanca [Mexico], but their chances are not strong if they go that route. Instead, we guide them through Saltillo, but that is subject to change.

What remains dubious is that pastors are benevolently shepherding migrants to specific smugglers without profiting themselves. Several evangelical churches in Almolonga are, in fact, openly serving as remittance houses for migrants, taking anywhere from 7 to 15 percent of remittances before distributing the funds to migrants' families. In Almolonga, only 22 percent of families received remittances, and these were received either monthly (39 percent, averaging $40) or biannually (7 percent), annually (32 percent), or sporadically (22 percent), ranging from $75 to $450 per transfer.

While customary in many K'iche' communities, the practice of *cuchubal* is no longer followed in Almolonga. As a community elder explained to me, *cuchubal* is a practice in which individuals contribute funds monthly and the funds are distributed to a rotating member, typically over the course of a year. As many families struggle to meet the needs of daily living, however, the availability of capital from friends and family members can be scarce. As banks, microcredit cooperatives, and additional actors aggressively advertise lending and create options for borrowing, some households reported turning to institutions rather than exclusively to neighbors or family, often with dire and enduring consequences.

Families in Almolonga utilize debt in a number of ways, not exclusively to fund migration. Over the prior five years (2011–2016), 36 percent of surveyed households reported utilizing loans. Families took a line of credit to invest in a family business; to fund agricultural products such as seeds, compost, and fertilizer at the start of a harvest; to purchase a household appliance or an auto-mobile; to pay for medical services, such as hospital stays, lab tests, or medica-tion; or to pay for funeral expenses. For many families, including Ana's, debts increasingly are incurred to recover from the effects of natural disasters resulting from climate change, such as prolonged droughts or excessive rains. In a national study conducted by Consejo Nacional de Áreas Protegidas (National Council on Protected Areas), Almolonga was ranked the third most severely impacted municipality due to climate change.[7] The study attributes Almolonga's vulner-abilities primarily to deforestation to make room for intensive agricultural pro-duction as well as to overfertilization and subsequent contamination of the soil. Nearby Santiaguito volcano poses the additional hazard of an overabundance of volcanic ash, which is detrimental to crops. For farmers utilizing loans to invest in agriculture, a failed harvest may quickly lead to debt and result in a search for alternative avenues for repayment. Depending on the size and conditions of the loan, farmers may turn to transnational migration as the only viable means to maintain their land that lenders—including banks, cooperatives, moneylend-ers, notaries, and lawyers—hold as collateral.

For those enlisting loans to fund transnational migration, the repayment of debt has both immediate and long-term impacts. If a migrant is able to arrive safely in the United States and secure employment quickly, families typically prioritize the repayment of debt from even modest remittances. That is, food, schooling, and other uses for remittances are secondary to the repayment of debt, which can take one to eight years depending on size of the loan, wages in the United States, and exchange rates. For those with outstanding loans, de-portation can have devastating effects on families, as debt repayment is prohibi-tively expensive relative to average monthly wages in Guatemala. This results in loss of land, vehicles, goods, and those of any *fiador* (cosigner, guarantor) as well. Some respondents confided that the pressures of financial debt lead to depression, alcoholism, family discord, intrafamilial violence, and homelessness.

Taken together, the proliferation of actors engaged in issuing credit, poorly regulated banking and lending practices, and usurious interest rates have served to expand the use of credit and debt as a means of navigating intergenerational, structural poverty. A failed harvest or business endeavor, illness, or death may have devastating consequences. In these ways, debt may also drive irregular mi-gration. Rather than the state addressing the underlying needs of Indigenous communities—or creating conditions that would allow people to exercise the right to not migrate—it has instead deregulated the financial industry, which benefits the private sector over its citizenry. While structural violence and forced migration has existed for centuries in Guatemala, the prevalence of lending to fund irregular migration amid growing rates of deportation has enhanced the precarity of Indigenous peoples.

A FAMILY AFFAIR

Dressed in jeans and work boots, Adrián was hunched over the outdoor sink washing the breakfast dishes alongside his fourteen-year-old daughter, Micaela. Together, they were responding to our survey questions. Adrián shared,

> I never felt the desire to migrate like my brothers. I had a decent life here in Almolonga—a small plot of land, my wife and daughter. Life had been good to me, so why would I leave? But then my wife got sick. She suffered from headaches and heart pain, and the doctors said if they didn't operate, she would die. She was hospitalized several times for two or three days; she couldn't get out of bed and couldn't care for Micaela. *Alquilamos dinero* (We "rented" money) from a local moneylender to cover the expenses. Thanks to God, she is alive today.

Initially seeking care at the local *centro de salud* (health center), Adrián described how the local doctor disparagingly treated his wife, Ixkik, so they sought out a private clinic in neighboring Xela. Many recognized that Almolonga was fortunate to have a health post, yet only 4.5 percent of community members report accessing health care there, citing lack of laboratory facilities and diagnostic tests, lack of confidence in the level of care, limited services in the K'iche' language, and derogatory and demeaning remarks by health-care providers toward Indigenous people, including yelling at women during childbirth. Instead, the majority of community members sought health care at private clinics (38 percent), at local pharmacies (30 percent), and with traditional healers (8.3 percent); utilized already-known treatments (5.5 percent); or forewent health care altogether (13.7 percent).

Adrián explained that he turned to a local moneylender to secure the funds necessary for Ixkik's care because of the urgency of their situation and because banks "do not understand our reality." As local bank employees elaborated, banks often require significant paperwork—including applications, legal documents, and evidence of collateral—and impose banking fees and prolonged waiting periods. For some community members, the inability of bank personnel to speak K'iche' was an additional deterrent to seeking bank services or loans. For those who lack the requisite paperwork, an additional *fiador* to cosign the banknote was required. While the terms of loans from lawyers, notaries, and moneylenders often were identified as riskier loans and with higher interest rates than banks, many nonetheless described banks as dishonest or untrustworthy.

In the survey, households described weighing the terms of loans from each lender. These include available principal, interest rate, annual percentage rate (APR), length of loan repayment, and potential for a revolving line of credit. Depending on an institutional determination of "creditworthiness," terms of loans from banks, microfinance cooperatives, and local moneylenders, notaries, or attorneys vary considerably, ranging from 10 to 50 percent APR. Several people pointed to banks repossessing goods or property more quickly than other sources of loans, such as moneylenders, cooperatives, and notaries, which are more willing to renegotiate the terms of the loan. Although many respondents identified loans as predatory and banks as dishonest, families such as Adrián's concurrently recognized that securing a loan was the only strategy to better their living conditions, respond to an acute crisis, or manage structural poverty.

We moved inside the family's home so as to include Ixkik in our conversation. Sitting on the edge of a bed, she appeared fragile with a scarf covering her head. Ixkik listened on as Adrián described how the family was unable to keep pace with repayments on their 40,000 quetzales (5,260 USD) loan plus 4 percent monthly interest to the local moneylender. "With medication, I improved," Ixkik whispered. "The daily pills and the operations cost a lot and then there was the debt, so Adrián migrated."

With remittances from his brothers, Adrián paid the 50,000 quetzales (6,580 USD) smuggling fee amid promises to repay his brothers. Deported twice from Mexico, on his third attempt, Adrián successfully arrived in New York, where his brother and cousin aided him in finding a place to stay, securing a job at a Mexican restaurant, and enrolling in English classes. "Nearly every cent I earned for four years went to my wife's health and to the debt. I don't have a house or a truck to show for my time over there, but she is still with us."

Micaela chimed in: "I left school so I could help my mother." Ixkik described how Micaela cared for her, tended the chickens, washed the clothes, sold cilantro and peppermint at the local market, and generally managed the household when Ixkik was too frail. "But then my mother was close to death the doctors said, so my father came home," Adrián returned by traversing the five thousand kilometers by bus from New York to Almolonga. Ixkik said, "I was dying, and I just wanted to see him one last time, so he came. Seeing him brought me peace when I needed it most. It gave me the will to survive."

The family's incursion into debt began with the need to access health care for Ixkik. They are not alone. In our survey, 8 percent of families utilized loans to pay for health care and an additional 4 percent of households enlisted migration as a means exclusively to support an ailing family member through remittances used for diagnostic tests, medication, treatment, and operations.

For nearly all families in our survey, debt is a family affair. Combining external sources, family remittances, local income, and loans, Adrián, Ixkik, and Micaela pieced together funds. Adrián reflected:

> At night, I don't sleep much. I think about the upcoming payments, and the debt is accumulating with interest. I worry about my wife's health. There is much we need in our house; it is a lot to consider. I've thought about migrating again, but I cannot leave her. The thought is too painful. My mother helps; she uses some of the remittances my brothers send to pay Micaela's school fees and clothes when she needs them, but [my mother] is getting older, and I don't know how long the remittances will keep coming. My brothers have families and responsibilities too.

The relationship between debt and migration experienced by Adrián, Ixkik, and Micaela cannot be understood in isolation. It must be contextualized by the conditions of poverty and the underperforming and often discriminatory health-care system that compel them to seek and to pay for more expensive care. Thus, it is not debt that initially drove Adrián's migration but rather a need to navigate a health-care system that repeatedly failed Ixkik while simultaneously shaming her for being K'iche'. In this way, structural violence directly impacts Ixkik's physical health and the family's well-being.

Now submerged in debt and with Ixkik's medical expenses accumulating, their family began to consider Micaela's migration. Ixkik shared, "I lament that she may have to migrate, but I do not know what other options we have. My daughter doesn't have anything, and this is my fault. I am the cause of so much suffering that many times I just wish to die so they do not have to care for me."

When asked about the prospect of migration, Micaela responded, "On Mother's Day, my father and I prepared Kaq'-ik [a traditional Maya Q'eqchi' stew] for my grandmother. We asked for her blessings and support. My grandmother is powerful, and I will only go if she supports me and believes that I can contribute. I want to help my family and my mother, but I will go only with her blessings. She says she will consider it." Amid everyday precarity, young people like Micaela are contributors on whom their families rely for moral support, caregiving, and paid and unpaid labor. When I returned to the family home six months later to invite Micaela to a workshop with youth in the community, Adrián shared that she was now cleaning homes in New York and caring for his brother's newborn.

Through the experiences of Adrián, Ixkik, and Micaela, we see how debt is acquired and utilized as well as the intergenerational impacts of debt—directly and indirectly—on the migration of young people. Just as care is familialized—that is, families undertake the responsibility to care for their members in the absence of the state—so, too, is debt. In most instances in Almolonga, assuming financial debt and ensuring repayment are understood as familial and often intergenerational obligations, rather than an individual's responsibility. The absence of health care for Ixkik spurred Adrián's migration and migratory debt; and the (in)ability to repay debt shapes the everyday lives, options, and futures of not only Adrián and Ixkik but also Micaela. In K'iche' culture, *dando mi palabra* (giving my word) is intertwined with one's trustworthiness, dependability, and respect as well as one's family's. In contrast to claims that Almolonga lacks a "repayment culture," the pressures of repayment are weighty and shared by extended, intergenerational kinship networks. For Micaela, this comprised her parents, grandmother, aunts and uncles, and cousins both in Guatemala and in the United States. Taken in context, Micaela's migration is a family affair, one that weaves together a complex web of factors and forces that shape the decision to migrate, the conditions of the journey, as well as social obligations across generations.

UNA GRAN ESTAFA

"Es pura necesidad" (It's pure necessity), Eulalia explains as the reason for her migration to New Jersey. At seventeen years old, Eulalia followed seasonal migration patterns to the Pacific coast of Guatemala and later to southern Mexico to harvest coffee alongside her father and elder brother. In Almolonga, 10 percent of families migrate seasonally within Guatemala, primarily to the Pacific coast and occasionally to Guatemala City. An additional 8 percent migrate regionally either to southern Mexico to harvest coffee or to El Salvador to labor on export crops. Of the households with seasonal and regional migrants, approximately 18 percent include household members like Eulalia who are under the age of eighteen. These data likely underrepresent national trends of child labor migration, as Almolonga is somewhat unique in that it maintains a strong import-export economy. At the same time, these rates are illustrative of the insufficiencies of the local labor market to garner livable wages for families, necessitating seasonal and regional migration to supplement household incomes. Wage-labor migration persists as a familial survival strategy, primarily for young men and boys who undertake the physically taxing labor.[8] As a young woman, Eulalia's participation in this labor migration spoke to her family's dire straits. In this context, transnational labor migration is one of multiple household survival strategies in which Maya children and youth actively participate by fulfilling social expectations and meeting economic needs.

When her father died in a car accident, the family income unexpectedly plummeted. Eulalia's family sought a bank loan of 40,000 quetzales (5,260 USD) at 3.5 percent monthly interest to cover funeral expenses *"para cumplir con la costumbre"* (to adhere to custom). Based upon one's collateral and financial position, the bank's interest rates can be as low as 3 percent compounded monthly, rates that are considerably lower than those offered by local moneylenders, notaries, or cooperatives. For those with limited collateral, a cosigner or *fiador* is required. Eulalia and her family enlisted a paternal uncle as a cosigner of their loan. Her uncle Edú, who ran a successful import-export business, maintained a line of credit that facilitated his ready access to funds for unexpected business expenses. Community members with lines of credit shared that this credit was particularly helpful in instances of emergency, such as a funerals, accidents, illness, lost wages, natural disasters, or failed harvests.

Those without established lines of credit and who likewise confront an urgent situation sought funds primarily from lawyers, notaries, and moneylenders, often at much higher interest rates (from 5 to 50 percent monthly) and stricter terms than bank rates and terms, which issue shorter repayment schedules and require greater collateral for lesser-resourced applicants.

Recognizing few options, Eulalia explained, "My aunt in El Norte [the United States] sent some remittances. We begged from neighbors to loan us a few quetzales. We sold our household furniture. My sisters and I sold our *güipiles* [traditional blouses]. We borrowed from the bank. We didn't bury my father properly; we just couldn't afford it. We used the money for me to travel *allá* [over there]."

Initially, Eulalia was proud that her family selected her to migrate to the United States. "I'm old enough, work hard, get good grades, and I speak Spanish. They trust me," she rationalized. Indeed, migration debt is not always negative or exclusively financial. Many youths view migration debt as a form of belonging and of trust, investment, and social obligation that binds them to their families. Indebtedness is a form of relationality, as debt in practice binds migrant youth to a wider community. The social indebtedness that youth experience toward their families bolsters their important positions within expansive kinship, communal, and ethnic networks—networks that offer emotional, spiritual, and financial support. Eulalia identified her migration as a collective investment in her family's future, a gesture of their trust in her to provide for them. After two deportations from Mexico, Eulalia expressed feelings of failure for not reaching the United States.

Eulalia also recognized that the consequences of debt extend beyond her immediate family to her uncle and his family. If they did not begin payment on the cosigned bank note, Eulalia elaborated, her uncle risked losing agricultural land and the season's harvest upon it. Hopeless and ashamed, Eulalia conceded that her fifteen-year-old sister, Sofia, might fare better. Perhaps recognizing the perils of multiple migrations as deterrents to young would-be clients, many smugglers now extend their offer of three attempts to a family rather than to a specific family member. Sitting in a courtyard with her sister and me, Sofia recounted: "I begged my mother to let me go. I want to help. I earn 25 quetzales [3.29 USD] a day and work four days a week. We don't have enough to eat, to pay for medicine. If I don't go, we will lose our home . . . And, if I die, at least I will die trying to help my family, rather than die here in misery."

Women and girls in Almolonga must navigate competing discourses on the ease with which they might migrate. Some men dismiss the threats facing women in claiming that women and children migrate more easily through Mexico and into the United States. *"Las mujeres entran fácilmente y los hombres sufren."* (Women enter easily, and the men suffer.) These dismissals diminish the risks that women and children face in Mexico. Young girls in particular shared that they found it challenging to convince family members to support their migration because the risks were seen as too great or women and girls were considered "too weak" to undertake the journey.

In Almolonga, women and girls readily identified the gendered risks of migration, including sexual violence, pregnancy resulting from rape, and sexually transmitted infections. Eulalia said, *"Lamentosamente, ahora la violación es un costo de migración; los costos de deportación todavía peores."* (Regretfully, rape is now a cost of migration, but the costs of deportation are still worse.) These additional risks associated with deportation include gendered stigma, rumors of promiscuity, and accusations of adultery—with problematic assumptions that women must sleep with someone "voluntarily" or coercively—in order to arrive in the United States. Accordingly, some young people do not tell their parents of their intentions to migrate for fear that their parents would not support their decision or that it would bring worry and concern. In other instances, families describe concealing their child's migration, claiming that they were "going on a trip," "visiting family in Guatemala City," or "working in the capital" so as to protect them from the social stigma if confronted with deportation. In both instances, family members articulate considerable anxiety about the migration of loved ones.

As with Micaela, the conditions that spurred Eulalia's migration are at once intergenerational and structural. Eulalia's seasonal migration alongside her father and brother is a well-worn strategy for many Guatemalans to manage precarity. As discussed in chapter one, historically, Indigenous families were coerced into providing labor on plantations in southern Guatemala. Although forced labor was abolished in 1940, the patterns of labor migration continue unabated. Researchers have documented how the labor of Indigenous workers is preferred due to racialized logics that claim Indigenous people are better suited for the physical demands of labor and that Indigenous people can be compensated less than their ladino counterparts.[9] In addition, there is a growing number of young people who are drawn to work in rural *maquilas*, or export apparel assembly factories. Together with the plantations along the Pacific coast, rural *zonas libres* (free trade zones) along the Pan-American Highway offer wage-labor opportunities for young people. These industries reinforce and intensify, rather than alleviate, existing social inequalities and intergenerational tensions while simultaneously instantiating powerlessness among Indigenous communities within the world economic system.[10] To understand the "pure necessity" that Eulalia describes, we must historicize it, linking wage labor and migration as a means of managing everyday structural violence across generations.

Following her father's death, income from wage labor became insufficient. Eulalia's family relied on any and all available credit to ensure survival, including the selling of their *traje*, arguably the most prominent visual marker of their Indigenous identity. Amid this intergenerational precarity, families turn to an increasing number of financial institutions and informal actors that are now in the business of loans. While some borrowers in Almolonga invested in their businesses, the returns only mitigated the short-term needs of families rather than providing future financial stability. In very few instances in the survey did families improve their economic situation over the long term. To the contrary, in 28 percent of households that utilized loans, financial interest quickly surpassed the principal, sinking families into financial ruin while financial institutions and actors flourished. For Eulalia and Sofia, it only ensured their survival for a few more months. In spite of banks and cooperatives advertising loans that claim to *"mejorar la calidad de vida"* (improve your quality of life) or *"satisfacer las necesidades de tu hogar"* (satisfy the needs of your home), ready access to credit, even within relatively more regulated financial industries such as banks and cooperatives, reinforces and at times exacerbates inequalities. Displaced and unsettled, Eulalia describes, "Now, my family is like a bird with nowhere to land."

While social networks in Almolonga have weakened, especially as credit among families is increasingly scarce, they have not entirely eroded. Eulalia's uncle Edú shared that he had observed the profound and disproportionate impact of loans on the community. Unbeknownst to his niece, he served as a cosigner to seven family members, friends, and neighbors because of their inability to pay interest rates on their loans. In some instances, he paid off the loans, most recently for his cousin who could not make payments on a loan of 45,000 quetzales (5,920 USD) with 18 percent *daily* interest. Another brother-in-law had not paid Edú for four years for the 38,000 quetzales (5,000 USD) Edú paid to Banrural so as to save the family's land from dispossession. Given this added economic hardship on Edú and his family, he explained his motivation:

> I hate to see them lose the land where our grandparents' grandparents lived. What will happen to their children if they lose their home? I stepped forward to pay them because I could not do *nothing* while the banks and lawyers and moneylenders take their children's inheritance and take over the town. *Es una gran estafa* [It's a big scam/fraud], not only by the banks but also by the rich and the corrupt in the government.

Edú recognized the injustice of these loans and their intergenerational impacts on Almolonga as a community. He laid blame on the banks, the elite, and corrupt government officials who collude to impoverish Indigenous peoples and dispossess them from their land.

LETHAL DEBTS

When their eldest son Tómas died from untreated diabetes at the age of thirty-four, Fernando and his wife Francesca welcomed Tómas's widow and their five grandchildren into their home. Their seventeen-year-old son Sebastián, with his own newborn on the way, felt compelled to migrate to support his new and growing family. Fernando was initially supportive. "We mortgaged our land and our home to the [cooperative] to support Sebastián. It was a difficult decision. My wife was sick, my knees and back are no good anymore. I cannot work like before. I didn't think we had another choice."

The 60,000 quetzales (7,895 USD) Fernando and Francesca received for the deed of their home would secure Sebastián's three attempts to cross Mexico into the United States, but he would never arrive. "Initially, he was worried but determined," his sister-in-law shared. For Sebastián, his first failed migration and deportation from Mexico to Guatemala signified not only an inability to provide for his family and his newborn son, but also the family's potential default on their loan from a nationally recognized cooperative. With no institutional follow-up or services for young people following deportation to Guatemala, the conditions that spurred Sebastián's migration were compounded by the financial debt his family enlisted for him to migrate irregularly. Rather than return to Almolonga, Sebastián remained in Malacatán, a Guatemalan municipality along Mexico's southern border, for twenty days before trying again.

Following his second failed attempt and with a quickly mounting debt, Sebastián migrated again almost immediately. "He was frantic. We told him to rest, to prepare himself. The journey requires strength, but he would not listen," Fernando commented. Sebastián's deportations placed considerable financial strain on their family. Unable to meet the interest payments on the loan, the cooperative began foreclosure proceedings on their home. After Sebastián's third failed attempt, the family was evicted from their land.

An attorney told me, "Mortgaging one's land is a civil process in which an individual administratively and free of coercion enters into a legal and financial contract. Because it does not fall in one's favor does not signify a crime has been committed." Rather than criminal or predatory behaviors on the part of moneylenders, notaries, or banks, the attorney points to "misfortune." In so doing, she collapses debt-driven migration into legal and political paradigms that distinguish *economic* or *voluntary* from *forced* migration, rather than recognizing the coercive role debt plays in driving migration.

Ashamed at what he viewed as a personal failure, Sebastián spiraled into depression and alcoholism over the next two years. His father sighed, "We lost our home, our land, our livelihood, and our son. *La deuda lo mató* [The debt killed him]." Sebastián died of alcohol poisoning at the age of twenty.

Now living in a two-room house with a corrugated metal roof, they struggled to survive. Unable to pay the 120 quetzales (16 USD) per month to their neighbor who loaned them electricity, Sebastián's family recently lost power. Still overcome with grief, Francesca mourned, "He went looking for life. He only found death."

In Almolonga, local understandings of migranthood are infused with social, cultural, and religious values and are influenced by kinship relations, economic precarity, and gender norms. For young men like Sebastián, migration is a rite of passage, one intimately rooted in notions of masculinity. In Guatemala, migration is often gendered, whereby young men are propelled by the desire to fulfill social expectations as providers. For some, migration may facilitate their changing social positions as heads of household, property owners, businessmen, and supporters of extended family networks, and even their prospects for courtship. Such were the aspirations of Sebastián who, according to his mother, wanted "to be someone" and "to have a future." As adolescents transitioning to adulthood, this rupture relegates youth to a prolonged period of "waithood" or "liminality"—waiting to get married, to have children, and to advance socially and financially.[11] Deportation marks the foreclosure of opportunities for upward mobility and serves as an often indefinite postponement of future plans. Moreover, for Indigenous youth, because giving one's word is intimately connected to identity, trustworthiness, and respect, the failure to repay migratory debts throws youth into profound moral and social turmoil, calling into question not only their trustworthiness and dependability but also that of their families within community life.

Migration and the performance of masculinity it enables, however, cannot be understood exclusively in financial terms. So, too, migration restructures masculinity in the ways it shifts scripts about the emotional lives of men and the meaning of fatherhood. Take, for example, Adrián, who contributes to domestic chores such as cleaning and washing dishes. During special occasions, he and his brothers gather together to cook Kaq'-ik for their mother, joking about how life in the United States forced them to learn new skills. "We either cooked or we starved," Adrián explained. At a family gathering, his brother who was deported from New York grinned as he took a bite of tamales. "I would trade with Adrián cooking for cleaning. I hated cooking but he's pretty good, no?" The interactions between Adrián and Micaela likewise reveal a tender and supportive bond as they navigate the emotional toll of Ixkik's illness and the uncertainty of their shared future.

The emotional ramifications of financial insecurity on the lives of young migrants and their families cannot be discounted. Sebastián's tragic death and the enduring impacts on his family leaves little closure and no happy ending. For many, migranthood is not simply a romanticized dream deferred or an elusive opportunity foreclosed. For Sebastián and his family; Ana and her son, Pedro; Adrián, Ixkik, and Micaela; and Eulalia and Sofia, it is a matter of life and death.

The ways migrant youth frame migranthood—as a rite of passage, as a fulfillment of gendered norms, as an escape from indebtedness, as a fulfillment of caregiver and care-provider roles, and as a form of familial obligation—exist alongside more disparaging, contradictory accounts of deportees—as scapegoats for crime, alcoholism, and drug use[12] or as cultural contaminates who pose a risk to the preservation of Indigenous culture and social values—that transform deported youth into a perceived social risk.[13] At the community level, Sebastián's depression and alcoholism were viewed as illustrative of the vagaries that deportees bring to the community, including alcohol, drugs, and sexually transmitted infections. *"Él era tal por cual"* (He was a good-for-nothing), a neighbor declared. Held as responsible and culpable for crime, violence, and social vices, community members identified deportees like Sebastián as "bringing problems," "trashing the town with beer bottles," "running clandestine bars," "selling drugs," "beating their wives," and generally "going down the wrong path." Migrants and deportees were also disparaged for their consumerist ways, with a "desire to have riches rather than work hard" as a common refrain. These stereotype are pervasive in Almolonga even while 13 percent of its households are impacted by forced removal of a household member, either from Mexico (32 percent) or from the United States (68 percent). Data from the department of Quetzaltenango judge who serves in Almolonga, however, do not corroborate assumptions that returned migrants were disproportionately responsible for crime in the community. According to the judge, 47 percent of the complaints presented to the Policía Nacional Civil (National Civil Police) involved violence directed toward women and were not disproportionately representative of deportees. As many Almolonguenses critically contend, while lauded nationally, migration does not bring development; it brings loss and suffering.

Given that the evangelical church maintains considerable power in Almolonga, narratives of migration and deportation also are assigned religious meanings. "If you do not arrive, you do not believe," declared an evangelical pastor during a Sunday sermon. If deportation is understood as an individual and spiritual failure, and often internalized as such, then the corresponding vices associated with it can only be remedied by conversion and religious practice, as another pastor, Luis Gonzálo, elaborated: "Since Almolonga's rebirth, we are a community of believers; we no longer drink." In part because church leaders have declared alcoholism incompatible with evangelism, deportees I met who sought to establish Alcoholics Anonymous in Almolonga described being driven from the community. In this view, conversion to evangelism is cast as the cure for addiction, physical illness, social ills, and consumerist desires. Yet, when asked about the most pressing issues in the community, the mayor and members of the COCODE agreed that clandestine bars and illicit drug use were the primary concerns. As the survey further revealed, even while 90 percent of the community self-identified as evangelical, 41 percent of households indicated that at least one household member currently suffers from alcoholism, a percentage that far exceeds households with deportees.

DEBT AND PRECARITY

Research on the diverse ways that Indigenous families enlist credit and debt to manage everyday precarity reveals that the causes of child migration are at once historical and emergently complex. While Indigenous families have relied upon social networks to navigate poverty and instability in the past, the availability of resources among communal and kinship networks is increasingly inadequate. Even in seemingly thriving communities like Almolonga, the availability of consistent and sufficient income is scarce, and subsequently, the reliance on credit is more prevalent. Families now turn to a diverse range of actors and financial institutions to navigate their everyday precarity. With little to no regulatory oversight, banks, cooperatives, moneylenders, notaries, attorneys, and even churches offer high-interest loans that, contrary to claims to better one's life circumstances, serve to compound poverty and instability. While families may seek loans to invest in businesses or to respond to short-term needs, the terms of the loans are such that they can quickly cascade into insurmountable debt serviceable only with U.S.-level wages.

Families have little recourse against predatory lenders. An attorney from La Procuraduría General de la Nación (Office of the Inspector General) in the department of Quetzaltenango recounted, "We've only had success in two cases [against moneylenders and notaries] taking land from migrants. It is a long and convoluted process that many victims abandon early on or are intimidated into ceasing to participate as the state's witnesses. In spite of our accompaniment throughout the process, it is a real and growing problem but with few positive outcomes for families."

The scale of this phenomenon is substantiated by survey data. Of the 148 surveyed households, 36 percent of households routinely enlisted loans from a diverse range of sources and for equally diverse reasons. At the time of our survey in 2016, 6 percent of loans had ended in default, including the loss of land and other collateral. Another 40 percent of borrowers were in the process of repayment, nearly half of whom already had renegotiated the terms of the loan at least once to extend its repayment ranging from two to thirty years, often with interest surpassing the principal. Only 53 percent of borrowers from any source had successfully repaid loans. When taken together, the likelihood of defaulting or extending the terms of the loan (with compounding interest rates) affected nearly half of all borrowers. Given that over 77 percent of borrowing households enlisted their land and homes as collateral, the real and potential loss of land affects a stunning portion of the community.

As Edú asserted, *"Es una gran estafa."* (It's a big scam/fraud.) In many ways, these predatory lending practices are the private sector's strategy to repress Indigenous communities in postconflict Guatemala. Debt keeps people marginalized, dependent, limited, restricted, controlled, and suffering. The deregulation of the banking industry and the lack of access to justice exacerbate poverty and dispossess Indigenous peoples of their lands, replicating historical patterns during colonialism, plantation labor, and armed conflict in Guatemala. One might argue that the banks should not loan money to people who are not capable of repayment or who risk becoming overly indebted. A local branch manager from Banrural asserted, "We are not here to take people's property from people but to support them." The credit serves an important function in terms of generating income for a *cosecha* (harvest) or purchasing goods on a payment plan that families might not otherwise be able to afford, but the risks and the prevalence of indebtedness are overwhelming. Assuming debt, even with risks of it spiraling out of control, is one of the few survival strategies available to the working poor, especially when the state systematically neglects Indigenous communities. Under the weight of structural violence, the networks of social support—in the form of traditional lending practices such as the *cuchubal,* or borrowing from neighbors—have given way to high-interest, unregulated loans that imperil the survival of Indigenous communities.

As the Almolonguenses with whom we spoke confirmed, the state's systematic neglect of Indigenous peoples is evidenced by the dearth of livable wages, a discriminatory health-care system, an ineffective justice system, and underresourced schools. While none of these factors in isolation is recognized as the sole cause of migration, when taken together, the structural violence they reinforce continues to displace Indigenous youth and their communities. To navigate structural violence and the everyday precarity it produces, community members turn to a deregulated financial industry to borrow money for survival. As the survey findings corroborate, this financial debt has acutely noxious and lasting effects on young migrants, their families, and entire communities—from homelessness and loss of land to family disintegration, intrafamilial violence, erosion of social ties, loss of cultural values and traditions, and even death. When taken in context, then, deportation and indebtedness leave deep wounds that will not heal for generations to come.

CHAPTER 7

EL DERECHO
A NO MIGRAR

NATIONAL AND REGIONAL securitization programs, border externalization policies, and detention and deportation are long-standing state practices intended to manage desired and undesired migrants.[1] They are practiced worldwide. Now, however, the public is becoming aware of the ways this global immigration dragnet increasingly traps children with devastating and long-lasting consequences. Indeed, children have become the face of the migration crises worldwide—the Syrian crisis, the European migration crisis, the humanitarian crisis at the U.S.-Mexico border. For many, migrant children are the most vulnerable of victims—their images spark moral outrage and societal despair with increasing depths and intensity. For others, youth on the move pose a criminal threat, warranting detention and removal from the state. Yet, in spite of the growing visibility of migrant children and the proliferation of discourses about their migranthood, the experiences of young people remain obscured. Their voices are silenced, and their experiences are relegated to shocking images splashed across national and international news media.

Within these migratory crises, development and security increasingly are conspicuously implicated. The European Union (EU) has fortified its Fortress Europe, interdicting migrants at sea and directing influxes of refugees to Turkey

and Hungary in exchange for entrance into the EU. Overcrowded and inhospitable camps on the Greek islands of Samos and Lesvos and on the Italian
islands of Lamepdusa and Sicily are now home to hundreds of thousands of
migrants, including children. Since 2017, the Italian government has enlisted
development aid for Libyan authorities to purchase equipment for patrolling
the high seas, all in an effort to push back would-be migrants from Europe's
gates, while simultaneously cracking down on humanitarian aid workers for
"intervening" in state maritime relief efforts.

Across the Atlantic, and as this book attests, securitized development has led
to increasingly costly and deadly migration journeys, arrivals, and returns. The
past thirty years in the United States have brought record levels of government
funding of immigration enforcement; the militarization of the U.S.-Mexico
border; the proliferation of partnerships between local police and immigration
authorities to enact immigration enforcement within the United States; and
the exponential growth of immigration detention facilities for adults, children,
and families. Meanwhile, the Trump administration has expanded categories of
individuals subject to deportation by attacking legal safeguards such as Deferred
Action for Childhood Arrivals (DACA) and Temporary Protective Status (TPS)
for Haitians, Hondurans, Nicaraguans, and Salvadorans, among others. While
categories of deportability have expanded, opportunities to arrive and remain
lawfully in the United States have been foreclosed, with fewer visas available
and family-reunification petitions lingering for decades. Domestic enforcement efforts have expanded through workplace raids and the policing of previously designated "safe spaces" such as schools, hospitals, places of worship, and
courthouses. In 2018, as CBP and ICE began forcibly removing children from
asylum-seeking parents, the U.S. government concurrently enlisted children
as a particular mode of "deterrence" to migration and as a political football in
efforts to repeal asylum protections and invest in further enforcement, including a border wall. By 2019, "Remain in Mexico" policies were well underway,
policies in which the Border Patrol began turning away asylum seekers at border
crossings, systematically violating U.S. and international law.

Once touted as a model for reception of deported youth, Guatemalan authorities now struggle to keep pace with the reception of deportees from Mexico
and the United States.[2] At the same time, they are under pressure to thwart
the through-migration of neighboring Salvadorans and Hondurans, among

others, en route to the United States. In 2018, the public caught a glimpse of this reality as a caravan of five thousand Honduran migrants attempted to cross Guatemala's border with Mexico. Clad in riot gear, Mexican and Guatemalan police attempted to halt those proceeding through immigration checkpoints in Tecún Umán, obstructing their entry into Mexico with chain-link fences and brute intimidation. Just as the U.S. border is moving south through Mexico with programs like the Southern Border Program, Guatemalan authorities are ensnared in the U.S. efforts to externalize borders. By assuming that migration management is a question of security rather than humanitarianism, nation-states around the globe attempt to relinquish their responsibilities to asylum seekers through outsourcing—effectively moving the border spectacle discursively and physically south. Meanwhile, the bodies of migrants pile up in morgues, decompose in the desert, or disappear at sea.

The narratives of young people challenge the ways that policy homogenizes and makes invisible the complex, multifaceted, and varied experiences of migranthood. Take, for example, the sociolegal production of the "unaccompanied child" status. The vast majority of the young people whose voices and experiences fill the pages of this book are legally categorized as unaccompanied children, yet the diversity of their experiences and trajectories attest to the considerable variation in reasons for migration, resources available to facilitate mobility, experiences of return, and long-term trajectories. So, too, the policy responses to child migration thus far have dehistoricized Indigenous migration. Forcibly displaced for generations through colonial violence, U.S. foreign intervention, migration management regimes, the securitization of development aid, and extractive industries, Indigenous peoples bear the brunt of globalized social inequality and misguided conceptions of development. By failing to recognize that the majority of young migrants from Guatemala are displaced from their Indigenous communities, we are ignoring the disproportionate impact of securitization policies and development violence on Indigenous peoples. The erasures of indigeneity negate the discrimination and violence Indigenous peoples encounter in Guatemala as well as in zones of transit through Mexico and upon arrival in the United States.

In so doing, this decontextualization and dehistoricization make individuals ostensibly responsible for their migranthood rather than the historical and contemporary systems that inflict violence and displace Indigenous communities. A seasoned Minnesota-based legal advocate, Anabel, illustrates:

> I am representing an Ixil unaccompanied child in immigration court. The ba-
> sis of my argument is that this child was repeatedly abused by his father who
> is an alcoholic, but you know why his father drinks? Because he was tortured
> by the paramilitary for six months, a paramilitary financially supported and
> trained by the U.S. government. He drinks to forget as a way of dealing with
> his unspeakable traumas. But I can't make *that* argument. I can't place blame
> on U.S. foreign policy or even on the Guatemalan government [for him to be
> granted asylum]. I have to pin it on his father.

For Anabel, the reasons for her young client's legal claim are intimately linked
to the violence and torture inflicted by U.S. foreign policy and its empowerment of Guatemalan security forces to commit genocide against Indigenous
Guatemalans. Yet, Anabel is unable to make a viable legal claim that implicates
the U.S. government in the contemporary displacement of her young Indigenous client. By interrogating how violence is produced and practiced across
borders and generations and how Indigenous youth navigate this violence, I
have sought to rethink how and why youth are on the move.

POLICY LESSONS

If, as I have argued, the migration of Indigenous youth is a policy-made crisis,
generations in the making, it follows that there are policy solutions. In the fall
of 2017, I returned to the U.S. Department of State along with four of my
students to present findings from the household survey in Almolonga in the
far-flung hopes of informing policy decisions that were becoming increasingly
draconian under the Trump administration. As I looked around the room at the
eighteen representatives from the U.S. Department of State, USAID, and the
U.S. Organized Crime Drug Enforcement Task Force, I recognized only two
people from my previous presentation just three years prior. Since the election
of Donald Trump, there had been a mass exodus of senior Foreign Service officers, including simultaneous resignations of the entire senior administrative
team earlier that year. By the presentation's end, I learned that only three of the
eighteen individuals sitting in the conference room had ever traveled to Central
America, only two of them spoke Spanish fluently, and only one—and perhaps
unsurprisingly, the narcotics officer—had ever traveled beyond Guatemala City.
Nonetheless, the people sitting around the mahogany conference table were in
charge of steering U.S. foreign policy in the region.

As an engaged public anthropologist, I aspire to ensure the accessibility of my research to decision makers, as this work is critical to creating effective policies and to bypassing adverse consequences in the communities where I work. Ethnographic research with Indigenous youth and their families, for example, reveals that the causes of child migration are historically rooted and multifaceted; yet in spite of this complexity, states continue to turn to the 1951 Refugee Convention and its 1967 Protocol as the templates for providing protections for migrants. The convention and its protocol do not reflect the new realities of migration and instead narrowly define refugees as those forced to leave their countries as a result of individual persecution based on specific grounds such as race, religion, nationality, political opinion, or membership in a social group. While states maintain the latitude to expand this definition to consider other forms of forced migration, such as natural or environmental disasters, chemical or nuclear disasters, famine, or development projects, few do. As national borders are increasingly externalized in the United States and Europe, national immigration laws fail to account for the regional implications of and accountability for states' foreign policies. New social realities such as development violence, climate change, transnational gangs, narcotrafficking networks, debt-driven migration, and child migration do not readily correspond to laws that never imagined the existence of these realities nor to nation-states that are unwilling to recognize their role in creating these realities. In contrast, research with migrant youth suggests they are engaged in complex, multilayered negotiations around collective and individual survival and betterment in a context of growing global inequity. Indigenous youth manage and employ transnational migration as a collective and historically rooted survival strategy, which responds to both historical and present-day violence and marginalization of Indigenous communities in Guatemala. Examining the migration of Indigenous youth over time productively problematizes established migratory typologies (economic migrants or refugees, for example) under international refugee law and U.S. immigration law and simultaneously compels consideration of the enduring consequences of deportation on young people and their families. It likewise reveals the reach of public policy—across geopolitical space and generations. Only with research-informed policies may we begin to create policies, programs, and institutional practices that are responsive to migrants' needs.

Research alone, however, is insufficient. In the wake of the 2014 influx of Central American children migrating to the United States, there was a flurry of visits to Central America from then Vice President Joe Biden, the U.S. Department of State, and USAID to meet with Central American officials and stakeholders. I interviewed an executive director of an NGO working with homeless youth in Guatemala City who was a key informant to these policy discussions. Upon entering his spacious office in Guatemala City's ritzy Zona 10, his secretary handed me a ten-page double-sided packet with pictures and quotes from the director in the local, national, and international news and invited me to sit in a plush, brown-leather chair overlooking a garden veranda. In the interview, I learned that he had never met a child who migrated nor a child who had been deported. In fact, in these high-level meetings, none of the organizations working with young migrants and their families were invited to participate. Only two of the organizations worked in the highlands of Guatemala where the overwhelming majority of young migrants originate. Moreover, only a handful of Guatemalan scholars who research migration or childhood, and none of Indigenous identity, participated. Instead, NGOs headquartered in Guatemala City entered the proverbial halls of power vying for development aid. A year later, this NGO that had no experience working with young migrants or returnees would receive a sizable grant from USAID to provide "migration interventions," as the NGO marketed it. These examples (of the many I might share here) serve as reminders of the importance of meaningfully engaging not only researchers, especially Central American and Indigenous researchers, but also young people themselves in the discussions about policies and programs designed for them.

As a white, English-speaking professor with U.S. citizenship, my privilege allowed me to catch a small glimpse of the decision-making process and to provide a modest platform to inform policymakers, futile as it felt. With this privilege, I have learned of the importance of centering the voices of Central American and Indigenous scholars so that they might share their expertise and knowledge directly and by creating platforms to reach often exclusively English-speaking audiences in academic publishing. Recognizing that higher education and research itself is an endeavor often accessible only to the elite, I must likewise create opportunities for research—from conceptualization to implementation to dissemination—to be collaborative and participatory with young people, especially when they are structurally disadvantaged. In so doing, we might begin to realize that young migrants possess wisdom and expertise by experience and to recognize how knowledge is produced and by whom. Only then will we have the right people sitting at the table.

There are, of course, more deliberate and sustained opportunities for engaged public research. It is not enough to critique the intended and unintended consequences of public policy; our response must be to harness our experiences and the expertise of the communities with which we collaborate to remedy or avoid these consequences. This includes participating in broad national and international networks, training in engaged public policy, and even bringing our work and anthropological understandings into public view across genres—blogs, podcasts, photo journals, digital stories, community events, art exhibits, poetry, public lectures, and op-eds—by which we can reach broader and more diverse publics, which in turn might pressure lawmakers to enact compassionate policies that recognize the dignity and humanity of Indigenous communities and migrants.[3] In recent years, mounting public pressure has led to investigations of abuses in Office of Refugee Resettlement (ORR) facilities for unaccompanied minors, the closing of the Tornillo detention facility in west Texas that housed over 2,500 migrant children (now slated to reopen as an adult detention center), and dozens of lawsuits against ORR, CBP, ICE, and the Trump administration around children's access to attorneys, reproductive rights, religious freedom, specialized protections, and freedom from indefinite detention. An informed public can be a powerful ally to im/migrant communities.

POSSIBILITY OF DREAMING

After two decades working with im/migrants in the United States, Mexico, and Central America, I am often personally and professionally overwhelmed by the totality of destructive policies and their repetition and proliferation to the detriment of Indigenous communities. At my most dejected, I wonder: Are we destined for those in power to repeat and reinforce this oppression for generations to come? Is it ignorance or historical amnesia or simply nefarious motives on the part of policymakers? Is racism and discrimination so systemically embedded in social, political, and economic institutions across the region that there is little hope of upending these systems of power? How are we not able to recognize that the proliferation of global migration crises is, at its core, policy made and exacerbated? In a context that privileges the economic and political interests of the elite (individuals, companies, and nations), how can we enlist research to inform public policy in ways that attend to the needs of individuals and communities—especially when policy erases their identities?

Yet, when I am at my most downcast by what I see as systemic, global oppression, I encounter activists, community leaders, and young people who remind me that change, slow and invisible as it sometimes may be, is possible. People who are daily and intimately impacted by the ways policy inflicts violence continue to struggle and to challenge their oppressors. They do so through daily tactics and strategies critical to navigating structural violence and poverty, and likewise through creating a different future. Once again, I return to the experiences of young people and the ways they imagine an alternative future—one that does not command them patronizingly to "Stay!" but that addresses their needs and rights as well as those of their families and communities. Many youths articulate a process of transformation—one that begins with decolonizing the ways systemic and historic oppression have been internalized within Indigenous communities and that aspires to *el buen vivir,* a movement toward living conscientiously rooted in the worldview of their ancestors.

As we sat on a park bench in San Marcos's town square watching men load trucks with produce, meat, and dried goods destined for Mexico, Gustavo, a youth activist, sipped from a cup of steaming *atol.* Following his deportation five years earlier, Gustavo had become involved with several Indigenous organizations advocating for the environmental rights of communities and the resignification of Indigenous identity, particularly among young people. He starkly explained:

> In Guatemala, the violence will kill you. Yes, there is organized crime and gangs and police that sow fear into us. It teaches us: if I don't have a job and nothing to eat, if my family is sick, I have to go out and rob people to survive. On the other hand, if I have a job and food for me and my family, I won't break into your house to steal things and it's for me and mine, not for others to benefit. This is what the system here teaches us—to look out for our own interests, that the rich are born rich and we as Maya are born poor, destined to thieve and die. We *must* unlearn this.

Gustavo went on to recognize the ways that political discourse in Guatemala, combined with the education system and mundane institutional encounters, reinforces the message that the Maya people are born poor, "like animals," and violently inclined. Over time, Gustavo explains, these messages become internalized. "Many believe God left us poor because we are Indigenous. This is what the pastors repeat from the altar. The government bakes it into their decrees. The television stations splash it on their bloody twitter feeds. We must resist these 'lessons' [and learn] that to be Indigenous is not something to be embarrassed about; it is our strength and our pride."

The reasons young people cite for their migration—"to have a future," "to get ahead," and "to look forward"—are intimately bound up in meanings assigned to indigeneity and migranthood over time and space. The migration of Indigenous youth cannot be dismissed as simple economic migration in response to limited finances or opportunities; rather, it is cloaked in historical violence and racism that young people encounter daily within and beyond Guatemala. For Gustavo and others, resisting the ways that society disparagingly frames Indigenous people is a critical step in seeking social transformation.

So, too, is reclaiming and revalorizing Indigenous identity. Following the completion of the survey in Almolonga, I returned several months later to present the preliminary findings in a series of community forums, meetings, and workshops; to collaboratively interpret the data; to discuss ways the community might enlist the findings; and to seek permission to present the findings in meetings with policymakers in Guatemala and the United States. In one such workshop, I partnered with a local Indigenous organization to discuss youth migration with a group of fifteen teenaged Almolonguenses. In discussing the varying messages of indigeneity that young people encounter in school, church, and other institutions, fifteen-year-old Anahí shared: "I get so fed up with school because we are learning someone else's history. We will never learn to change the way we think if we don't learn K'iche' and our own cultures. It is important to value our past so that we know that we are not alone."

Ignacio, a young man sitting beside her, nodded. He shared how he always felt unimportant and undervalued, even refraining from speaking K'iche' in public so as to avoid others rejecting him. "I'm never as good as ladinos. I don't have the education, the money, the big house; but is money really so important to happiness? We don't need all of these things; we can produce and survive like our grandparents and their grandparents." Globalization, remittances, and consumerist capitalism have changed the nature of daily life within rural communities like Almolonga. Young people have some, albeit limited, opportunities to acquire the latest technology or fashions. Youth describe navigating these multiple messages about "the good life," which they often associate with consumerism and self-interest. As Ignacio reminds us, however, these items do not ensure happiness. His reference to the ways his grandparents and great-grandparents lived alludes to a collective well-being in which communities cultivated shared land and provided mutual support.

Since the start of the workshop, Neri had been drawing quietly in her red spiral notebook, her long, black hair draped over the sides of her face. Sitting next to her in the circle, one of my collaborators asked what she thought. Putting her pen down, Neri took a deep breath. Quietly at first, she unhurriedly shared,

> I used to be embarrassed to speak K'iche', to tell people my last name, to wear *traje*. It's what I've been taught in school and on the street— *"Soy pobre porque soy india"* [I'm poor because I'm an Indian]. But we can't be that way; we can't think like ladinos. We have to value our grandparents, our people, and Maya culture—our history, land, and our connection to the cosmos. Only when we've changed inside our hearts and inside our minds, can there be change. I must first value who I am and what I contribute as Maya, only then will society change.

By resisting the aggressive narratives that disparage Indigenous peoples and devalorize Indigenous culture and identity, Neri describes a process of internal and collective decolonization. For Neri, she must actively unlearn these pervasive, violent messages that inundate her daily. In reflecting on the meanings of and connections to her *pueblo*, the land, and the universe, she recognizes that she must assign value to herself and her Maya identity, and only then will the larger society change.

This is not easy. Just as shifting social valuations and beliefs at a national level is challenging, so too is resignification of identity in a global context. Reflecting on what being Indigenous means to her and the possibilities for the future, another young woman, Ixchel, shared:

> Being K'iche' is not just about how I dress or weave or dance . . . I am not folk-
> lore. I am not for sale in the market when the tourists come to take our pictures
> without asking or to buy the scarves we weave. For me, it is about participating
> in activities where I can learn our history or our language that will help me to
> know that we as Maya matter. Only then can we can imagine *un futuro en lo
> cual convivencia sea posible* [a future in which coexistence is possible].

Throughout my research, young people describe their reasons for migration as
linked to their aspirations for the future—*"tener un futuro"* (to have a future),
"salir adelante" (to get ahead), and *"buscar una vida mejor"* (to seek a better
life). I encountered many young people who assume that they cannot "have a
future" in Guatemala particularly because of entrenched poverty and the scarcity of livable wages.

I asked the group to describe how they might "have a future" in Guatemala, or, in other words, what the right to not migrate might it look in practice? They explained:

> This is my home and I have to make the best of what I have. There is so much
> richness. I don't want to leave, even when it gets difficult. The right to not
> migrate? It's having the conditions in which I can choose to stay just like I can
> choose to leave, but you see the difference? It is a choice.

> A future without the suffering that our parents and grandparents endured.

> It's a *sueño familiar* [family dream].

> It's the possibility of dreaming.

These aspirations do not belie the violence and precarity that young people and
their families encounter. They do, however, offer a path forward in which young
people have pride in their Indigenous identities and can imagine futures in which
the well-being of each of us is interconnected with the well-being of others.

With remarkable clarity and hard-fought wisdom, Anahí, Ignacio, Neri,
and Ixchel articulate the desire and, indeed, the imperative to decolonize how
society has taught them to think, and to reclaim their Indigenous identity. They
recognize the need to resignify the meanings of indigeneity and to reignite their
connectivity to their ancestors, the natural world, and the universe. For Ixchel
and indeed for other youths in the room, *convivencia* (coexistence) signifies

living in a society where Indigenous culture is acknowledged, respected, and valued. For many Indigenous peoples throughout Latin America, the concept of *el buen vivir* likewise critiques Western models of development and the Euro-American values that underpin them. It demands that we actively work against policies of forgetting and impunity—by the U.S., Mexican, and Guatemalan states—and redress historical abuses, while simultaneously compelling us to rethink what is and who benefits from "development." As the experiences of Indigenous Guatemalan youth and their families illustrate, policies that privilege security and extractive development over social, political, and economic conditions serve only to produce new crises.

Young people link internal and community-based decolonizing projects as critical to broader social and, even, global transformation. This does not signify, however, that Indigenous peoples are responsible for transforming the views of those in power and those with privilege; that imperative falls squarely to each of us to educate ourselves and others on the historical and contemporary ways violence is inflicted upon Indigenous peoples. It requires us to listen. By attending to the perspectives and insights of Indigenous youth, we learn how they are as contributors to household well-being, local practices, and global processes and how their lived experiences might—and *must*—inform public policy. Only with recognition that every action and reaction, including public policies, are intricately linked to our collective well-being can we collaboratively enact "the possibility of dreaming."

APPENDIX

APPENDIX 1: Unaccompanied Children Encountered in the U.S. by Guatemalan Department of Origin, by Fiscal Year (2007–2017)

Department	2007	2008	2009	2010	2011
QUETZALTENANGO	121	272	216	68	386
HUEHUETENANGO	36	127	102	114	185
QUICHÉ	10	52	40	23	75
GUATEMALA	65	163	129	74	186
SANTA ROSA	33	88	67	18	94
SAN MARCOS	26	51	41	79	68
TOTONICAPÁN	34	57	58	24	76
ESCUINTLA	16	50	54	30	53
SOLOLÁ	14	34	33	12	47
CHIMALTENANGO	7	20	20	42	47
JALAPA	10	40	29	9	29
IZABAL	5	31	26	19	34
BAJA VERAPAZ	4	23	10	2	23
CHIQUIMULA	10	41	18	20	28
JUTIAPA	3	32	10	90	16
PETÉN	7	25	15	6	12
SUCHITEPÉQUEZ	8	9	15	14	18
RETALHULEU	5	11	12	12	11
ZACAPA	2	14	10	11	12
ALTA VERAPAZ	2	2	0	10	0
EL PROGRESO	2	5	9	5	5
SACATEPÉQUEZ	1	4	0	8	6
Total	421	1151	914	690	1411

2012	2013	2014	2015	2016	2017	TOTAL
1038	2156	3732	2536	3493	2265	16283
415	914	3040	2616	3169	1679	12397
167	541	1266	1803	1966	1229	7172
418	800	1668	1111	1389	915	6918
209	470	1017	634	945	775	4350
167	443	958	784	1059	600	4276
195	361	600	459	675	421	2960
119	227	492	301	416	420	2178
127	239	408	301	427	351	1993
82	178	314	284	424	321	1739
54	132	302	185	427	264	1481
74	190	327	296	281	150	1433
70	99	190	308	390	247	1366
81	127	302	201	306	191	1325
43	93	231	110	274	227	1129
36	97	243	136	263	178	1018
40	71	192	91	167	113	738
23	50	116	85	122	99	546
24	38	129	44	119	68	471
14	17	39	15	48	36	183
11	10	42	21	41	27	178
2	7	13	13	17	15	86
3409	7260	15621	12334	16418	10591	70220

NOTES

PREFACE

1. Following disciplinary custom, I enlist pseudonyms for all research participants. I conducted all interviews in Spanish or English with occasional interpretation from Mam and K'iche to Spanish. All Spanish translations are my own.

INTRODUCTION

1. Under U.S. immigration law, a family unit "represents the number of individuals (either a child under 18 years old, parent, or legal guardian) apprehended with a family member by the U.S. Border Patrol." "U.S. Border Patrol Southwest Family Unit Subject and Unaccompanied Alien Children Apprehensions," 2016, U.S. Customs and Border Protection, https://www.cbp.gov/newsroom/stats/southwest-border-unaccompanied-children/fy-2016.

2. Hernández 2014.

3. A bipartisan legislation under George W. Bush, the TVPRA permitted unaccompanied children from noncontiguous territories to reunite with parents or a sponsor while they pursue legal relief in immigration court. Public Law 106-386.

4. See galleries of http://www.youthcirculations.com for an analysis of images and materials about unaccompanied children from media and nonprofit organizations.

5. Heidbrink and Statz 2017.

6. Heidbrink 2014: 41–42.

7. "Facts and Data: General Statistics," n.d., U.S. Dept. of Health and Human Services, Office of Refugee Resettlement (ORR), https://www.acf.hhs.gov/orr/about/ucs/facts-and-data.

8. Butler 2004: 25.

9. Burrell and Moodie 2012, LeVine 2007, Stephens 1995, Woodhead and Montgomery 2002.

10. Recognizing the power of language and terminology (such as humanitarian crisis, refugee versus migrant, or child versus youth) to frame social phenomena in particular ways, throughout the book I enlist terms that youth themselves utilize to narrate their varied experiences of return and the ways their physical return may alter their relationships to people and places, their own identities, sentiments of belonging, and importantly, their imagined futures.

11. DACAmented youth refers to the beneficiaries of President Obama's executive order, Deferred Action for Childhood Arrivals (DACA).

12. Gonzales 2011, 2015.

13. Berger Cardoso et al. 2017, Patler and Gonzales 2015.

14. Christie 1986: 18.

15. Crea, Lopez, Taylor, and Underwood 2018; Zayas et al. 2017.

16. Ensor and Gozdziak 2010, Uehling 2008.

17. Bhabha and Schmidt 2008, Georgopoulos 2005, Zatz and Rodriguez 2015.

18. Heidbrink 2014, Terrio 2015.

19. Roth and Grace 2015, Zayas 2015.

20. De Genova 2005, Peutz 2006.

21. "U.S. Border Patrol Southwest Border Apprehensions by Sector FY 2019," n.d., U.S. Customs and Border Protection, https://www.cbp.gov/newsroom/stats/sw-border-migration.

22. Ibid.

23. These data have considerable limitations as many children evade apprehension and pass irregularly into the United States. Other child migrants may successfully pass through official points of entry with false documents or without inspection. Still other migrants enter the United States with valid documents but overstay their tourist or student visas, thereby shifting their status to unaccompanied minor once their visas expire.

24. A limitation of U.S. data is its failure to reflect the diversity of family formations that do not adhere to heteronormative notions of the nuclear family.

25. Rosenblum and Ball 2016: 1.

26. See also, "Closed Doors: Mexico's Failure to Protect Central American Refugee and Migrant Children," 2016, Human Rights Watch, March 31, 2016, https://www.hrw.org/report/2016/03/31/closed-doors/mexicos-failure-protect-central-american-refugee-and-migrant-children.

27. Knippen, Boggs, and Meyer 2015: 31; Seelke 2016: 22; Seelke and Finklea 2011.

28. Dickerson, C., 2018, "Trump Administration Moves to Sidestep Restrictions on Detaining Migrant Children," *New York Times,* September 6, 2018, https://www.nytimes.com/2018/09/06/us/trump-flores-settlement-regulations.html.

29. Lytle Hernández, K., 2017, "America's Mass Deportation System Is Rooted in Racism," *The Conversation,* February 26, 2017, http://theconversation.com/americas-mass-deportation-system-is-rooted-in-racism-73426. See also Lytle Hernández 2010.

30. U.S. Customs and Border Protection, n.d., "Southwest Border Unaccompanied Alien Children Statistics FY 2016," https://www.cbp.gov/site-page/southwest-border-unaccompanied-alien-children-statistics-fy-2016#. See also Rietig and Villegas 2015.

31. Personal communication, July 2016.

32. Dirección General de Evaluación e Investigación Educativa, 2013, "Reporte General: Primaria 2010," Guatemala City: Ministerio de Educación. Accessed May 1, 2018, http://www.mineduc.gob.gt/digeduca/documents/informes/Reporte_Primaria_2010.pdf.

33. Little and Smith 2009, Lovell and Lutz 1995, Lutz and Lovell 2000.

34. Bilsborrow and Stupp 1997, Gauster and Isakson 2007, Katz 2000, McAllister and Nelson 2013, Moran-Taylor and Taylor 2010, Stoll 2012.

35. Bhugra and Becker 2005.

36. Ong 1999: 10.

37. De Genova and Peutz 2010: 14; Coutin 2005, 2007, 2010; Menjívar 2006, 2011.

38. Gonzales and Chavez 2012: 255; Agamben 2005; Rosas 2006; Willen 2007.

39. Ku and Matani 2001, Kullgren 2003, McLeigh 2010.
40. Zimmerman and Fix 2014.
41. Reynolds 2013.
42. Menjívar and Abrego 2012.
43. Baum, Jones, and Berry 2010; Hall 2011; Lykes, Brabeck, and Hunter 2013.
44. Rojas-Flores et al. 2016.
45. Dreby 2012.
46. Boehm 2016; Peutz 2006; Khosravi 2018; Zilberg 2007, 2011.
47. Curran and Saguy 2001.
48. Hondagneu-Sotelo 2011.
49. Anderson, Gibney, and Paoletti 2011.
50. Gomberg-Muñoz 2016: 3.
51. Bloch and Schuster 2005, Galvin 2015: 617.
52. Byrne and Miller 2016: 26.
53. See also Khosravi 2018: 9.
54. Coutin 2016.
55. Heidbrink 2014.
56. Ingold and Vergunst 2008.
57. Ramakrishnan and Viramontes 2010, Sites and Vonderlack-Navarro 2012.

CHAPTER I. YOUTH AS AGENTS, CAREGIVERS, AND MIGRANTS

1. Parreñas 2000: 560.
2. Parreñas 2000: 561.
3. Hochschild 2000b.
4. Choy 2003.
5. Kilkey 2010, Scrinzi 2010.
6. Hochschild 2000a, Parreñas 2005, Yeates 2009. A notable exception includes Coe et al. 2011.
7. Leinaweaver 2008, 2013.
8. Van Hear 1998: 42.
9. Heidbrink 2018.
10. Handy 1984: 17.
11. Lutz and Lovell 2000: 15.
12. Foxen 2007: 32.
13. Lovell 1992, McCreery 1990, Warren 2018.
14. Burns 1986: 18.
15. Foxen 2007: 32.
16. Ibid.
17. Castillo and Casillas 1988.
18. Taylor, Moran-Taylor and Ruiz 2006: 44.
19. Foxen 2007: 76.
20. Gírón 2010: 251.
21. Gobierno de México 2005.
22. Fischer 2001: 147.

23. See also Nititham 2017.

24. World Bank, n.d., "Personal Remittances, Received (% of GDP)," https://data.worldbank.org/indicator/BX.TRF.PWKR.DT.GD.ZS?locations=GT.

25. Herrera, M., 2007, "Guatemalan Leader Visits," *Sun Sentinel,* February 18, 2007, https://www.sun-sentinel.com/news/fl-xpm-2007-02-18-0702170241-story.html.

26. Moran-Taylor and Taylor 2010.

27. Guyer 2004.

28. Yeates 2009: 5.

29. Foner 2009; Moran-Taylor 2008; Smith, Lalonde, and Johnson 2004.

30. Baldassar and Merla 2013: 8.

31. Yarris 2017.

CHAPTER 2. WIDENING THE FRAME

1. U.S. Customs and Border Protection, n.d., "CBP Commissioner Discusses Dangers of Crossing U.S. Border, Awareness Campaign," https://www.cbp.gov/newsroom/national-media-release/cbp-commissioner-discusses-dangers-crossing-us-border-awareness.

2. Yu-Hsi Lee, E., 2014, "Border Patrol Agency Launches Campaign to Stop Central American Kids from Coming to U.S.," *Think Progress,* July 3, 2014, https://thinkprogress.org/border-patrol-agency-launches-campaign-to-stop-central-american-kids-from-coming-to-u-s-1c6ba1839728.

3. Hiskey, J., et al., 2016, "Understanding the Central American Refugee Crisis: Why They Are Fleeing and How U.S. Policies Are Failing to Deter Them," American Immigration Council, February 1, 2016, https://www.americanimmigrationcouncil.org/research/understanding-central-american-refugee-crisis.

4. Schmidt and Buechler 2017, Vogt 2013, 2018.

5. "Widespread Abuse Against Migrants Is Mexican 'Human Rights Crisis.'" Amnesty International, April 28, 2010, https://www.amnesty.org/en/press-releases/2010/04/widespread-abuse-against-migrants-mexican-e28098human-rights-crisise28099/.

6. For discussions of the gendered violence in zones of transit, see Brigden 2018, Valencia 2017.

7. Galemba 2018.

8. Musalo, Frydman, and Cernadas 2015.

9. U.S. Department of Homeland Security 2017.

10. Jarvie, J., 2017, "Immigrant Rights Groups Denounce New ICE Policy that Targets Parents of Child Migrants," *LA Times,* June 30, 2017, http://www.latimes.com/nation/la-na-immigration-daca-20170630-story.html.

11. Dickerson, C., 2017, "Trump Administration Targets Parents in New Immigration Crackdown," *New York Times,* July 1, 2017, https://www.nytimes.com/2017/07/01/us/trump-arrest-undocumented-immigrants.html.

12. Statz, M., and L. Heidbrink, 2017, "Threatening Parents? What DHS Reminds Us About Unaccompanied Youth," Youth Circulations, July 20, 2017, http://www.youthcirculations.com/blog/2017/7/18/threatening-parents-what-dhs-policies-remind-us-about-unaccompanied-youth.

13. Herrera-Sobek 2012.

14. Ibid.

15. "EEUU paga a México millones para 'represión feroz' contra los migrantes," 2015, *La Opinion,* October 12, 2015, https://laopinion.com/2015/10/12/nyt-eeuu-paga-a-mexico-millones -para-represion-feroz-contra-los-migrantes/.

16. Cárdenas 2017.

17. "Learn more," n.d., https://www.colibricenter.org/history/.

18. "Central American Migration," 2016. Movimiento Migrante Mesoamericano, July 13, 2016, https://movimientomigrantemesoamericano.org/2016/07/13/central-american -migration.

19. De León 2015; Slack, Martinez, Lee, and Whiteford 2016.

20. Citroni 2018, Squire 2017.

21. Mbembé and Meintjes 2003.

22. De Graeve and Bex 2017, Prout and James 2003.

23. Caneva 2014, Moskal and Tyrrell 2016, White et al. 2011.

24. Heidbrink and Statz 2017.

25. Hardy and Thomas 2015.

26. Diamond and Quinby 1988: 185.

CHAPTER 3. THE MAKING OF A CRISIS

1. Nader 1972.

2. Bourgois 2001.

3. De Haas 2010.

4. Massey 1988: 383.

5. Boehm 2008.

6. Bourbeau 2011.

7. See also Reyes and Curry Rodríguez 2012.

8. Freire 2005.

9. Foxen 2007: 12.

10. Handy 1984; Jonas 1991; Lovell 1992, 2010; Manz 2004; Sanford 2003.

11. Costello 1997: 10.

12. Ibid.: 11.

13. Jonas and Rodríguez 2015, McAllister and Nelson 2013.

14. del Valle Escalate 2009: 58.

15. Little and Smith 2009, Green 2010.

16. Bannan 1986. See also Zong, J., and J. Batalova, 2015, "Central American Immigrants in the United States," Migration Policy Institute, September 2, 2015, https://www .migrationpolicy.org/article/central-american-immigrants-united-states-3.

17. *American Baptist Churches v. Thornburgh,* 760 F. Supp. 796 (N.D. Cal. 1991).

18. Ibid.

19. Illegal Immigration Reform and Immigrant Responsibility Act of 1996, Division C of Public Law 104-208, 110 Stat. 3009-546.

20. Public Law 105-100, title II.

21. Moran-Taylor 2008: 111, García 2006.

22. Menjívar and Abrego 2012.

23. "Global Study on Homicide: Understanding Homicide," 2019, U.N. Office on Drugs and Crime, https://www.unodc.org/documents/data-and-analysis/gsh/Booklet_3.pdf.

24. Arana 2005, Cruz 2010.

25. Méndez Arriaza and Mendoza 2013.

26. Bourgois and Scheper-Hughes 2004, Bourgois 2009, Galtung 1969, Tyner and Inwood 2014.

27. Farmer 2004: 306.

28. Holmes 2013, Horton 2016.

29. Ibid.

30. Stenzel 2009.

31. Zarsky and Stanley 2013.

32. Fulmer, Godoy, and Neff 2008; Nolin and Stephens 2011.

33. Ferdman, R. A., 2014, "The Ugly Truth Behind Guatemala's Fast-Growing, Super-Efficient Palm Oil Industry," April 3, 2014, https://qz.com/194593/the-ugly-truth-behind-guatemalas-fast-growing-super-efficient-palm-oil-industry/.

34. Batz 2017.

35. Canel, Idemudia, and North 2010; Dougherty 2011; Pedersen 2014.

36. Krznaric 2006.

37. O'Connor and Nolan García 2015.

38. Fulmer, Godoy, and Neff 2008.

39. Sassen 2016, Walter and Urkidi 2017.

40. Sassen 2016: 205.

41. Isaacs, A., and R. Schwartz, 2013, "Repression, Resistance, and Indigenous Rights in Guatemala," *Americas Quarterly,* Winter 2013, http://www.americasquarterly.org/content/repression-resistance-and-indigenous-rights-guatemala.

42. Fulmer, Snodgrass Godoy, and Neff 2008.

43. Seelke, C. R., 2016, "Mexico's Recent Immigration Enforcement Efforts," Congressional Research Service, March 9, 2016, https://www.centerforhumanrights.org/PFS_Petition/Ex18_CRS_PFS_Report030916.pdf.

44. Partlow, J., and N. Miroff, 2018, "U.S. Gathers Data on Migrants Deep in Mexico, a Sensitive Program Trump's Rhetoric Could Put at Risk," *Washington Post,* April 6, 2018, https://www.washingtonpost.com/world/national-security/us-gathers-data-on-migrants-deep-in-mexico-a-sensitive-program-trumps-rhetoric-could-put-at-risk/2018/04/06/31a8605a-38f3-11e8-b57c-9445cc4dfa5e_story.html.

45. Vega 2017.

46. Secretaría de Gobernación, 2015, "Coordinación para la Atención Integral de la Migración en la Frontera Sur: Informe de Actividades," July 2014–July 2015," Mexico: CAIMFS, https://www.wola.org/sites/default/files/MX/WOLAFUNDAR/CAIMFS%20%20Informe%20de%20Actividades%20JULIO%202014%20A%20JULIO%202015%20%20.pdf.

47. Ibid: 3–4.

48. Vega 2016.

49. Ibid.

50. Vega 2017.

51. Kopan, T., 2017, "DHS Ends Program for Central American Minors," *CNN,* August

16, 2017, http://edition.cnn.com/2017/08/16/politics/trump-ending-central-american-minors-program/index.html.

52. "Asylum Refugees and Applications in Mexico," n.d., *WorldData.info,* https://www.worlddata.info/america/mexico/asylum.php.

53. "Costa Rica," n.d., *WorldData.info,* https://www.worlddata.info/america/costarica/asylum.php; "Panama," n.d., *WorldData.info,* https://www.worlddata.info/america/panama/asylum.php;

"Mexico," n.d., *WorldData.info,* https://www.worlddata.info/america/mexico/asylum.php.

54. Office of the Secretary, 2016, "Fact Sheet: The United States and Central America: Honoring Our Commitments," The White House, January 14, 2016, https://obamawhitehouse.archives.gov/the-press-office/2016/01/15/fact-sheet-united-states-and-central-america-honoring-our-commitments.

55. Governments of El Salvador, Guatemala, and Honduras, 2014, "Plan of the Alliance for the Prosperity of the Northern Triangle: A Road Map," September 2014, http://idbdocs.iadb.org/wsdocs/getdocument.aspx?docnum= 39224238.

56. Grandin and Oglesby 2011.

57. Consolidated Appropriations Act 2016 (*Public Law 114-113*).

58. To view the statement in English, visit http://cispes.org/sites/default/files/wp-uploads/2015/04/Final-Letter-to-Presidents-at-Summit-of-the-Americas.pdf.

59. Veltmeyer, Petras, and Vieux 2016; Morley 1995.

60. Ybarra 2016: 60.

CHAPTER 4. ¿QUÉDATE Y QUÉ?

1. Soichet, C. E., and C. Merrill, 2018, "Ice Air: How US Deportation Flights Work," *CNN,* January 17, 2018, https://edition.cnn.com/2017/05/26/us/ice-air-deportation-flights-explainer/index.html.

2. Santos, F., 2017, "The Road, or Flight, from Detention to Deportation," *New York Times,* February 20, 2017, https://www.nytimes.com/2017/02/20/us/the-road-or-flight-from-detention-to-deportation.html.

3. DHS Office of Inspector General, 2015, "ICE Air Transportation of Detainees Could Be More Effective," U.S. Department of Homeland Security, April 9, 2015, https://www.oig.dhs.gov/assets/Mgmt/2015/OIG_15-57_Apr15.pdf.

4. Inter-American Commission on Human Rights, 2015, "Situation of Human Rights in Guatemala: Diversity, Inequality, and Exclusion," Organization of American States, http://www.oas.org/en/iachr/reports/pdfs/Guatemala2016-en.pdf.

5. "Central America: Guatemala," n.d., CIA, https://www.cia.gov/library/publications/the-world-factbook/geos/print_gt.html.

6. Koser and Kuschminder 2015: 1.

7. Kanstroom 2007: 208; *Yamataya v. Fisher* 189 U.S. 86 (1903).

8. De Genova and Peutz 2010.

9. Khosravi 2016: 172.

10. Dreby 2010.

11. See also Khosravi 2018.

12. Burrell 2013, Burrell and Moodie 2015, Clouser 2009, Levenson 2013.

13. Sanford, V., 2013, "Victory in Guatemala? Not Yet," *New York Times,* May 14, 2013,

https://www.nytimes.com/2013/05/14/opinion/its-too-soon-to-declare-victory-in-guatemalan
-genocide.html.

14. Congreso de la República de Guatemala, 2016, "Decreto Número 44-2016," *Diario de Centro América,* October 18, 2016, http://igm.gob.gt/wp-content/uploads/2017/09/10978.pdf.

CHAPTER 5. NEGOTIATING RETURNS

1. Turnbull 2018: 42.

2. Heidbrink and Statz 2017.

3. Parreñas 2005, Suarez-Orozco and Suarez-Orozco 2001.

4. Gao et al. 2010, Falicov 2005.

5. Asis 2006, McGovern and Devine 2016.

6. Cebotari and Mazzucato 2016.

7. Haagsman and Mazzucato 2014.

8. Olwig 1999: 267, 281.

9. Grabel, J., 2017, "Sold for Parts," Propublica, May 1, 2017, https://www.propublica.org/article/case-farms-chicken-industry-immigrant-workers-and-american-labor-law.

10. Montesanti 2015.

11. Zayas 2015.

12. Wessler 2011.

13. Congressional Research Service, 2019, "The Trump Administration's 'Zero Tolerance' Immigration Enforcement Policy," Washington, DC: Congressional Research Service, February 26, 2019, https://fas.org/sgp/crs/homesec/R45266.pdf.

14. Linthicum, K., 2016, "Nearly Half a Million U.S. Citizens Are Enrolled in Mexican Schools," *LA Times,* September 13, 2016, http://www.latimes.com/world/mexico-americas/la-fg-mexico-return-migration-schools-20160913-snap-story.html.

15. Brabeck, Lykes, and Hershberg 2011, Zúñiga and Hamann 2009.

16. For a discussion of de facto deportation, see Kanstroom 2012.

17. Registro Nacional de las Personas (RENAP, National Registry of Persons) is the Guatemalan entity responsible for issuing identification documents and for the registry of birth, marriage, and death certificates.

18. Dirección General de Evaluación e Investigación Educativa (DIGEDUCA), 2013, "Reporte General: Primaria 2010," Guatemala: Ministerio de Educación. Accessed October 30, 2017, http://www.mineduc.gob.gt/digeduca/documents/informes/Reporte_Primaria_2010.pdf.

19. Calculations based on annual statistics from 2014 to 2018 on sheets 3.2.2 and 3.2.5 found at "Boletin estadístico anual" SEGOB, http://www.gobernacion.gob.mx/es_mx/SEGOB/Boletines_Estadisticos.

20. Heidbrink 2014: 110–34.

21. Cacho 2012: 32.

CHAPTER 6. DEBT AND INDEBTEDNESS

1. Tsing 2015: 2.

2. According to a local historian, prior to the Spanish conquest, Almolonga was called Sakpolia, or the place where the water streams. In the early 1500s, Mexican Indians who ac-

companied the Spanish conquistador Pedro de Alvarado renamed the community Almolonga, which is derived from the Nahuatl words *alt* (water) and *molo* (forms), an apocopate form of *molini* (the place where water flows).

3. See Katz 2000, Gauster and Isakson 2007, Moran-Taylor and Taylor 2010.

4. Stoll 2012.

5. Morduch 2000: 620.

6. Epstein and Yuthas 2010.

7. INAB-CONAP 2015, Regalado et al. 2010.

8. Foxen 2007.

9. Bossen 1982, Green 2003, Oglesby 2004.

10. Green 2003.

11. Honwana 2014, Turner 1987.

12. See also Kanstroom 2012.

13. Hasselberg 2018, Schuster and Majidi 2013.

CHAPTER 7. EL DERECHO A NO MIGRAR

1. Notably, the externalization of immigration enforcement is not new. Rather, in the United States it builds upon past histories of intercepting Haitian refugees at sea in the 1990s to thwart their asylum claims at offshore detention facilities such as the infamous Guantanamo Bay.

2. Argueta, A., N. Hesse, M. Johnson, and W. Newton, 2015, "The Realities of Returning Home: Youth Repatriation in Guatemala," Washington, DC: Wilson Center, https://www.wilsoncenter.org/sites/default/files/Guatemala%20Repatriation_June%202015-%20v4%20-%20draft%20disclaimer.pdf.

3. See, for example, Anthropologist Action Network for Immigrants and Refugees (www.anthropologistactionnetwork.org) and Youth Circulations (www.youthcirculations.com).

REFERENCES

Agamben, G. 2005. *State of Exception,* vol. 2. Chicago: University of Chicago Press.

Anderson, B., M. J. Gibney, and E. Paoletti. 2011. "Citizenship, Deportation and the Boundaries of Belonging." *Citizenship Studies,* 15(5): 547–63.

Arana, A. 2005. "How the Street Gangs Took Central America." *Foreign Affairs,* 84(3): 98–110.

Asis, M. M. 2006. "Living with Migration: Experiences of Left-Behind Children in the Philippines." *Asian Population Studies,* 2(1): 45–67.

Baldassar, L., and L. Merla, eds. 2013. *Transnational Families, Migration, and the Circulation of Care: Understanding Mobility and Absence in Family Life.* Abingdon, UK: Routledge.

Bannan, R. S. 1986. "The World as Sanctuary." *Cross Currents,* 36(1): 110–12.

Batz, G. 2017. "The Fourth Invasion: Development, Ixil-Maya Resistance, and the Struggle Against Megaprojects in Guatemala." PhD diss., University of Texas, Austin.

Baum, J., R. Jones, and C. Berry. 2010. *In the Child's Best Interest? The Consequences of Losing a Lawful Immigrant Parent to Deportation.* Collingdale, PA: Diane.

Berger Cardoso, J., K. Brabeck, D. Stinchcomb, L. Heidbrink, O. A. Price, Ó. Gil-García, T. M. Crea, and L. H. Zayas. 2017. "Integration of Unaccompanied Migrant Youth in the United States: A Call for Research." *Journal of Ethnic and Migration Studies,* 45(2): 1–20.

Bhabha, J., and S. Schmidt. 2008. "Seeking Asylum Alone: Unaccompanied and Separated Children and Refugee Protection in the U.S." *Journal of the History of Childhood and Youth,* 1(1): 126–38.

Bhugra, D., and M. A. Becker. 2005. "Migration, Cultural Bereavement and Cultural Identity." *World Psychiatry,* 4(1): 18–24.

Bilsborrow, R. E., and P. Stupp. 1997. "Demographic Processes, Land, and Environment in Guatemala." *Progress in Human Geography,* 33(3): 355–78.

Bloch, A., and L. Schuster. 2005. "At the Extremes of Exclusion: Deportation, Detention and Dispersal." *Ethnic and Racial Studies,* 28(3): 491–512.

Boehm, D. A. 2008. "'For My Children': Constructing Family and Navigating the State in the U.S.-Mexico Transnation." *Anthropological Quarterly,* 81(4): 777–802.

Boehm, D. A. 2016. *Returned: Going and Coming in an Age of Deportation.* Berkeley: University of California Press.

Bossen, L. 1982. "Plantations and Labor Force Discrimination in Guatemala." *Current Anthropology*, 23(3): 263–68.

Bourbeau, P. 2011. *The Securitization of Migration: A Study of Movement and Order.* London: Taylor and Francis.

Bourgois, P. 2001. "The Power of Violence in War and Peace: Post–Cold War Lessons from El Salvador." *Ethnography*, 2(1): 5–34.

Bourgois, P. 2009. "Recognizing Invisible Violence: A Thirty-Year Ethnographic Retrospective." In *Global Health in Times of Violence,* edited by L. Whiteford, B. Rylko-Bauer, P. Farmer, 18–40. Santa Fe, NM: School for Advanced Research Press.

Bourgois, P., and N. Scheper-Hughes. 2004. "Comment on 'An Anthropology of Structural Violence,' by Paul Farmer." *Current Anthropology*, 45(3): 317–18.

Brabeck, K. M., M. B. Lykes, and R. Hershberg. 2011. "Framing Immigration to and Deportation from the United States: Guatemalan and Salvadoran Families Make Meaning of Their Experiences." *Community, Work and Family*, 14(3): 275–96.

Brigden, N. K. 2018. "Gender Mobility: Survival Plays and Performing Central American Migration in Passage." *Mobilities*, 13(1): 111–25.

Burns, E. B. 1986. *Eadweard Muybridge in Guatemala, 1875: The Photographer as Social Recorder.* Berkeley: University of California Press.

Burrell, J. L. 2013. *Maya After War: Conflict, Power, and Politics in Guatemala.* Austin: University of Texas Press.

Burrell, J. L., and E. Moodie. 2012. *Central America in the New Millennium: Living Transition and Reimagining Democracy.* New York: Berghahn Books.

Burrell, J. L., and E. Moodie. 2015. "The Post–Cold War Anthropology of Central America." *Annual Review of Anthropology*, 44: 381–400.

Butler, J. 2004. *Precarious Life: The Powers of Mourning and Violence.* London: Verso.

Byrne, O., and E. Miller. 2016. *The Flow of Unaccompanied Children Through the Immigration System: A Resource for Practitioners, Policy Makers, and Researchers.* New York: Center on Immigration and Justice.

Cacho, L. M. 2012. *Social Death: Racialized Rightlessness and the Criminalization of the Unprotected.* New York: NYU Press.

Canel, E., U. Idemudia, and L. L. North. 2010. "Rethinking Extractive Industry: Regulation, Dispossession, and Emerging Claims." *Canadian Journal of Development Studies/ Revue canadienne d'études du développement*, 30(1–2): 5–25.

Caneva, E. 2014. "Intolerant Policies and Discourses in Northern Italian Cities." *Journal of Immigrant and Refugee Studies*, 12(4): 383–400.

Cárdenas, M. 2017. "A Central American Wound: Remapping the U.S. Borderlands in Oscar Martinez's *The Beast*." In *Symbolism 17: Latina/o Literature: The Trans-Atlantic and the Trans-American in Dialogue,* edited by R. Ahrens, F. Kläger, K. Stierstorfer, 13–30. Berlin: DeGruyter.

Castillo, M. Á., and R. R. Casillas. 1988. "Características básicas de la migración guatemalteca al Soconusco chiapaneco." *Estudios demográficos y urbanos*, 3(3): 537–62.

Cebotari, V., and V. Mazzucato. 2016. "Educational Performance of Children of Migrant Parents in Ghana, Nigeria and Angola." *Journal of Ethnic and Migration Studies*, 42(5): 834–56.

Choy, C. C. 2003. *Empire of Care: Nursing and Migration in Filipino American History.* Durham, NC: Duke University Press

Christie, N. 1986. "The Ideal Victim." In *From Crime Policy to Victim Policy,* edited by E. A. Fattah, 17–30. New York: Springer.

Citroni, G. 2018. "The First Attempts in Mexico and Central America to Address the Phenomenon of Missing and Disappeared Migrants." *International Review of the Red Cross,* 99(905): 1–23.

Clouser, R. 2009. "Remnants of Terror: Landscapes of Fear in Post-Conflict Guatemala." *Journal of Latin American Geography,* 8(2): 7–22.

Coe, C., R. R. Reynolds, D. A. Boehm, J. M. Hess, and H. Rae-Espinoza, eds. 2011. *Everyday Ruptures: Children, Youth, and Migration in Global Perspective.* Nashville, TN: Vanderbilt University Press.

Costello, P. 1997. "Historical Background." In *Negotiating Rights: The Guatemalan Peace Process,* edited by R. Sieder and R. Wilson, 10–17. *Accord: An International Review of Peace Initiatives,* vol. 2. London: Conciliation Resources.

Coutin, S. B. 2005. "Being en Route." *American Anthropologist,* 107(2): 195–206.

Coutin, S. B. 2007. *Nations of Emigrants: Shifting Boundaries of Citizenship in El Salvador and the United States.* Ithaca, NY: Cornell University Press.

Coutin, S. B. 2010. "Confined Within: National Territories as Zones of Confinement." *Political Geography,* 29(4): 200–208.

Coutin, S. B. 2016. *Exiled Home: Salvadoran Transnational Youth in the Aftermath of Violence.* Durham, NC: Duke University Press.

Crea, T. M., A. Lopez, T. Taylor, and D. Underwood. 2017. "Unaccompanied Migrant Children in the United States: Predictors of Placement Stability in Long Term Foster Care." *Children and Youth Services Review,* 73: 93–99.

Cruz, J. M. 2010. "Central American Maras: From Youth Street Gangs to Transnational Protection Rackets." *Global Crime,* 11(4): 379–98.

Curran, S. R., and A. C. Saguy. 2001. "Migration and Cultural Change: A Role for Gender and Social Networks?" *Journal of International Women's Studies,* 2(3): 54–77.

De Genova, N. 2005. *Working the Boundaries: Race, Space, and "Illegality" in Mexican Chicago.* Durham, NC: Duke University Press.

De Genova, N., and Peutz, N. 2010. *The Deportation Regime: Sovereignty, Space, and the Freedom of Movement.* Durham, NC: Duke University Press.

De Graeve, K., and C. Bex. 2017. "Caringscapes and Belonging: An Intersectional Analysis of Care Relationships of Unaccompanied Minors in Belgium." *Children's Geographies,* 15(1): 80–92.

De Haas, H. 2010. "Migration and Development: A Theoretical Perspective." *International Migration Review,* 44(1): 227–64.

De León, J. 2015. *The Land of Open Graves: Living and Dying on the Migrant Trail.* Berkeley: University of California Press.

del Valle Escalante, E. 2009. *Maya Nationalisms and Postcolonial Challenges in Guatemala: Coloniality, Modernity, and Identity Politics.* Santa Fe, NM: School for Advanced Research.

Diamond, I., and L. Quinby. 1988. *Foucault and Feminism: Reflections on Resistance.* Boston: Northeastern University Press.

Dougherty, M. L. 2011. "The Global Gold Mining Industry, Junior Firms, and Civil Society Resistance in Guatemala." *Bulletin of Latin American Research,* 30(4): 403–18.

Dreby, J. 2010. *Divided by Borders: Mexican Migrants and Their Children.* Berkeley: University of California Press.

Dreby, J. 2012. "The Burden of Deportation on Children in Mexican Immigrant Families." *Journal of Marriage and Family,* 74(4): 829–45.

Ensor, M., and E. Gozdziak, eds. 2010. *Children and Migration: At the Crossroads of Resiliency and Vulnerability.* New York: Palgrave Macmillan.

Epstein, M. J., and K. Yuthas. 2010. "Microfinance in Cultures of Non-Repayment." *Journal of Developmental Entrepreneurship,* 15(1): 35–54.

Falicov, C. J. 2005. "Emotional Transnationalism and Family Identities." *Family Process,* 44(4): 399–406.

Farmer, P. 2004. "An Anthropology of Structural Violence." *Current Anthropology,* 45(3): 305–25.

Fischer, E. F. 2001. *Cultural Logics and Global Economies: Maya Identity in Thought and Practice.* Austin: University of Texas Press.

Foner, N., ed. 2009. *Across Generations: Immigrant Families in America.* New York: NYU Press.

Foxen, P. 2007. *In Search of Providence: Transnational Mayan Identities.* Nashville, TN: Vanderbilt University Press.

Freire, P. 2005. *Pedagogy of the Oppressed* (revised). New York: Continuum.

Fulmer, A. M., A. Snodgrass Godoy, and P. Neff. 2008. "Indigenous Rights, Resistance, and the Law: Lessons from a Guatemalan Mine." *Latin American Politics and Society,* 50(4): 91–121.

Galemba, R. B. 2018. "'He Used to Be a Pollero': The Securitization of Migration and the Smuggler/Migrant Nexus at the Mexico-Guatemala Border." *Journal of Ethnic and Migration Studies,* 44(5): 870–86.

Galtung, J. 1969. "Violence, Peace, and Peace Research." *Journal of Peace Research,* 6(3): 167–91.

Galvin, T. M. 2015. "'We Deport Them but They Keep Coming Back': The Normalcy of Deportation in the Daily Life of 'Undocumented' Zimbabwean Migrant Workers in Botswana." *Journal of Ethnic and Migration Studies,* 41(4): 617–34.

Gao, Y., L. P. Li, J. H. Kim, N. Congdon, J. Lau, and S. Griffiths. 2010. "The Impact of Parental Migration on Health Status and Health Behaviours Among Left Behind Adolescent School Children in China." *BMC Public Health,* 10(1): 56–66.

García, M. C. 2006. *Seeking Refuge: Central American Migration to Mexico, the United States, and Canada.* Berkeley: University of California Press.

Gauster, S., and S. Ryan Isakson. 2007. "Eliminating Market Distortions, Perpetuating Rural Inequality: An Evaluation of Market-Assisted Land Reform in Guatemala." *Third World Quarterly,* 28(8): 1519–36.

Georgopoulos, A. 2005. "Beyond the Reach of Juvenile Justice: The Crisis of Unaccompanied Immigrant Children Detained by the United States." *Law and Inequality,* 23: 117–55.

Girón, C. 2010. "Migrantes Mam entre San Marcos (Guatemala) y Chiapas (México)." In *Niñez indígena en migración. Derechos en riesgo y tramas culturales,* edited by S. Caggiano, L. Caicedo, and C. Girón. Quito, Ecuador: FLACSO/AECID/UNICEF.

REFERENCES   201

Gomberg-Muñoz, R. 2016. "Criminalized Workers: Introduction to Special Issue on Migrant Labor and Mass Deportation." *Anthropology of Work Review*, 37(1): 3–10.

Gonzales, R. G. 2011. "Learning to Be Illegal: Undocumented Youth and Shifting Legal Contexts in the Transition to Adulthood." *American Sociological Review*, 76(4): 602–19.

Gonzales, R. G. 2015. *Lives in Limbo: Undocumented and Coming of Age in America*. Berkeley: University of California Press.

Gonzales, R. G., and L. R. Chavez. 2012. "'Awakening to a Nightmare': Abjectivity and Illegality in the Lives of Undocumented 1.5-Generation Latino Immigrants in the United States." *Current Anthropology*, 53(3): 255–81.

Grandin, G., and E. Oglesby. 2011. *The Guatemala Reader: History, Culture, Politics*. Durham, NC: Duke University Press.

Green, L. 2003. "Notes on Mayan Youth and Rural Industrialization in Guatemala." *Critique of Anthropology*, 23(1): 51–73.

Green, L. 2010. *Fear as a Way of Life: Mayan Widows in Rural Guatemala*. New York: Columbia University Press.

Guyer, J. 2004. *Marginal Gains: Monetary Transactions in Atlantic Africa*. Chicago: University of Chicago Press.

Haagsman, K., and V. Mazzucato. 2014. "The Quality of Parent-Child Relationships in Transnational Families: Angolan and Nigerian Migrant Parents in the Netherlands." *Journal of Ethnic and Migration Studies*, 40(11): 1677–96.

Hall, C. E. 2011. "Where Are My Children . . . and My Rights? Parental Rights Termination as a Consequence of Deportation." *Duke Law Journal*, 60: 1459–1503.

Handy, J. 1984. *Gift of the Devil: A History of Guatemala*. Toronto: Between the Lines.

Hardy, C., and R. Thomas. 2015. "Discourse in a Material World." *Journal of Management Studies*, 52(5): 680–96.

Hasselberg, I. 2018. "Fieldnotes from Cape Verde: On Deported Youth, Research Methods, and Social Change." In *After Deportation*, edited by S. Khosravi, 15–35. New York: Springer.

Heidbrink, L. 2014. *Migrant Youth, Transnational Families, and the State: Care and Contested Interests*. Philadelphia: University of Pennsylvania Press.

Heidbrink, L. 2017. "Assessing Parental Fitness and Care for Unaccompanied Children." *Journal of the Social Sciences*, 3(4): 37–52.

Heidbrink, L. 2018. "Circulation of Care Among Unaccompanied Migrant Youth from Guatemala." *Children and Youth Services Review*, 92: 30–38.

Heidbrink, L. 2019. "The Coercive Power of Debt: Migration and Deportation of Guatemalan Indigenous Youth." *Journal of Latin American and Caribbean Anthropology*, 24(1): 263–81.

Heidbrink, L., and M. Statz. 2017. "Parents of Global Youth: Contesting Debt and Belonging." *Children's Geographies*, 15(5): 545–57.

Hernández, C. C. 2014. "Immigration Detention as Punishment." *Immigration and Nationality Law Review*, 35: 1346–414.

Herrera-Sobek, M. 2012. "The Border Patrol and Their *Migra Corridos*: Propaganda, Genre Adaptation, and Mexican Immigration." *American Studies Journal*, 57. DOI 10.18422/57-06.

Hochschild, A. R. 2000a. "Global Care Chains and Emotional Surplus value." In *On the Edge: Living with Global Capitalism*, edited by W. Hutton and A. Giddens, 130–46. New York: Vintage Books.

Hochschild, A. R. 2000b. "The Nanny Chain." *American Prospect*, 11(4): 32–36.

Holmes, S. 2013. *Fresh Fruit, Broken Bodies: Migrant Farmworkers in the United States*. Berkeley: University of California Press.

Hondagneu-Sotelo, P. 2011. "Gender and Migration Scholarship: An Overview from a 21st-Century Perspective." *Migraciones Internacionales*, 6(1): 219–33.

Honwana, A. 2014. "Youth, Waithood, and Protest Movements in Africa." In *African Dynamics in a Multipolar World: 5th European Conference on African Studies—Conference Proceedings*, 2428–47. Lisbon: Centro de Estudos Internacionais do Instituto Universitário de Lisboa (ISCTE-IUL).

Horton, S. B. 2016. *They Leave Their Kidneys in the Fields: Illness, Injury, and Illegality Among U.S. Farmworkers*. Berkeley: University of California Press.

INAB-CONAP. 2015. "Mapa forestal por tipo y subtipo de bosque, 2012, Guatemala: Informe técnico." Guatemala City: Instituto Nacional de Bosques/Consejo Nacional de Areas Protegidas. http://www.sifgua.org.gt/Documentos/Cobertura%20Forestal/Cobertura%202012/Informe_de_Cobertura_Forestal_20_julio_15.pdf.

Ingold, T., and J. L. Vergunst, eds. 2008. *Ways of Walking: Ethnography and Practice on Foot*. Farnham, UK: Ashgate.

Jonas, S. 1991. *The Battle for Guatemala: Rebels, Death Squads, and U.S. Power*. Abingdon, UK: Routledge.

Jonas, S., and N. Rodríguez. 2015. *Guatemala-U.S. Migration: Transforming Regions*. Austin: University of Texas Press.

Kanstroom, D. 2007. "Post-Deportation Human Rights Law: Aspiration, Oxymoron, or Necessity?" *Stanford Journal of Civil Rights and Civil Liberties*, 3: 195–231.

Kanstroom, D. 2012. *Aftermath: Deportation Law and the New American Diaspora*. Oxford: Oxford University Press.

Katz, E. G. 2000. "Social Capital and Natural Capital: A Comparative Analysis of Land Tenure and Natural Resource Management in Guatemala." *Land Economics*, 76(1): 114–32.

Khosravi, S. 2016. "Deportation as a Way of Life for Young Afghan Men." In *Detaining the Immigrant Other: Global and Transnational Issues*, edited by R. Furman, D. Epps, and G. Lamphear, 169–81. Jericho, UK: Oxford University Press.

Khosravi, S., ed. 2018. *After Deportation: Ethnographic Perspectives*. New York: Springer.

Kilkey, M. 2010. "Men and Domestic Labor: A Missing Link in the Global Care Chain." *Men and Masculinities*, 13(1): 126–49.

Knippen, J., C., Boggs, and M. Meyer. 2015. *An Uncertain Path: Justice for Crimes and Human Rights Violations Against Migrants and Refugees in Mexico*. Washington, DC: Washington Office on Latin America.

Koser, K., and K. Kuschminder. 2015. *Comparative Research on the Assisted Voluntary Return and Reintegration of Migrants*. Geneva: International Organization for Migration Publications.

Krznaric, R. 2006. "The Limits on Pro?Poor Agricultural Trade in Guatemala: Land, Labour and Political Power." *Journal of Human Development*, 7(1): 111–35.

Ku, L., and S. Matani. 2001. "Left Out: Immigrants' Access to Health Care and Insurance." *Health Affairs*, 20(1): 247–56.

Kullgren, J. T. 2003. "Restrictions on Undocumented Immigrants' Access to Health Services: The Public Health Implications of Welfare Reform." *American Journal of Public Health*, 93(10): 1630–33.

Leinaweaver, J. B. 2008. *The Circulation of Children: Kinship, Adoption, and Morality in Andean Peru*. Durham, NC: Duke University Press.

Leinaweaver, J. B. 2013. *Adoptive Migration: Raising Latinos in Spain*. Durham, NC: Duke University Press.

Levenson, D. T. 2013. "*Adiós niño: The Gangs of Guatemala City and the Politics of Death*. Durham, NC: Duke University Press.

LeVine, R. A. 2007. "Ethnographic Studies of Childhood: A Historical Overview." *American Anthropologist*, 109(2): 247–60.

Little, W. E., and T. J. Smith. 2009. *Mayas in Postwar Guatemala: Harvest of Violence Revisited*. Tuscaloosa: University of Alabama Press.

Lovell, W. G. 1992. *Conquest and Survival in Colonial Guatemala: A Historical Geography of the Cuchumatán Highlands, 1500–1821*. Kingston, Ontario: McGill-Queen's University Press.

Lovell, W. G. 2010. *A Beauty that Hurts: Life and Death in Guatemala*. Austin: University of Texas Press.

Lovell, W. G., and C. H. Lutz. 1994. "Conquest and Population: Maya Demography in Historical Perspective." *Latin American Research Review*, 29(2): 133–40.

Lutz, C. H., and W. G. Lovell. 2000. "Survivors on the Move: Maya Migration in Time and Space." In *The Maya Diaspora: Guatemalan Roots, New American Lives*, edited by J. Loucky, 11–34. Philadelphia: Temple University Press.

Lykes, M. B., K. M. Brabeck, and C. J. Hunter 2013. "Exploring Parent-Child Communication in the Context of Threat: Immigrant Families Facing Detention and Deportation in Post-9/11 USA." *Community, Work and Family*, 16(2): 123–46.

Lytle Hernández, K. (2010). *Migra! A History of the U.S. Border Patrol*. Berkeley: University of California Press.

Manz, B. 2004. *Paradise in Ashes: A Guatemalan Journey of Courage, Terror, and Hope*. Berkeley: University of California Press.

Massey, D. S. 1988. "Economic Development and International Migration in Comparative Perspective." *Population and Development Review*, 14: 383–413.

Mbembé, J. A., and L. Meintjes. 2003. "Necropolitics." *Public Culture*, 15(1): 11–40.

McAllister, C., and D. M. Nelson. 2013. *War by Other Means: Aftermath in Post-Genocide Guatemala*. Durham, NC: Duke University Press.

McCreery, D. 1990. "State Power, Indigenous Communities, and Land in Nineteenth-Century Guatemala, 1820–1920." In *Guatemalan Indians and the State, 1540–1988*, edited by C. A. Smith with M. M. Moors, 96–115. Austin: University of Texas Press.

McGovern, F., and D. Devine. 2016. "The Care Worlds of Migrant Children—Exploring Inter-Generational Dynamics of Love, Care and Solidarity Across Home and School." *Childhood*, 23(1): 37–52.

McLeigh, J. D. 2010. "How Do Immigration and Customs Enforcement (ICE) Practices Affect the Mental Health of Children?" *American Journal of Orthopsychiatry*, 80(1): 96–100.

"Memorandum: Implementing the President's Border Security and Immigration Enforcement Improvements Policies." February 20, 2017. U.S. Department of Homeland Security. https://www.dhs.gov/sites/default/files/publications/17_0220_S1_Implementing-the-Presidents-Border-Security-Immigration-Enforcement-Improvement-Policies.pdf.

Méndez Arriaza, C., and C. Mendoza. 2013. "Siete mitos sobre la violencia homicida en Guatemala." *El Periódico,* February 4, 2013. http://www.elfaro.net/es/201302/internacionales/10873.

Menjívar, C. 2006. "Liminal Legality: Salvadoran and Guatemalan Immigrants' Lives in the United States." *American Journal of Sociology,* 111(4): 999–1037.

Menjívar, C. 2011. *Enduring Violence: Ladina Women's Lives in Guatemala.* Berkeley: University of California Press.

Menjívar, C., and L. Abrego. 2012. "Legal Violence: Immigration Law and the Lives of Central American Immigrants." *American Journal of Sociology,* 117(5): 1380–421.

Montesanti, S. R. 2015. "The Role of Structural and Interpersonal Violence in the Lives of Women: A Conceptual Shift in Prevention of Gender-Based Violence." *BMC Women's Health,* 15(93). DOI 10.1186/s12905-015-0247-5.

Moran-Taylor, M. 2008. "Guatemala's Ladino and Maya Migra Landscapes: The Tangible and Intangible Outcomes of Migration." *Human Organization,* 67(2): 111–24.

Moran-Taylor, M. J., and M. J. Taylor. 2010. "Land and Leña: Linking Transnational Migration, Natural Resources, and the Environment in Guatemala." *Population and Environment,* 32(2–3): 198–215.

Morduch, J. 2000. "The Microfinance Schism." *World Development,* 28(4): 617–29.

Morley, S. A. 1995. *Poverty and Inequality in Latin America: The Impact of Adjustment and Recovery in the 1980s.* Baltimore: Johns Hopkins University Press.

Moskal, M., and N. Tyrrell. 2016. "Family Migration Decision-Making, Step-Migration and Separation: Children's Experiences in European Migrant Worker Families." *Children's Geographies,* 14(4): 453–67.

Musalo, K., L. Frydman, and P. C. Cernadas, eds. 2015. *Childhood and Migration in Central and North America: Causes, Policies, Practices and Challenges.* Hastings Research Paper no. 211. San Francisco: Center for Gender and Refugee Studies, University of California Hastings Law College. Social Science Research Network. https://papers.ssrn.com/sol3/papers.cfm?abstract_id=2834141.

Nader, L. 1972. "Up the Anthropologist: Perspectives Gained from 'Studying Up.'" In *Reinventing Anthropology,* edited by D. Hyms, 284–311. New York: Random House.

Nititham, D. S. 2017. *Home in Diasporic Communities.* London: Routledge

Nolin, C., and J. Stephens. 2011. "'We Have to Protect the Investors': 'Development' and Canadian Mining Companies in Guatemala." *Journal of Rural and Community Development,* 5(3): 37–70.

O'Connor, E., and K. A. Nolan García. 2015. "The Effectiveness of Trade-Based Clauses in Improving Labor Rights Protections: The Case of the CAFTA-DR Labor Clause." Mexico City: Centro de Investigación y Docencia Económicas.

Oglesby, E. 2004. "Corporate Citizenship? Elites, Labor, and the Geographies of Work in Guatemala." *Environment and Planning D: Society and Space,* 22(4): 553–72.

Olwig, K. F. 1999. "Narratives of the Children Left Behind: Home and Identity in Globalised Caribbean Families." *Journal of Ethnic and Migration Studies*, 25(2): 267–84.

Ong, A. 1999. *Flexible Citizenship: The Cultural Logics of Transnationality*. Durham, NC: Duke University Press.

Parreñas, R. S. 2000. "Migrant Filipina Domestic Workers and the International Division of Reproductive Labor." *Gender and Society*, 14(4): 560–80.

Parreñas, R. S. 2005. *Children of Global Migration: Transnational Families and Gendered Woes*. Stanford, CA: Stanford University Press.

Patler, C., and R. G. Gonzales. 2015. "Framing Citizenship: Media Coverage of Anti-Deportation Cases Led by Undocumented Immigrant Youth Organisations." *Journal of Ethnic and Migration Studies*, 41(9): 1453–74.

Pedersen, A. 2014. "Landscapes of Resistance: Community Opposition to Canadian Mining Operations in Guatemala." *Journal of Latin American Geography*, 13(1): 187–214.

Peutz, N. 2006. "Embarking on an Anthropology of Removal." *Current Anthropology*, 47(2): 217–41.

"Plan of the Alliance for the Prosperity of the Northern Triangle: A Road Map." September 2014. Governments of El Salvador, Guatemala, and Honduras. http://idbdocs.iadb.org/wsdocs/getdocument.aspx?docnum=39224238.

Prout, A., and A. James. 2003. *Constructing and Reconstructing Childhood: Contemporary Issues in the Sociological Study of Childhood*. London: Routledge.

Ramakrishnan, S. K., and Viramontes, C. 2010. "Civic Spaces: Mexican Hometown Associations and Immigrant Participation." *Journal of Social Issues*, 66(1): 155–73.

Regalado, O., X. Villagrán, G. Pérez Irungaray, E. Castellanos, G. Martínez, K. Incer, V. H. Ramos, O. Molina, C. Beltetón, and J. Gómez. 2012. "Mapa de cobertura forestal de Guatemala 2010 y dinámica de la cobertura forestal 2006–2010." https://www.researchgate.net/publication/281861610.

Reyes, K. B., and J. E. Curry Rodríguez. 2012. "Testimonio: Origins, Terms, and Resources." *Equity and Excellence in Education*, 45(3): 525–38.

Reynolds, J. F. 2013. "(Be)laboring Childhoods in Postville, Iowa." *Anthropological Quarterly*, 86(3): 851–89.

Rietig, V., and R. D. Villegas. 2015. *Stopping the Revolving Door: Reception and Reintegration Services for Central American Deportees*. Washington, DC: Migration Policy Institute.

Rojas-Flores, L., M. L. Clements, J. Hwang Koo, and J. London. 2017. "Trauma and Psychological Distress in Latino Citizen Children Following Parental Detention and Deportation." *Psychological Trauma: Theory, Research, Practice, and Policy*, 9(3): 352–61.

Rosas, G. 2006. "The Thickening Borderlands: Diffused Exceptionality and 'Immigrant' Social Struggles During the 'War on Terror.'" *Cultural Dynamics*, 18(3): 335–49.

Rosenblum, M. R., and I. Ball. 2016. *Trends in Unaccompanied Child and Family Migration from Central America*. Washington, DC: Migration Policy Institute.

Roth, B. J., and B. L. Grace. 2015. "Falling Through the Cracks: The Paradox of Post-Release Services for Unaccompanied Child Migrants." *Children and Youth Services Review*, 58: 244–52.

Sanford, V. 2003. *Buried Secrets: Truth and Human Rights in Guatemala*. New York: Springer.

Sassen, S. 2016. "A Massive Loss of Habitat: New Drivers for Migration." *Sociology of Development*, 2(2): 204–33.

Schmidt, L. A., and S. Buechler. 2017. "'I Risk Everything Because I Have Already Lost Everything': Central American Female Migrants Speak Out on the Migrant Trail in Oaxaca, Mexico." *Journal of Latin American Geography*, 16(1): 139–64.

Schuster, L., and N. Majidi. 2013. "What Happens Post-Deportation? The Experience of Deported Afghans." *Migration Studies*, 1(2): 221–40.

Scrinzi, F. 2010. "Masculinities and the International Division of Care: Migrant Male Domestic Workers in Italy and France." *Men and Masculinities*, 13(1): 44–64.

Seelke, C. R. 2016. *Mexico's Recent Immigration Enforcement Efforts*. March 9, 2016. Washington, DC: Congressional Research Service.

Seelke, C. R., and K. M. Finklea. 2011. *U.S.-Mexican Security Cooperation: The Mérida Initiative and Beyond*. Washington, DC: Congressional Research Service.

Sites, W., and Vonderlack-Navarro, R. 2012. "Tipping the Scale: State Rescaling and the Strange Odyssey of Chicago's Mexican Hometown Associations." In *Remaking Urban Citizenship: Organizations, Institutions, and the Right to the City*, edited by M. P. Smith and M. McQuarrie, 151–69. Comparative Urban and Community Research, vol. 10. New Brunswick, NJ: Transaction.

Slack, J., D. E. Martinez, A. E. Lee, and S. Whiteford. 2016. "The Geography of Border Militarization: Violence, Death and Health in Mexico and the United States." *Journal of Latin American Geography*, 15(1): 7–32.

Smith, A., R. N. Lalonde, and S. Johnson. 2004. "Serial Migration and Its Implications for the Parent-Child Relationship: A Retrospective Analysis of the Experiences of the Children of Caribbean Immigrants." *Cultural Diversity and Ethnic Minority Psychology*, 10(2): 107.

Squire, V. 2017. "Governing Migration Through Death in Europe and the U.S.: Identification, Burial and the Crisis of Modern Humanism." *European Journal of International Relations*, 23(3): 513–32.

Stenzel, P. L. 2009. "Free Trade and Sustainability Through the Lens of Nicaragua: How CAFTA-DR Should Be Amended to Promote the Triple Bottom Line." *William and Mary Environmental Law and Policy Review*, 34: 653–743.

Stephens, S. 1995. *Children and the Politics of Culture*. Princeton, NJ: Princeton University Press.

Stoll, D. 2012. "*El Norte or Bust! How Migration Fever and Microcredit Produced a Financial Crash in a Latin American Town*. Lanham, MD: Rowman and Littlefield.

Suárez-Orozco, C., and M. M. Suárez-Orozco. 2009. *Children of Immigration*. Cambridge, MA: Harvard University Press.

Taylor, M. J., M. J. Moran-Taylor, and D. R. Ruiz. 2006. "Land, Ethnic, and Gender Change: Transnational Migration and Its Effects on Guatemalan Lives and Landscapes." *Geoforum*, 37(1): 41–61.

Terrio, S. J. 2015. *Whose Child Am I? Unaccompanied, Undocumented Children in U.S. Immigration Custody*. Berkeley: University of California Press.

Tsing, A. L. 2015. *The Mushroom at the End of the World: On the Possibility of Life in Capitalist Ruins*. Princeton, NJ: Princeton University Press.

Turnbull, S. 2018. "Starting Again: Life After Deportation from the UK." In *After Deportation,* edited by S. Khosravi, 37–61. New York: Springer.

Turner, V. 1987. "Betwixt and Between: The Liminal Period in Rites of Passage." In *Betwixt and Between: Patterns of Masculine and Feminine Initiation,* edited by C. C. Crocker, 3–19. Chicago: Open Court.

Tyner, J., and J. Inwood. 2014. "Violence as Fetish: Geography, Marxism, and Dialectics." *Progress in Human Geography,* 38(6): 771–84.

Uehling, G. 2008. "Children's Migration and the Politics of Compassion." *Anthropology News,* 49(5): 8–10.

Valencia, Y. 2017. "Risk and Security on the Mexico-to-U.S. Migrant Journey: Women's Testimonios of Violence." *Gender, Place and Culture,* 24(11): 1530–48.

Van Hear, N. 1998. *New Diasporas: Mass Exodus, Dispersal and Regrouping of Migrant Communities.* Seattle: University of Washington Press.

Vega, L. A. 2016. *Mexico's Not-So-Comprehensive Southern Border Plan.* Issue Brief for the Mexico Center, Baker Institute for Public Policy, Rice University, Houston.

Vega, L. A. 2017. *Policy Adrift: Mexico's Southern Border Program.* Baker Institute for Public Policy, Rice University, Houston.

Veltmeyer, H., J. Petras, and S. Vieux. 2016. *Neoliberalism and Class Conflict in Latin America: A Comparative Perspective on the Political Economy of Structural Adjustment.* New York: Springer.

Vogt, W. A. 2013. "Crossing Mexico: Structural Violence and the Commodification of Undocumented Central American Migrants." *American Ethnologist,* 40(4): 764–80.

Vogt, W. A. 2018. *Lives in Transit: Violence and Intimacy on the Migrant Journey.* Berkeley: University of California Press.

Walter, M., and L. Urkidi. 2017. "Community Mining Consultations in Latin America (2002–2012): The Contested Emergence of a Hybrid Institution for Participation." *Geoforum,* 84: 265–79.

Warren, K. B. 2018. "Interpreting *la violencia* in Guatemala: Shapes of Mayan Silence and Resistance." In *The Violence Within,* edited by K. B. Warren, 25–56. Abingdon, UK: Routledge.

Wessler, S. F. 2011. *Shattered Families: The Perilous Intersection of Immigration Enforcement and the Child Welfare System.* New York and Oakland: Center for Racial Justice Innovation. Applied Research Center (now Race Forward) https://www.raceforward.org /research/reports/shattered-families?arc=1.

White, A., C. Ní Laoire, N. Tyrrell, and F. Carpena-Mendez. 2011. "Children's Roles in Transnational Migration." *Journal of Ethnic and Migration Studies,* 37(8): 1159–70.

Willen, S. S. 2007. "Exploring 'Illegal' and 'Irregular' Migrants' Lived Experiences of Law and State Power." *International Migration,* 45(3): 2–7.

Woodhead, M., and H. Montgomery. 2002. *Understanding Childhood: An Interdisciplinary Approach.* Hoboken, NJ: Wiley.

Yarris, K. E. 2017. *Care Across Generations: Solidarity and Sacrifice in Transnational Families.* Stanford, CA: Stanford University Press.

Ybarra, M. 2016. "'Blind Passes' and the Production of Green Security Through Violence on the Guatemalan Border." *Geoforum,* 69: 194–206.

Yeates, N. 2009. *Globalizing Care Economies and Migrant Workers: Explorations in Global Care Chains*. Basingstoke, UK: Palgrave Macmillan.

Zarsky, L., and L. Stanley. 2013. "Can Extractive Industries Promote Sustainable Development? A Net Benefits Framework and a Case Study of the Marlin Mine in Guatemala." *Journal of Environment and Development*, 22(2): 131–54.

Zatz, M. S., and N. Rodriguez. 2015. *Dreams and Nightmares: Immigration Policy, Youth, and Families*. Berkeley: University of California Press.

Zayas, L. H. 2015. *Forgotten Citizens: Deportation, Children, and the Making of American Exiles and Orphans*. Oxford, UK: Oxford University Press.

Zayas, L. H., K. M. Brabeck, L. C. Heffron, J. Dreby, E. J. Calzada, J. R. Parra-Cardona, and H. Yoshikawa. 2017. "Charting Directions for Research on Immigrant Children Affected by Undocumented Status." *Hispanic Journal of Behavioral Sciences*, 39(4): 412–35.

Zilberg, E. 2007. "Refugee Gang Youth: Zero Tolerance and the Security State in Contemporary U.S.-Salvadoran Relations." In *Youth, Globalization, and the Law*, edited by S. A. Venkatesh and R. Kassimir, 61–89. Stanford, CA: Stanford University Press.

Zilberg, E. 2011. *Space of Detention: The Making of a Transnational Gang Crisis Between Los Angeles and San Salvador*. Durham, NC: Duke University Press.

Zimmermann, W., and M. Fix. 2014. "Immigration and Welfare Reforms in the United States Through the Lens of Mixed-Status Families." In *From Immigration Controls to Welfare Controls*, edited by S. Cohen, B. Humphries, and E. Mynott, 59–79. New York: Routledge.

Zúñiga, V., and E. T. Hamann. 2009. "Sojourners in Mexico with U.S. School Experience: A New Taxonomy for Transnational Students." *Comparative Education Review*, 53(3): 329–53.

INDEX